LLEWELLYN'S

2014

HERBAL

ALMANAC

Cover Design: Kevin R. Brown
Editing: Andrea Neff

Cover images:
Chamomile: iStockphoto.com/mikosca
Aroma herbs: iStockphoto.com/iadamson
Branches and leaves of parsley:
iStockphoto.com/Viktor Blazhuk
Green hummingbird:
iStockphoto.com/Rony Graphics
Green tea: iStockphoto.com/spline_x
Fresh mint leaves:
iStockphoto.com/Serhiy Zavalnyuk

Interior Art: © Fiona King

You can order annuals and books from *New
Worlds*, Llewellyn's catalog. To request a free
copy, call toll free: 1-877-NEW WRLD or
visit http://www.llewellyn.com.

ISBN 978-0-7387-2152-1
Llewellyn Worldwide Ltd.
2143 Wooddale Drive
Woodbury, MN 55125-2989

Printed in the United States of America

Contents

Herbs for Health and Beauty

Herb Crafts

Herb History, Myth, and Lore

Moon Signs, Phases, and Tables

Introduction to
Llewellyn's Herbal Almanac

More and more people are using herbs, growing and gathering them and studying them for their enlivening and healing properties. Whether in the form of a refreshing herbal infusion, a "golden years" garden, or a new favorite recipe, herbs can clearly enhance your life.

In the 2014 edition of the *Herbal Almanac*, we once again feature some of the most innovative and original thinkers and writers on herbs. We tap into practical, historical, and just plain enjoyable aspects of herbal knowledge—using herbs to help you reconnect with the earth, enhance your culinary creations, and heal your body and mind. The twenty-nine articles in this almanac will teach you everything from how to host your own herbal spa night to how to develop and sell an entire herbal product line. You'll also learn how to grow a curry or avocado tree, craft your own herbal vinegars and liqueurs, and tap into the vibrational healing power of flowers. Enjoy!

Note: The old-fashioned remedies in this book are historical references used for teaching purposes only. The recipes are not for commercial use or profit. The contents are not meant to diagnose, treat, prescribe, or substitute consultation with a licensed health-care professional. Herbs, whether used internally or externally, should be introduced in small amounts to allow the body to adjust and to detect possible allergies. Please consult a standard reference source or an expert herbalist to learn more about the possible effects of certain herbs. You must take care not to replace regular medical treatment with the use of herbs. Herbal treatment is intended primarily to complement modern health care. Always seek professional help if you suffer from illness. Also, take care to read all warning labels before taking any herbs or starting on an extended herbal regimen. Always consult medical and herbal professionals before beginning any sort of medical treatment—

this is particularly true for pregnant women. Herbs are powerful things; be sure you are using that power to achieve balance.

Llewellyn Worldwide does not participate in, endorse, or have any authority or responsibility concerning private business transactions between its authors and the public.

Growing
and
Gathering
Herbs

Create a Golden Years Garden

⤞ by Dallas Jennifer Cobb ⤝

With a large percentage of the population belonging to the baby-boom generation, you might be interested in creating a "golden years garden" for yourself or someone else.

A golden years garden is an herb garden designed specifically for the aging adult. It contains herbs with beneficial effects for aging adults, and is designed for easy access and care.

Whether you're a boomer yourself, or the neighbor, family, or friend of a boomer, take a little time to help design the perfect garden—one that older adults can care for independently, and that contains herbs they can, and will, use.

Accessible Garden Design

Good garden design for older adults is much like garden design for anyone else. The most successful gardens are those that take individual needs and preferences into consideration and result in an accessible, easy-to-maintain garden that is pleasing and useful.

Gardens need to be planned before being laid out, in order to ensure that they are accessible. For older adults, accessible can mean many different things, depending on the person. It might mean that garden beds need to be up high, at waist height, to minimize bending and stooping, or that gardens have wide paths to accommodate wheelchairs and/or walkers. It could also mean that gardens are in a smaller, contained space that is limited in scope and easy to care for, like a deck or balcony, or that gardens grow in pots on windowsills in apartments.

These small spaces, like windowsills, balconies, decks, and miniscule back yards, can make great gardens for older adults, yielding a good amount of a wide variety of herbs. Consideration for the size of the space can help to maximize the use of these small spaces.

Good garden design builds on personal needs and preferences, adds an accessible layout plus plants to suit the size and scope of the garden, and results in an easily maintained, healthy, and productive garden.

Simple Considerations

The size of space that you have for your garden will impact your garden design. If you have a small deck, you won't need to worry about paths and walkways. But in a larger area, this should be your first consideration. Make paths at least three feet wide to accommodate wheelchairs and walkers, and allow for only a slight slope. No stairs, curbs, or other obstructions that could deter accessibility should be in the garden.

Construct level, wide paths with hard, even surfaces like asphalt and crushed stone to make them barrier-free for wheelchairs, walkers, and people with limited mobility. Plan for a safe garden, and keep the path clear of growth. Don't plant aggressive vines anywhere near the path.

Plant manageable-size beds that are easy to maintain. Place smaller plants in the front of the bed, and larger, more ornamental plants—that require less care—in the back. Reaching and stretching are hard on backs of all ages.

Many older adults, with or without mobility restrictions, will find raised beds, container gardens, and table planters easier to work with. They will be able to tend to their plants, get their hands dirty, and avoid bending, kneeling, and stooping. When constructing raised beds, table planters, and containers, be sure to position them where they will be rained on. They dry out quickly and require lots of water.

Table planters allow folks in wheelchairs to roll up close, with their legs underneath, much like sitting at a table. Raised beds and containers can be constructed in a variety of heights to bring the garden up closer to the gardener. The most common heights are 15, 20, and 24 inches. These are accessible from a seated or standing position. Containers come in a wide variety of shapes, colors, and designs.

Hanging baskets also allow for increased accessibility. They can be placed on cords for raising and lowering them or attached to chains to position them at the correct height.

Purchasing long-handled tools can make weeding and pruning easier. Look for tools with easy-grip handles that are lightweight and comfortable to use. For anyone with arthritis, look for the larger-grip handles, which are easier on the hands.

For older adults with deteriorating vision, think about creating themed sections of the garden for easy organization, and planting contrasting colors and textures for easy identification.

Herbs Helpful to Aging Adults

There are so many herbs that are beneficial to boomers that this could be a book instead of an article. For the sake of brevity, I will focus on a few common herbs that also happen to be easy to grow, and include culinary, medicinal, and growing information for each one.

Garlic (*Allium sativum*)

Because it is a bulb and grows underground, most people think that garlic is a vegetable, but it is an herb. Garlic is used widely as a culinary herb because of its great taste, easy preparation, and versatility. In combination with other herbs, garlic can be rubbed on meat, sautéed with vegetables, baked with potatoes and root vegetables, added to soups, and even used in fresh salad dressings. On its own, garlic can be baked and spread on bread, boiled and puréed to make soup, and sliced on toast to make a garlic sandwich.

The medicinal qualities of garlic include its ability to reduce cholesterol and lower blood pressure, keeping the heart and blood vessels healthy. Garlic is a diuretic, and promotes urination. It is used to treat gastrointestinal parasites and has antibacterial, antiviral, antimicrobial, and antifungal qualities for both internal and external use. Garlic has been studied extensively, and the research shows it is an all-around excellent booster to immune-system health and has sulfur-containing compounds that help to prevent stomach cancer. Recent research indicates that garlic is also an effective repellent of flies, insects, and spiders.

Growing garlic is easy. Plant it in the mid-fall before the ground freezes, placing cloves "root" side down, pointy tips up. Do not peel the cloves, and only one is needed per plant. Cover with about two inches of fertile soil over the top of the tips. If you get growth in the fall, and see green tips above the soil, mulch around them with straw, and don't worry. Frost will kill those little shoots, but the mulch will protect the bulbs.

In the spring, you will see new green shoots. Carefully remove the layer of mulch, and give the shoots lots of fresh compost to stimulate growth. The shoots will grow up and form a little bulb on the top, which is called a scape. Trim these to focus the plant's energy on the root development. Scapes can be used in salads or sautéed with other vegetables and make beautiful garnishes. It is also common to purée them with basil and olive oil to make garlic-scape pesto, which is great with pasta and on crusty bread.

Garlic likes regular watering, but never pour water directly on top of the bulbs. Use a sprinkler or watering can to make it more like a gentle rainfall.

Harvest garlic early in the fall, when growth slows down and a few brown leaves form. These leaves are an indicator that the bulbs are ready. It is easiest to harvest garlic when the soil is dry. Dig near the garlic to loosen the soil, and, holding the leaves and stock, gently lift the bulb out.

Garlic can be cured by laying it out in the sun. It is perfect when the outer layer of skin is papery. Brush off all the dirt that you can, and store bulbs in a cool, dry location—a wicker basket in a cool cupboard or a rolled-down paper bag makes a nice little garlic nest. Never put garlic in the fridge or in a plastic bag.

Thyme *(Thymus vulgaris)*
A versatile herb, thyme can be used with breads, meats, roasted vegetables, casseroles, and soups. The flavor of thyme is especially complementary to chicken and is often rubbed on the skin for roasting or added liberally to chicken soup. Many Caribbean dishes call for a sprig of thyme in the pot while rice or beans are slow-cooking.

Medicinally, thyme is valued for its antiseptic properties and works well both internally and externally. It can treat ulcers, aid in digestion, and even help with gas. For centuries, thymol, the active ingredient in thyme, has been used in surgical dressings and wound disinfectants.

Thyme is commonly used for gargling and treating tonsillitis and sore throats. It helps to clear phlegm and was used historically to treat any ailment of the lungs.

Thyme is easy to grow. A tender perennial, it can come back year after year in moderate climates or where protected from the harsh effects of winter. It likes a light, sandy soil, with good drainage, where the soil can dry thoroughly between watering. Because it is a low, creeping plant, thyme doesn't like lots of neighbors, and does well on the edge of a garden bed or climbing over the edge of a pot.

Sage *(Salvia officinalis)*

A strongly flavored herb, common sage is often used with pork, in sausage, and in stuffing prepared for chicken or turkey. Many Mediterranean recipes for pasta, pizza, and flatbread call for sage, and in North America, sage is used in a wide range of bread, biscuit, scone, and cornbread recipes. With the large number of varieties of sage, you could have an entire garden filled with only it. There are orange, pineapple, apple, rose, and even chocolate sage.

Sage has historically been used to treat sprains, strains, swelling, ulcers, and contusions. It is antimicrobial and is effective against both salmonella and candida. Sage is an anti-inflammatory and is beneficial in treating inflammatory conditions like rheumatoid arthritis. It strengthens the nervous system, restores clarity, improves memory, and sharpens the senses.

Sage is useful for restoring health to the liver and the digestive system. You can crush a few leaves, steep them in boiling water, and drink a calming cup of sage tea to help with digestion after a fatty meal. Research shows that gargling with sage fights the bacteria that causes bad breath, reduces gingivitis, and relieves the pain of a sore throat. While the research on the effects of sage on blood pressure has only been done with animals, the results show that it is an effective antihypertensive.

Sage can be started from seed, root cuttings, or transplants. It takes a long time to establish itself, so purchasing an older plant will enable you to use the herb the first year. Sage loves full sun, dry soil, and being pruned after flowering. Sage grows well in pots, especially in clay pots, which help the soil to dry thoroughly between watering.

Rosemary *(Rosmarinus officinalis)*

Rosemary is commonly used in baking bread and biscuits and seasoning roasted meat and root vegetables. Because of its strong flavor, rosemary is often used to season lamb and pork and in the preparation of herb vinegars and oils.

Medicinally, rosemary helps to relieve headaches, high blood pressure, and lethargy. A gentle stimulant, rosemary helps to open up the small capillaries, improving circulation, sharpening the senses, and facilitating concentration. Those garlands worn by Roman and Greek students were made of rosemary. Rosemary is renowned for promoting digestion and relieving gas, indigestion, and flatulence.

Used externally, the essential oil of rosemary has anti-bacterial and antifungal properties. With a high antioxidant content, it protects against free radicals that damage cells and cause skin cancer and tumors. Often used in massage oil, rosemary can relieve arthritis and rheumatism with its anti-inflammatory qualities and relax spasms and muscle cramps.

While not exactly a medicinal result, rosemary is said to be effective in maintaining youthful skin, slowing down the aging process, and preventing hair loss.

Like a small cedar bush, rosemary branches out from a bark-covered trunk. It loves full sun and grows well in clay pots and soil that drains well. Like many herbs, rosemary doesn't like to be watered too frequently and needs to dry out thoroughly in between. An annual, you can bring a big pot of rosemary indoors in the fall and use it fresh all winter long. Alternatively, pick rosemary near the end of the summer, dry well, and store in jars. Because of its high oil content, rosemary maintains a strong taste and scent even when dried.

Basil *(Ocimum basilicum)*

Originating in India, basil loves full sun. Commonly grown alongside tomatoes, it helps to add flavor to neighboring plants and keeps the bugs away. An annual, basil can be taken indoors in pots and kept carefully pinched so it doesn't flower and seed, but it usually won't last a full winter. Outdoors, basil is very sensitive to the cold, and will wilt and turn black with the slightest touch of frost.

If allowed to flower, basil will produce seeds that can be gathered and sown the following year, or you can pick leaves and dry them in the sun, keeping the dried basil in jars for use in cooking. My favorite way to preserve basil is to gather the leaves at their peak, place them in the food processor with olive oil and garlic, and purée. I pour the mixture into ice cube trays and freeze, then pop the cubes out and keep them in a bag in the freezer. When I need the taste of basil, I add one or two cubes to whatever I'm cooking.

Basil is used in many Mediterranean and Thai dishes. It can be used in pasta sauce, pesto, bread, dips, and sauces.

Medicinally, basil has many therapeutic qualities. Taken internally, it aids digestion, lowers blood sugar levels, and produces neurological calm. It is an anti-inflammatory useful in the relief of arthritis, rheumatism, and even bowel inflammation. Basil has antibacterial properties and is an effective treatment for colds, flu, and herpes viruses.

The fresh leaves of basil are very high in antioxidants, and essential oil produced from basil is effective externally, protecting the skin from free radical damage and the potential of skin cancer.

Peppermint *(Mentha piperita)*

Were you ever given a peppermint candy when you had nausea on a long car ride? Peppermint is widely used to flavor candy, gum, mints, cookies, cakes, and even ice cream.

Peppermint is known to relieve nausea and is an effective remedy for indigestion. A cup of peppermint tea can treat the effects of a common cold, soothing a sore throat, loosening phlegm, and clearing sinus passages.

Used externally, peppermint is effective in treating inflammation and itchiness, easing cramps and spasms, and stimulating circulation. Menthol, a derivative of peppermint, is used in topical cold remedies like Vicks VapoRub, and in ointments that relieve muscle pain, arthritis, rheumatism, and neuralgia.

Always grow peppermint in a pot or container, because it spreads rapidly, with roots creeping underground, and can be really pervasive. A hardy perennial, it likes full sun and a nutrient-rich soil that can hold water.

Lemon Balm *(Melissa officinalis)*

Another fast-spreading herb, lemon balm is best grown in containers or pots. This hardy perennial likes well-drained soil and moderate amounts of sunlight.

Like mint, lemon balm is often used in the preparation of alcoholic drinks. The liqueurs Benedictine and Chartreuse are both flavored with lemon balm. Found in a wide variety of herbal tea preparations, lemon balm is highly scented and very tasty, but it gets bitter if steeped too long. It is widely used in cooking, and complements fish, chicken, fruit salads, and vegetables. Chopped finely, it is added to green salads and used in salad dressings. Lemon balm leaves are often candied and used in fine baking.

Called a "balm," lemon balm is known to relieve depression, dispel anxiety, and generally improve mood. It is known to relieve tension and restlessness. Recent research suggests that lemon balm helped to stimulate the memory in young adults and Alzheimer's patients.

Enjoying Your Golden Years

Choose a few herbs to start with, and plan your ideal golden years garden. Incorporate several of the common herbs mentioned here, focusing on those that you like, use, or could benefit from healthwise.

Though aging brings changes to the body and mind, many of the effects of aging can be lessened by a golden years garden. In addition to the therapeutic effects of using natural herbal remedies, there are also a lot of positive side effects to the exercise required in daily garden maintenance. Regular physical activity promotes strength, flexibility, balance, and increased mobility, all of which lessen the risk of falling. Exercise can help to stave off osteopenia and osteoporosis and improve bone density. It can help reduce cholesterol and lessen the risk of diabetes and obesity. Exercise lowers blood pressure and reduces the risk of a stroke. Best of all, regular exercise has been shown to increase feelings of well-being and improve mood.

A golden years garden can help make life taste great, treat minor ailments, and relieve some of the effects of aging. So start planning, designing, and dreaming, and this spring, get out and enjoy your golden years garden.

Invaders in the Garden

☙ by Elizabeth Barrette ❧

A s gardeners, we often choose to move plants to areas where they do not grow naturally. When taken outside their natural habitat—and especially outside the reach of the controls with which they evolved— they can spread so rapidly that they cause problems. Some herbs just have aggressive habits in general. Even if they are not officially counted as invasive, they may have similar effects on a local scale and respond to some of the same remedies. These are important concerns in planning or maintaining an herb garden. To a lesser extent, they also influence buying herbs, if you want to avoid supporting practices that worsen problems with invasive plants.

What Does "Invasive" Mean?

"Invasive" describes a plant that is not native to the problem area and that is spreading out of control in a way that causes problems. Some native plants grow aggressively, but do not count as invasive in their home range. They are prone to become invasive if moved elsewhere, and are better left in their natural habitat. Some plants spread more slowly or are downright difficult to propagate. Even if moved elsewhere, they are less likely to spread so fast that they create difficulties.

Therefore, "invasive" is a purely contextual description. A plant may be counted as invasive in some areas but not others. Wherever you live, you need to check the list of invasive species for your home, and ideally the surrounding areas. This will help reduce the opportunity of species spreading with human assistance.

Invasive plants share some common features, although not every species will have all of these.

Invasive Plants Reproduce in Large Numbers

This may include producing many seeds, or sprouting new plants from fragments of the original.

Invasive Plants Spread Fast and Far

They may have windblown seeds, buoyant seeds, hooked parts to catch on animal fur, delicious fruit, or beautiful flowers that make humans want to grow them. Some have enthusiastic features such as seedpods that pop and fling seeds a long distance.

Invasive Plants Outcompete Other Plants

They usually grow faster and may have denser growth that crowds out the competition. Some invasive plants secrete chemicals that discourage or even kill other plants. Some devour nutrients, although a few invasives are actually "bandage" plants that help heal disturbed areas by drawing up nutrients from deep soil. Look at how much damaged earth there is, and you can see why those helper plants can spread so far.

Invasive Plants Are Very Tough and Versatile
Some specialize in a type of habitat that few plants can tolerate. Others adapt to a wide range of soil and climate conditions.

Invasive Plants Spread Vigorously
Outside Their Home Range
Invasive plants spread vigorously once outside their home range where natural pests and other controls keep them from dominating. They may be unpalatable or even toxic to a majority of herbivores. Some have very high disease resistance, another factor that may appeal to humans.

If you encounter species with these features, don't plant them, even if they do something you otherwise like. They are more trouble than they're worth, and in some areas they may be illegal. Check to make sure plants you buy are not invasive, because some are still for sale. Watch for descriptions such as "thrives in poor soil," "drought-resistant," "good ground-cover," and "low maintenance." Unless those apply to native plants, they can mean trouble. The recognition of invasive species is an ongoing process. For maximum safety, only plant species native to your area. Since most of us want more variety than that, first try to find a native species that does what you want, and only plant an exotic species if necessary.

Invasive plants cause many problems. First, they take up space, light, water, and nutrients that other plants need. Because they grow and spread so fast, they tend to crowd out milder native species. Since they don't belong there, native insects and animals find them less useful or even harmful. So they diminish the habitat, sometimes a little, other times so much that it becomes almost a wasteland. Kudzu is famous for turning formerly healthy forests into something that looks like a shambling row of monsters draped in strangling vines and leaves. Invasive species can also damage infrastructure, such as by clogging water pipes or tearing down utility poles. It costs millions of dollars each year in attempts to control invasives, repair the damage done, and educate people about them.

Herbs That Can Be Invasive

Some popular herbs tend to be aggressive in the garden. Outside their native habitat, they may turn invasive. If you choose to grow these, take precautions to avoid future problems.

Artemisia includes an assortment of closely related herbs. Mugwort (*Artemisia vulgaris*) is used to wash scrying bowls and mirrors. Wormwood (*Artemisia absinthium*) is used for pesticides and repellents, but also for flavoring absinthe and other beverages. Silver Mound and Dusty Miller are two of the smaller, tamer cultivars usually grown as ornamentals. All types of artemisia serve as a symbol of the moon. They have gray-green leaves. Mugwort can grow over six feet tall, but most other varieties reach only two to three feet high. Due to their bitter taste and toxic compounds, many types of artemisia have few herbivores that will eat them. Deep, woody roots make artemisia difficult to eradicate, and the small seeds propagate readily. Grow this herb in containers, deadhead it, and/or treat it as an annual.

Basil is a leafy, bright green herb used to flavor sauces and salads. It grows approximately one foot tall. Plenty of insects and animals enjoy eating basil, but it can produce masses of tiny seeds that scatter everywhere. Don't allow it to flower, as that isn't good for the flavor anyhow. You can pick leaves individually, or just cut the whole plant to make pesto.

Bee balm grows about two feet tall, with a bushy shape and dark green leaves. Bees like the pink and purple flowers, while hummingbirds prefer the scarlet ones. The leaves and flowers are used in salads; the leaves are also used in cooked foods. Medicinally, bee balm treats colds and many other complaints. It can spread by seed and by creeping rhizomes. It is susceptible to a mold, so it can be controlled with wet bark mulch. Growing it in a container is also a good idea.

Comfrey is a tall plant with fuzzy green leaves and tiny pink to blue bell-shaped flowers. It attracts bees. It draws nutrients up from deep soils and makes a terrific compost mulch; you can mow or slash-and-drop it in place. The drawback is that once you put it somewhere, there it stays. It can propagate from the tiniest fragment of root. So if you need to kill it, don't dig. Smother it with a massive layer of something impenetrable, or use herbicide.

Cranberry is primarily a bog plant, although some types grow in drier areas. The low shrub has leathery green leaves. The sour red berries make excellent sauce and tea. Cranberry assists the female reproductive system and the urinary system. Birds may eat the fruit and spread this plant in favorable habitats. To kill cranberry, pull it out of soft soil, or cut back the stems and then use herbicide or a weedburner torch.

Daylily produces slender pale green leaves and large flowers. The wild type is yellow to orange, but many cultivars in other colors also exist. The flowers are edible, and are usually fried in batter. Daylily has thick, fleshy roots excellent for retaining soil on slopes—but that is also how it spreads. Control daylily with root barriers. It can survive in small harsh places like road medians, or slopes where nothing else will grow.

Echinacea is a beautiful prairie plant with pink to purple daisylike flowers. Cultivated varieties have more colors. Butterflies love the flowers in bloom. Finches and other birds love the seeds, and drop them everywhere to sprout. Medicinally, echinacea boosts the immune system. To control the plant, pick off the flowers before they set seeds. This plant will survive hot, dry conditions that will kill most other plants.

Feverfew has lovely frilly leaves and cute little daisylike flowers. It's popular for treating headaches. However, it produces a great many seeds. Grow it in a container if you don't want to spend a lot of time picking off all the flowers.

Horseradish is a scraggly plant grown primarily for its large root with a hot flavor. It also has a variety of internal and external medicinal uses. Grow it in a container. If it's in the ground, dig it up very thoroughly—the roots are edible, after all—because a large enough piece of root can regrow. For this reason, this plant is difficult to remove entirely once established.

Lamb's ear puts out soft, fuzzy gray-green leaves. They are among the most popular "toilet paper" plants in the wilderness; they have also been used as bandages. They are often grown in herb gardens or children's gardens just because they feel nice to touch. Lamb's ear can seed and creep, so remove the flowers and keep it in a firmly edged border. Because it grows in rocky habitat, it's susceptible to too much moisture; wet mulch can kill it.

Lemon balm belongs to the mint family and is as enthusiastic as its relatives. It grows one to two feet high, with crinkly dark green leaves. It has a brilliant lemon fragrance and flavor, used in potpourri and tea. Its many tiny flowers attract bees quite strongly. Grow lemon balm in a pot, preferably on a patio or other surface. It rambles vigorously by seed or spreading clumps. Smothering is an effective way to get rid of it.

Marjoram belongs to the Origanum genus and is related to oregano. Wild marjoram (*Origanum vulgaris*) can be extremely invasive, creeping and seeding; there are domesticated cultivars sold as Greek oregano. Sweet marjoram (*Origanum majorana*) is more genteel, but buy it from a reputable supplier. There are many varieties, which resemble one other closely, and it's easy to get the wrong thing even if you're trying to be careful. Sweet marjoram has a delicate, spicy-sweet flavor that works splendidly with mild foods such as eggs or chicken. It's a good idea to grow plants from this group in containers, just in case you wind up with something more aggressive than you wanted.

Mint spans a wide range of sizes, leaf shapes, and flavors but usually has a fresh smell and taste. Most mints grow one to two feet tall. Their tiny flowers attract bees. Mint makes excellent tea and jelly. Medicinally, it soothes the digestive system. It also tries to take over the entire yard, by tiny seeds and extremely vigorous surface runners. Grow it in containers on a patio, or better yet a wall. One advantage is that the fancy flavored mints—which come in everything from apple to cinnamon—are almost always more delicate and less vigorous than the basics like spearmint or peppermint. Pennyroyal is a type of mint used as a pest repellent, but is very prone to rambling. Never mow mint; that can make it spread worse. It creeps past most barriers or smothering agents. It can be dug up if you're willing to work for it, because the roots run wide rather than deep. But if it gets loose, consider using herbicide.

Raspberry is a woody, thorny briar that produces delicious berries. The leaves make excellent tea that can relieve menstrual cramps. Raspberries spread by surface runners, tall arching canes, and birds distributing the fruit. This combination can be impossible to control. The canes can be dug up. Netting helps keep the birds out of your edible berries. Yellow raspberries tend to lack the arching canes and are the most controllable. Red raspberries are less aggressive than black ones. The wild-type black raspberries often have the best disease resistance and splendid flavor...and will obey no law but their own. Plant at your own risk.

Soapwort has airy foliage and white to pink flowers. Its root produces saponin for washing. It spreads through a creeping root system. Grow it in containers. Ideally, choose a less aggressive variety, like Bressingham.

Sweet woodruff is a low-growing ground cover for shady areas and spreads by creeping. It has whorls of dark green leaves. Sweet woodruff is traditionally used to flavor wine. It can be contained with solid borders, or kept to manageable growth by mowing.

Tansy is a huge ferny plant with brilliant yellow flowers. Butterflies like the flowers. Tansy is somewhat toxic, and is used in insect repellents. It produces many seeds, and also spreads from the roots. Grow it in containers on a patio. It's very hard to pull up, and a nuisance to deadhead because there are so many flowers. To get rid of it, cut the plant close to the ground and then use herbicide.

Thyme comes in many varieties, all with a spicy-musky flavor that goes well with many foods. The white to pink flowers attract bees. Choose a bushy, upright variety, such as English thyme, or one of the more delicate lemon thymes. Those are usually safe to plant in the ground. Ramblers like creeping thyme and mother of thyme can get loose. Keep them in containers or firmly edged borders.

Wild strawberry produces tiny, exquisitely flavored red berries and treble leaves. It's a charming woodland plant. It spreads by surface runners and can get into places where it's not welcome. For best results, mulch around it and remove the runners. It can also get into new areas if birds spread the seeds. Put netting over the berry patch to discourage this.

Yarrow grows about one to two feet tall, with spicy, ferny leaves. It produces large panicles of flowers in white, yellow, or red tones. Butterflies love them. Yarrow is popular as a wide-spectrum healing herb, so it appears in many blends. The flowers produce a lot of seeds, which like disturbed areas, but they require light to germinate. Deep mulch discourages this.

How to Control Invasive Plants

There are three broad ways to get rid of invasive plants: mechanical, biological, and chemical. Mechanical methods remove the plant by cutting, pulling, digging, smothering, etc. Biological methods involve introducing a natural enemy of the invasive species, such as an insect that eats only that plant. Chemical methods feature herbicides and other substances that destroy plants. These can be used selectively if aggressive garden plants threaten to get out of bounds.

Mechanical methods are reliable and minimally destructive to the environment. However, they are more labor-intensive than other methods. Some methods are not ideal for obnoxious plants with thorns, contact toxins, or other hazards. Many plants can simply be pulled up by the roots or dug out. Woody plants may need to be cut; small ones can be mowed. Never mow or dig anything that spreads by vegetative propagation! Mowing mint can fling viable runners clear across your yard. Digging comfrey just chops the roots into dozens of little plants. "Try mulching with concrete blocks" has been said as a joke, but a heavy layer of something will in fact kill plants underneath it. Blocks, bricks, newspapers, plastic—use what you have. A thick enough layer of mulch, or better yet raw manure, also works. Chicken, horse, and sheep manure are "hot" and will kill plants when applied fresh; but after the manure breaks down, the ground is safe and fertile for replanting. Heat kills plants, too, such as with a "weed-burner" torch or boiling water.

Biological methods are less work, but are erratic in effect and sometimes cause more trouble. You have to find a very good match between the plant and what will eat or kill it. But for those invasives where that is already available, it's a good bet. It works with nature to control nature.

Chemical methods require moderate work and are expensive, but can be used over wider areas more efficiently. You can spray a whole field if you have to—if it's been taken over by something horrid—and then replant later. Chemicals also work well for spot-killing of noxious plants, things you don't want to touch or just can't quite reach. An excellent way of removing woody brush is to cut it close to the ground and then spray the cut stumps with herbicide. The main drawback is that chemicals are nasty; they're bad for the environment and for people. You have to be very careful using them. However, nature has tricks of her own! There are a few plants that produce their own herbicides, like black walnut trees. Take the soft outer hulls off the nuts once they turn black, and use that as herbicidal mulch. Almost nothing will survive it. This is best for creating a barrier around aggressively spreading plants, or for preventing plants from growing someplace you want barren.

Remains of invasive plants should be burned or taken to a landfill. Don't put them in a brush pile or compost heap; they are just too stubborn. Some communities have services that will dispose of invasive remains for you, if there is a target plant causing serious problems locally.

However, not all control methods need to kill. Plants that are aggressive but not downright harmful may be contained for their useful qualities. First, choose bushy rather than creeping or spreading varieties (i.e., English thyme rather than mother of thyme) and other mild-mannered cultivars (Bressingham soapwort and many of the fancy-flavored mints are more delicate) to reduce the aggression level. For species that produce male and female flowers on separate plants or that are not self-fertile, keep only one sex or only one plant.

Next, put aggressive plants where they can't get into trouble easily. Grow them in pots on a patio, or sink lengths of pipe vertically into the garden soil. This works well for many herbs such as artemisia, creeping thyme, marjoram, mint, tansy, and wild strawberry. Use root barriers to block underground runners or spreading clumps of roots; these are long, thin pieces of metal or plastic that get pounded into the ground. Use solid borders such as concrete scallops to block surface runners.

Limit the plant's reach while it is growing. Harvest herbs early before they flower; with annuals you can just cut or pull the whole plant. This works great for some of the basils that will self-seed like mad if they like their habitat. Pick off flowers before they can set seed; deadheading works well on plants that produce many seeds, such as echinacea, lamb's ear, feverfew, and yarrow. Mow or shear harshly after flowering to control shallow-rooted plants, such as soapwort and sweet woodruff. Hoe or pull up seedlings and shoots to contain species like cranberry and daylily.

Finally, don't pamper aggressive plants; let them survive on their own. Avoid watering or fertilizing them. If they still misbehave, move them to a spot where nothing else will grow and they barely survive. This is a good way to cover bare spots in shade or baking hot spaces between a house and sidewalk.

Enchanting Primroses

❧ by James Kambos ❧

It's March. The frost is still in the ground, but the day is bright and sunny. I can feel the pulse of spring. It's time to take my first walk of the season around my garden. I walk past a shrub border filled with mountain laurel, rhododendron, and deutzia. Most of my garden is still cloaked in the neutral tones of late winter, but as I turn a corner I come upon a patch of bright colors. My primroses are blooming! Their white, red, and yellow flowers are held on short stems in clusters above a rosette of crinkled green leaves. The chilly March wind still has the bite of winter in it, but the cheery flowers of my primroses tell me spring—and summer—are close at hand.

Primroses are charming plants that have been grown in gardens and found in the wild for centuries. They belong to the family Primulaceae and the genus *Primula*. The common name primrose is derived from the Latin *primula*, which means "first" or "early," and they are among the first flowers to brighten the garden in late winter or early spring.

Herbalists have used all parts of the primrose over the years for treating ailments such as coughs, arthritis, migraines, and sleeplessness.

Primroses deserve at least a small spot in every herb garden. They're easy to care for, come in many colors, and, as you'll see, have a rich history in folklore. I planted my primroses on the north side of my house at the base of some yew shrubs, and they've bloomed reliably for years with very little help from me.

Growing Conditions and Botanical Information

There are over four hundred species of primroses and about one thousand hybrids. They can be found in the wild throughout Asia, Europe, and North America. Basically, primroses grow in moist, woodsy locations, but there are a few species that prefer rocky hillsides. Most primroses you'll encounter at nurseries and garden centers like slightly acidic, rich humus soil, moisture, and some shade. Primroses are usually hardy in USDA zones 5 to 9. They may droop in heat and humidity, but they bounce back when the weather cools.

Primroses can range in height from six to twelve inches and about eighteen inches wide. Some "candelabra" types send up flower stalks twelve to twenty-four inches high from a base of leaves. Foliage is usually small and oval and can be crinkly or fuzzy in texture.

To plant primroses in your garden, select a lightly shaded area. The north side of your house, around a tree, or at the base of acid-loving shrubs such as rhododendron would be ideal. Work up the soil and add leaf mold or compost. Plant so the crown is level with the soil. You may plant them in mass or tuck here and there around shrubs. I've also seen them mingled in with hostas and ferns, which is very charming. Water until they're established; once settled in, I seldom water them, except during extreme drought.

Primroses aren't invasive, but some do seed themselves and form lovely colonies. I usually plant primroses in the spring, and they can be planted while blooming. Clumps can be divided in spring or fall.

Experts say primroses may be damaged by snails or slugs, but I've found primroses to be rugged and pest-free. I'm also happy to tell you I have never had deer or rabbits eat my primroses!

Growing Primroses as Houseplants

Primroses can make attractive houseplants. To be successful, keep temperatures cool, no higher than 65 degrees; keep plants away from fireplaces, woodstoves, and other heat sources. Light should be bright but indirect, and soil should be moderately moist, with good drainage. For an attractive indoor display, try placing them together with African violets. I should mention here that some nurseries sell a small flowering houseplant commonly called Cape Primrose, but it is not a primrose. It is actually a *Streptocarpus*. This is a very desirable and attractive plant to group with your primroses, but just be aware it isn't a primrose.

When the weather warms, you may set your potted primroses outdoors for the summer in a sheltered location. Bring them indoors at the end of the growing season before temperatures cool too much.

If you wish to place your primroses permanently in the garden, in early spring transition your plants slowly outside—setting them on a porch is a good idea—then follow the outdoor planting instructions I've given, and you should be fine.

In late winter you may see beautiful displays of primroses in full bloom in many stores. These are hybrids or "supermarket" varieties bred for the mass market. Most experts agree that these aren't as hardy as other primroses, but they make lovely houseplants and I've had good luck placing them into the perennial border by following a few easy steps. First, remove any decorative wrapping that probably covered the pot, as this will aid drainage. Don't fertilize, since this has already been done by the grower. Follow the other instructions I've given for primrose houseplants. After flowering, in the early spring, plant in a sheltered outdoor location such as near a foundation or beneath shrubs. I've done this and have had them return for several years.

Primrose Varieties

Out of the hundreds of primrose species and even more hybrids, I've selected a few here that you might like to try. Most are hardy in USDA zones 5 to 9. Check with your nursery for specific gardening instructions. If any nursery says they're selling "wild" primroses, check to be sure that they've responsibly collected the seed and raised these primroses instead of plundering the woodland to obtain the plants.

Primula acaulis

These are five to eight inches in height and retain the qualities of the old strains, but are more hardy. They come in white, pink, blue, and red. One of my favorites is Harbinger. This white variety is ideal for an heirloom garden; it was discovered in the 1880s. Acaulis are frequently called English primroses (*P. vulgaris*).

Primula elatior

This is the true "oxlip" primrose used by herbalists years ago to cure coughs by extracting a substance from the roots. The flowers produced a relaxing herbal tea. Found in damp wooded areas, its creamy yellow flowers bloom before the leaves appear. It originated in southern Scandinavia and the British Isles.

Primula japonica

This is the Japanese primrose, which is a candelabra-type primrose. It sends up flower stalks about a foot high, rising above crinkled green foliage. The flowers, which are pink, red, or white, bloom in whorls along the upper part of the stem. This primrose likes moist places—along a stream, pond, or wetland would be perfect—and attracts butterflies. It blooms later, in May or perhaps June, and if it's happy, it will form a nice colony.

Primula juliae

This primrose is named Julia after the Russian naturalist who discovered it in 1900 growing wild in the Caucasus Mountains. It's a ground-cover type, reaching about two inches tall. The flowers are purple/pink, with a yellow eye. The pollen is frequently used to create other hybrids. This species is not easy to find but is worth the effort.

Primula polyanthus

These are not English primroses. Instead, these are usually the hybrid primroses that come in a large array of colors. The primroses you're likely to find in supermarkets and large retail garden centers are probably some type of polyanthus. They are bred quickly for fast flowering and aren't as hardy as other strains, but they are beautiful and inexpensive and I have had good luck with them. Even if they aren't long-lived for you, they make a nice annual and are pretty when planted with pansies.

Primula veris

Growing throughout much of Europe and Asia, this is the true "cowslip" strain of primrose. It's sometimes confused with *P. vulgaris* (English primrose), but *P. veris* grows in more open areas such as meadows and pastures. The word *veris* means "spring," and it does bloom in April/May, with yellow flowers. It's known by other folk names, such as Herb Peter and Fairy Cups. This is another small, low-growing variety, six to eight inches high. Its leaves are sometimes used as a salad green. Cowslip makes a wonderful addition to a wildflower border.

Evening Primroses

This is a good time to mention a word of warning about evening primroses. For starters, they are *not* primroses at all. They belong to the genus *Oenothera* and are invasive. I spent one summer removing them entirely from my garden. The appearance is quite different: it either forms a spreading mat or sends up flower stalks four feet high, with bright yellow flowers. So if you come across the name online or in a catalog, don't be fooled. It's not a primrose.

Herbal Uses of Primrose

The primrose has been a favorite medicinal plant at least since the days of ancient Rome. Remedies using substances obtained from the roots were used in wet compresses to relieve arthritis and paralysis. Salves containing the leaves and flowers were said to heal wounds and burns and soften the skin.

Teas made from the flowers were used to treat migraines and anxiety and as a non-addictive sleep aid. Today, extracts from the roots may be added to cough remedies, since the plant is a good expectorant. In cuisine, some cooks in Europe add primrose to wine, vinegar, and jam.

Before using primrose medically or in food, check first with a health professional. Primrose shouldn't be used by people who are sensitive to aspirin and who are on blood thinners. In some people, primroses can cause skin irritation when touched.

The Primrose in Folklore

For such a small plant, the primrose holds an important place in history. It was believed that the ancient Scandinavian goddess Freya used the primrose as the "key" to open the gates for spring to begin. In Eastern Europe, it was thought that if a girl was the first to find a primrose on Easter, she would marry that year. In old English lore, primroses were believed to attract fairies and that the fairies would live in them, especially when it rained.

Primroses are ruled by the planet Venus. As such, the plant and oil derived from it were used in many love spells and sachets.

It took Shakespeare to give the primrose an enduring place in the field of literature. In *Hamlet*, Shakespeare coined the phrase "primrose path" in the words Ophelia spoke to her brother:

> *Do not, as some ungracious pastors do,*
> *Show me the steep and thorny way to heaven;*
> *Whiles, like a puff'd and reckless libertine,*
> *Himself the primrose path of dalliance treads;*
> *And recks not his own rede.*

We may never know why Shakespeare chose this metaphor, but Ophelia is warning her brother to take his own advice and not follow the easy path of sin.

By the Victorian era, however, the primrose was a highly favored magical plant. Planted near doorsteps, it was used to attract fairies so that they'd bless the house. And when worn or carried, it was a symbol of status and wealth.

Few herbs offer such a combination of beauty, low maintenance, and rich history. To create some magic of your own, try planting a few of these enchanting flowers. Use them to brighten a shady nook in your herb garden. Or, better yet, plant them to create your own primrose path.

For Further Information

Visit www.americanprimrosesociety.org, the American Primrose Society's website. It has a wealth of information about primrose plants, seeds, and local chapters you may join.

Cultivating Curry for Health, Wealth, and History

❧ by Esthamarelda McNevin ❧

Ask any health guru in America and they'll tell you that in the West we've gone "curry crazy," as it is commonly dubbed. After nearly five hundred years of war, colonialism, and trade with the civilizations of the East, Asian curry has finally swept the globe. Curry-spiced dishes are curative foods with healthful properties, resulting in "Curry Friday" and other wholesome gastronomic trends. Curry dishes are also an amazing way to bring flavor and flair to all cuisine styles—vegan, vegetarian, and carnivorous alike.

The exotic blanket term *curry* pays homage to the many beloved and regionally spiced meals served throughout Asia. It was the overeager

entrepreneurial British colonialists who first marketed blended spice powders from India, calling them *madras*. These were combined to quickly re-create favorite Indian cuisines back home. As a result, curry spice powder became the ubiquitous flavor of globalization, filled with a wide range of other seasonings, in addition to actual curry leaf, such as garlic, asafetida, fenugreek, fennel, ginger, cinnamon, cardamom, mace, and red pepper powders. It's true: no two curries are alike. So especially in the West, it can be hard to untangle the true South Asian herb from the medicinal Mediterranean shrub, used commonly by medieval monks to treat warts!

Regalia, Pomp, and Circumstance

Murraya koenigii, or *kadi patta* in Hindi, is a modest queen of the Rutaceae, or citrus family, a beloved and cultivated native species found throughout the Indian subcontinent. She is a curry to conquer all curries! Her classification name honors the Baltic botanist and physician Johann Gerhard König, who worked tirelessly as a naturalist for the British East India Trading Company, the strong arm of Western Imperial colonialism throughout Asia. König was posted to the Nawab of Arcot in southern India during the 1770s. Once there, he helped to catalogue and document the pharmacology of the diverse ecosystem of the Carnatic region. As a result of his extensive botanical writing and research, he became one of the foremost academics and translators of Vedic Hindu texts. König wrote extensively on daily life, Western medicine, and the classical Hindu systems of health and healing.

His namesake, *Murraya koenigii*, is an unimposing tree that grows four to six meters (thirteen to twenty feet) tall and is reminiscent of her distant cousin, the mountain ash. With a trunk that grows up to forty centimeters (sixteen inches) in diameter, the leaves and fruit of the curry tree are prized as key ingredients in many dishes throughout South and East Asia. They impart a sweet and subtle citrus flavor that is suggestive of thyme; the leaves are often used as a key ingredient in stewed and pan-fried dishes. The leaves themselves excrete saccharine essential oils and are aromatic and pinnate, with eleven to twenty-one leaflets per stem; each leaflet grows two to four centimeters long and one to two centimeters broad. The bursting clusters of flowers are small, white, and intoxicatingly fragrant. *Murraya koenigii* also produces small early-autumn berries that form orange or red, ripening to black. They are shiny and edible, with a distinct flavor reminiscent of a honeyed resin, although the seeds are poisonous and should never be consumed.

Thriving Vedic Medicine

For many Hindus, curry leaves are an important feature of Ayurvedic medicine and ritual ceremonialism. They act as a substitute for *tulsi* (holy basil) when used in home, land, and shrine blessings. When used in food, the dried leaves (both crushed and whole) are valued for their aroma, although the flavor is inferior to garden-picked green leaves. Curry is often used fresh when included in Vedic healing poultices. It acts as an antimicrobial and anti-inflammatory medicine, preventing the spread of infection and disease.

The strong association of curry with health has ensured its position as an omnipresent spice in its native South Asian tropics. The Indian curry tree is also recognized as "sweet neem," in contrast to *Azadirachta indica*, or "bitter neem," which is also a common pharmacological source within Ayurvedic medicine.

Both are valued in Indian cultures and cuisines because they are ecologically abundant and closely linked with health and religion. Curry especially is viewed as a beneficial spice and a dietary supplementing crop as well as an ornamental hedge for parks, orchards, plantations, and shared gardens.

As a healthful food, curry spice is treasured for its ability to lower cholesterol and glycemic index levels. Consequently, the leaves of the *Murraya koenigii* are considered an instrumental part of the equatorial diet throughout much of tropical Asia. The species even thrives in the northern foothills of the Himalayas and is often cultivated along with other viable crops like sugar and tea. The curry tree is so beloved that it has traveled with Mother India's immigrants as they've journeyed and settled across the globe.

An Exotic Import

Cultivating curry is easy-peasy on the subcontinent, as verdant and diverse as India's tropical ecosystem is. In the West, however, curry planted from seed is a specially cultivated and often pampered jewel of well-tended greenhouses and lavish southern garden patios. Though many rush to buy curry from the nearest Indian grocer or food importer, small curry trees can be cultivated from seed and are especially hearty when grown from clippings, so much so that they will take off even if left to their own devices in water! This is because *Murraya koenigii* grows effortlessly in the humid monsoon belt of tropical Asia, where she is near enough to the equator to be protected from harsh snows and seasonal dieback. Most cultivators in the north are forced to turn to indoor methods to stave off pests as well as the weather conditions that wreak havoc on tender pinnate leaves.

Like any other royal, curry is particular about her soil. The young trees especially need a warm and humid environment with good drainage, but thrive best when they receive water both at the soil level and also through a humid atmosphere. I'm a committed fan of mimicking the ecosystem of origin when it comes to the cultivation of any living thing, so I follow the advice of many gardeners from Asia who recommend a specific routine. It's a method that requires compassionate devotion, but if you do love a good curry, it is well worth the work.

The common method includes watering at the base of the tree and misting the leaves once each week until the wet monsoon season. From June to September, trees need mist and water once daily. This is essential for leaf and flower development, especially if they are often picked or over-pruned. After the fruits have been produced and harvested, from October to December, *Murraya koenigii* must observe a post-monsoonal half-season, just as they do in southern India. Mimicking this natural phase demands attention to detail and watering only once a week. At this stage, they need little to no misting— just every other week or so, nothing more. Such an essential change simulates the dry, arid conditions that often encourage slow growth and woody fiber development in the trunk and branches.

To Pamper a Monarch

To cultivate this exotic treasure, a rich and diverse supply of nutrients is recommended. Curry trees flourish in acidic soil. They love freshly cracked and crushed eggshell, used tea leaves, coffee grounds, Epsom salts, potash, diluted seaweed emollition, and black loam. Yet *Murraya koenigii* should be fed only from June to September and should never receive nutrients during their dormant period from late October to early March. The most important thing for potted curry trees is to have healthy and well-maintained soil.

Layering the bottom of a large tree pot or garden bed with bulky rocks, gravel, peat moss, and black sand is ideal. This provides drainage when it is placed under three feet or more of healthy soil, and such techniques give a moist underlayer for roots to reach toward. Employing such planting methods for trees additionally increases fruit yield, because it helps the soil retain the heat of the day. Salvaged warmth facilitates the absorption of more nutrients by lengthening daily growth cycles during the hours of dawn and dusk. Methods like this stimulate new shoot and branch development by encouraging leaf production with fertilizers. Proper layering during planting maintains healthy growth by also giving nutrients a "sweet spot" of sand and peat moss to settle into until the tree is able to absorb them.

Murraya koenigii is at her best in full sun, but only once young trees have developed branches. In areas where frost occurs, the trees must be insulated or brought in for the winter. Clippings and starts from seed require delicate care and attention to detail because they thrive best in moist, partial shade, as one would expect of a lush tropical species. Once mature, curry trees will grow prolifically and spread new shoots, or "suckers," as they age. Pinch-pruning is beneficial for growth year round. Any harvesting should be done as needed. Fresh leaves should be used immediately as medicine or for cooking because they only keep for a matter of days, and the dried leaves have a short and temperamental shelf life of six to eight months.

No Two Curries, Indeed!

In sharp contrast, Italian curry, *Helichrysum italicum*, is a hearty annual shrub native to the dry sand and rocky landscapes of the sun-drenched Mediterranean. The leaves are favored for their healing medicinal value and are cherished in regionally celebrated salves, medicines, and robust wild game stews. Italian curry is more widely known as rosemary's tussie-mussie cousin, because its golden clusters of bright yellow flowers keep both their color and form with age, like any good lady should. Accordingly, they are favored in wreaths and dried flower arrangements, and to our Victorian forebears they were equated with everlasting light, agelessness, consciousness, and knowledge.

Italian curry has been cultivated since the days of early Greece. Its name comes from the Greek *Helisso*, meaning "to turn around," alongside *Chrysos*, meaning "gold." Though native to Africa, it has been used extensively throughout the Mediterranean as an anti-inflammatory. The Xhosa and Zulu tribes in Africa considered it sacred and burned the leaves of the plant to honor and appease the spirits present in their tribal ceremonies. Even today, *Helichrysum italicum* continues to keep the demons at bay, as it is still a notable and effective treatment for common cold and flu symptoms, including fever, cough, headache, colic, and open sores.

The shrub itself is hearty, with a woody base that reaches 60 to 90 centimeters (23 to 36 inches) in height, and can prolifically overtake any dry area of the garden, transforming it into a lush herbal oasis of healing and survival. A member of the Asteraceae, or Compositate, family, Italian curry is a distant cousin of marigold, echinacea, and chrysanthemum. The small needle-shaped leaves grow one to two centimeters along bushy base stalks. Though reminiscent of rosemary, it is the rich spicy aroma that makes *Helichrysum italicum* so easily mistaken for *Murraya koenigii*—not just because of the folk name alone!

The essential oil of the Italian curry shrub was of great significance to medieval medicine. It gained extensive popularity as an antifungal treatment for warts and sores. This was due largely to its ability to promote healthy tissue repair and reduce skin discoloration. The leaves and stem are still used to improve skin conditions and increase circulatory function. Though not entirely safe for women who may be expecting, it is safe enough to use on infants and children. The Department of Botany at the University of Pretoria in South Africa has found it to be especially effective against herpes simplex virus type 1 (HSV-1) in vitro. Recently, Italian curry has also been used in naturopathic medicine with some success. Many have found it effective in the fight against liver cancer and disease. Some modern herbalists even profess its powers as a practical aphrodisiac.

Mirror, Mirror, on the Wall …

Both varieties of curry offer a healthful and flavorful look at herbal medicine and take me back to that time-honored tradition of "mother's home-cooked medicine." Both *Murraya koenigii* and *Helichrysum italicum* are revered curative foods that have long been incorporated into the human diet for their beneficial and supplemental qualities. Like all herbs that make it into the pot, there is a distinct flavor and purpose to every curry, regardless of which one is reached for. The real benefit of hashing out any identity crisis is the wisdom of experience and experimentation. Even in our modern times, a mere shrubbery could dethrone no queen, even if *Helichrysum italicum* could heal the world. When it comes to curry, *Murraya koenigii*, with her pinnate floral regalia and equatorial pedigree, remains the true sovereign of the world of spices.

Curry Recipes

HRH Golden Curry

This is a mild curry dish that takes only 30 minutes to prepare. It is a simple way to make a homemade vegetarian meal for 4 to 6 people. Curry is a favored meal throughout Asia, and though some dishes are made with meat curry, it is more often kept vegan or vegetarian. This recipe teaches you how to make a healthy medicinal meal without letting a compound spice take all the fun out of it! Why use a store-bought curry when making one at home can be so magical and delicious? Enjoy!

  2 tablespoons canola oil

  1 teaspoon mustard seeds

  1 teaspoon sesame seeds

  1 fresh *Murraya koenigii* curry leaf

  1 pinch asafetida

  ¼ cup golden raisins

  1 jalapeño, all seeds removed and julienne-sliced

1. In a large wok or skillet, fry the ingredients listed above in oil on medium heat until the sesame and mustard seeds begin to pop. Do not overheat or brown the herbs or golden raisins, as this will impart a bitter flavor.

2. Add:

  1 onion, sliced into quarter wedges

  1 cup carrots, peeled and diced into small cubes

3. Cover with a lid and let simmer until caramelized.

4. Add:

  2 teaspoons turmeric

  1 teaspoon fennel powder

  1 teaspoon fenugreek powder

  ¼ teaspoon nutmeg powder

  ¼ teaspoon ginger powder

  1 teaspoon mustard powder

  ¼ teaspoon cumin powder

  ¼ teaspoon coriander powder

  1 tablespoon garlic powder

5. Let simmer 1 minute, then add:

  2 cups broccoli

  1 cup zucchini, peeled and diced

  1 cup red bell peppers, cored and julienne-sliced

  2 cups mushrooms, sliced in quarters

  ½ cup vegetable stock

6. Simmer on medium-low heat for 10 minutes. Garnish with ½ cup chopped cilantro and 1 tablespoon sesame seeds.

7. Finally, salt to taste. This dish is at its best when served with jasmine rice.

Napoleon's Biryani

Rice is one of the jewels of the Orient that remains an African and Mediterranean staple. Italian cuisine rarely features rice if is not seasoned or flavored with herbs and spices of one variety or another. This simple rice dish is savory and healthful. With quick and easy prep work, it is ideal for a health-conscious family on the go, and meals like this one can help fend off the dreaded wiles of the cold and flu season. Enjoy!

> 3 tablespoons extra virgin olive oil
>
> 1 sprig *Helichrysum italicum* curry shrub
>
> 1 bay leaf
>
> 1 sprig fresh thyme
>
> 1 cup thinly sliced shallots
>
> 2 cloves garlic, finely diced
>
> 1 teaspoon mustard powder

1. In a large wok or skillet, fry the ingredients listed above in the oil on medium heat until the shallots begin to caramelize.

2. Add:

> 2 cups rice
>
> 5 sun-dried tomatoes, diced

3. Fry this on medium heat until the grains become opaque and begin to turn slightly golden.

4. Quickly add:

> 2½ cups chicken stock (from humanely treated local chickens, preferably)

5. Cover and let simmer on low for 15 minutes. This dish is best served hot with grilled fish and vegetables.

Resources

Griffin, Judith. *Mother Nature's Herbal: A Complete Guide for Experiencing the Beauty, Knowledge & Synergy of Everything That Grows*. Woodbury, MN: Llewellyn Publications, 2008.

Kowalchik, Claire, and William H. Hylton, eds. *Rodale's Illustrated Encyclopedia of Herbs*. Emmaus, PA: Rodale Press, 1987.

McGee, Harold. *On Food and Cooking: The Science and Lore of the Kitchen*. New York: Scribner, 2004.

Robuchon, Joël, and Prosper Montagné. *Larousse Gastronomique*. New York: Clarkson Potter, 2001.

Online Resources

BBC.com. "Food: Seasons." http://www.bbc.co.uk/food/seasons.

eHow.com. "How to Propagate Murraya." http://www.ehow.com /how_8585881_propagate-murraya.html.

Gardening Know How. "Curry Leaf Care—Growing Curry Leaf Tree in Your Garden." http://www.gardeningknow how.com/herb/growing-curry-leaf.htm.

Plant Cultures. "Curry Leaf—History." http://www.kew.org /plant-cultures/plants/curry_leaf_history.html.

Tarla Dalal. "Curry Leaves." http://www.tarladalal.com /glossary-curry-leaves-388i.

Wikipedia. "Curry Tree." http://en.wikipedia.org/wiki/Curry _Tree.

———. "*Helichrysum italicum*." http://en.wikipedia.org/wiki /Helichrysum_italicum.

A Joy to Come Home To: DIY Curb Appeal

ཤ by Emyme ཥ

It begins the first time you arrive home and the sight does not make you joyful. You think, "Maybe this place could use a little sprucing up." The next flicker comes while watching one of those home improvement television shows, the ones where they arrive in a neighborhood and overhaul the façades and front lawns/porches of several homes. You think, "Boy, I wish they would show up at my door." Finally, you notice a house along your usual commute actually getting an overhaul, be it full-scale or just a few potted plants by the front door. You think, "I can do this." And there you are: committing every summer weekend, and not just the evenings, to improving the curb appeal of your home on

the cheap. This is what happened to limited-budget me, a card-carrying member of both the Pennsylvania Horticultural Society and AARP.

When we purchased this home, the family pitched in one long weekend and overhauled the front, back, and side yards. Almost seven years later, the front is looking careworn and in need of more attention. My wish list includes what I can do myself and what has to be done by professionals. First on both lists is what I can afford. Complete replacement of all the hardscape—driveway, walkway, front porch? Out of the question. Removal of the broken, rickety front porch railing? Done.

The Final List
1. Remove and replace the planter, and some plants, under the front windows.
2. Replace the fencing, which faces the road, on both sides of the house.
3. Hire a lawn service, mowing and trimming only, to neaten up the appearance.
4. Paint the front door, and purchase or refurbish front porch décor.

June: Front Planter

The first thing to go is the dated planter under the windows of the master bedroom. Composed of bulky red bricks, it once was a tidy half-circle, but time has shifted the bricks, and weeds creep out of awkward spaces. Southern exposure brings full sun to the front all day. Four fast-growing evergreens had been planted for privacy and cooling. These are now just under six feet tall and provide the desired protection and shade. At the base of these trees grow three low yellowish evergreen bushes. I am embarrassed to say I have no idea of the names of this greenery—I did not pick them. However, they do provide an attractive backdrop of color, texture, and height to annuals. These evergreens and some thriving, aggressive, variegated vinca are the only perennials to really take hold in this bed. Just outside the planter, verging on the lawn, are three flat, prickly evergreen bushes and numerous stones.

With the help of four able-bodied young people, the flat, prickly bushes, stones, and planter are the first things to go. In their place goes a rectangular wooden enclosure originally intended for a vegetable garden. The footprint of the new planter is smaller, and most of the vinca is gone—although it may never truly be eliminated—and there is just enough room in the right front corner for a statue, a birdbath, or a sun-loving plant. The lawn will grow up to meet the planter in time, and now there is no curved bed around which to clumsily maneuver a lawn mower.

Potential mistake (or what I would do differently if I planned to stay in this house for more than three to five years): Use a more substantial material for the planter—the veggie garden structure will not last long.

July: Fencing

This job required professionals. A six-foot wooden stockade privacy fence encloses the back yard, and white vinyl privacy fences face the street on either side of the house. After seven-plus years, the elements have taken a toll, and the fence is dingy and claustrophobic. A fresh and airy look is created with white picket fencing. Along the western side yard are three large rose of Sharon bushes, the ownership of which is unclear. They create a cool and concealed space—which sounds lovely but is a potential problem due to a bedroom window facing those shrubs. Leaving that window open during the day never feels secure. With safety and privacy in mind, the new fence is moved forward to the front corner of the house. The rose of Sharon bushes arch gracefully over the pickets.

That reconfiguration makes the side yard now part of the back yard. Work remains to be done there; it is still full of the aforementioned stones and rocks. There is also a sad, scraggly azalea bush, which may revive when transplanted.

Potential mistake: I ordered an extra gate kit to provide an additional entrance to the back yard, but only one was sent, so I let it go.

August: Lawn Service

Over the years I have spoken proudly of mowing the lawn all by myself. Alas, the summers have become hotter and I have become slower. Keeping the edges neat has eluded me. So this year I hired a lawn service. After only two visits, the front is uniformly short and evenly edged. By the end of next summer I anticipate results I alone could never achieve.

Although this project is about front yard curb appeal, now that the side fencing is "see-through," the attractiveness of the back yard comes into play. What had started out as a little pile of limbs and some grass left to grow on its own had ended up as an eyesore of leaves and sticks and weeds too complicated and time-consuming for one woman of a certain age to handle—an experiment in naturalization gone awry. In just over one hour, three men accomplish what would have taken me three days (or more) to do, and they cart it all away. One can now see all the way to the back fence, neighbors do not have a messy yard to look down upon, and I discover that the critters that I thought lived in that habitat actually live underground—as evidenced by all the holes uncovered.

Potential mistake: Why did I wait so long to do this?

June, July, and August: Front Porch

The front porch is a rectangular concrete slab approximately fifteen by four feet. The brick-face front door to the left, the large window to the right, the shutters, and the brass carriage light create a typical early-1980s ranch-style façade. The thirty-year-old front door was replaced shortly after we moved in and painted a dun/mocha, providing a better look and draft protection. But it is time for a change—a big change. Cheerful pumpkin-yellow paint now highlights the door and brightens the porch. A salvaged metal lawn chair, painted glossy black, creates eye-catching contrast to the door, brick, white window trim and curtains, and musket brown shutters.

One of my favorite things to do is to peruse stores for slightly damaged or outdated lawn and garden decorations. During one of these outings I score a resin side table in the shape of a barrel, deep turquoise, with a crack and a chip. With a little spackle and two coats of the same warm yellow door paint, it is better than new. I also manage to talk down the price of a distressed-tan orphan bistro table. Chairs long gone, it matches the color of the siding. I add one brown and one green glazed, large, deeply discounted porcelain pot, filled with black-eyed Susan and bee balm. The final touch is an intentionally scruffy white, rectangular wooden planter filled with perennial ground covers. All of these items are light enough to be moved into a variety of configurations.

Potential mistake: None!

Earlier I wrote that I would commit to this project "every summer weekend." Well, it actually continued into the fall...

September: Tweaking the Final Product for the Fall

The air has turned crisp, and the hot, hot, HOT days of summer are behind us. The front yard is looking better than ever. The back yard, now visible through the new picket fence, looks better, but bare—a project for next summer. Time to decorate for Halloween. I set out for various family-owned farm markets and garden centers in my community. I pick up pumpkins and gourds, hay bale, and purple chrysanthemum at one place, corn stalk at another, decorative purple and black bow at the third, and ornamental peppers and cabbage at the last one.

After less than two hours of shopping and about an hour of arranging, the curb appeal project is finally complete. The pumpkins and gourds arranged on the hay bale and the black chair are decorated with purple fairy lights. Corn stalk is attached to the porch post, with ribbon in place and mums at the base. An inflatable witch ornament stands guard over all, and solar path lights lead the way to the front door.

The home improvement television show never did show up at my door, and there remain a few small, never-ending jobs to maintain this curb appeal: weeds grow, the mulch must be replaced almost every year, and the porch post needs freshening. But for a manageable cost, with some serious sweat and thanks to some rented "muscle," the house has been spruced up and I did it. It is a joy to arrive home now. Actually, that was the point: to create a sight that brings a smile when I pull in the driveway.

Overharvested Herbs and Their Substitutes

❧ by Diana Rajchel ❧

Endangered animals get all the attention, especially the cute ones. It's easy to motivate someone to save a cuddly panda or a tiny monkey. Plants, on the other hand, have to have some glamour. Majestic redwood forests prompt humans to climb them and live in them for months and years to protect them. But the smaller, greener creatures, the ones you can't imagine cuddling or hugging, also need help. Over 21 percent of the world's plants are an endangered species.

A disconnect between where and how we get our goods contributes to the lack of awareness about the sheer number of endangered plants. Because most people in the United

States and the United Kingdom rely heavily on imported goods, people can live their entire lives without knowing where plants they use regularly come from. They may not even realize that common items such as rubber tires are a plant material. We often don't stop to think what impact cultivation of a plant has on the global environment, and we may not realize that some of the most popular herbs cannot be cultivated.

Often when these issues of overuse arise, people raise the possibility of synthetics as a way of preserving endangered plants, especially among aromatherapists. In some ways, however, synthetics contribute to the overuse. These imitative molecules are often constructed using petroleum, by itself an environmental blight. Also, to make a convincing imitation, chemists often must still use the plant imitated in some small way.

This does not mean synthetics need throwing out altogether. There are cases where synthetics do create life-saving materials and alternatives. Synthetics, like the naturals they imitate, require very conscientious use. Synthetics work best for situations where use of the natural material has more negative environmental consequences than does the use of the synthetic material.

One plant that often comes up in the synthetics debate is sandalwood. True sandalwood *(Santalum album)* is disappearing from the world at a fast rate. This is not amyris, a tree that grows in Haiti and is used as a popular substitute (also now endangered), nor is it red sandalwood, a cultivar found mainly in Australia that has a similar scent but a different magical signature. So rare and valued is true sandalwood that thieves have stolen temple doors made of it. Because the plant is actually a parasite, changing cultivation techniques cannot save it. While there are attempts at greenhouse cultivation, at this time the bulk of sustainable sandalwood provision comes from the Australian reds.

Supplies of the resins frankincense and myrrh are dwindling daily, as are their popular alternatives of dragon's blood, copal, and benzoin. Not only are these trees stripped of wood and drained of sap, rendering them dead or unusable for years, but most myrrh and frankincense trees grow in extremely volatile regions such as Syria and Sudan. Even if harvesting techniques could improve, conditions of the countries often make it too dangerous and costly to propose any type of change.

It is not just resins and woods that face endangerment through overharvesting. Herbs useful in allopathic medicine also face disappearance. While any medical discovery is good news, the profit-protecting practices of the pharmaceutical industry can seriously warp the benefits of these discoveries, as the industry rarely pairs their corporate policy with protection of the resources used. If the pharmaceutical industry fixates on a wild plant, the plant dies off through overharvesting, competitive destruction of natural harvests of a plant, or manipulative regulations of a plant as a dangerous substance. Each occasion requires critical examination of the players involved. Sometimes an herb really does pose a danger. Often enough, however, it's a ploy to gain competitive control.

It is worth noting that while we assume corporate packaged herbs come from a farmed and hopefully sustainable source, all too often it is corporate interests and not individual herbalists that are the source of wild herb overharvesting. In some locations, gatherers are encouraged to collect herbs in the wild and then sell it to the corporations at a low fee. This adds fair trade justice issues to the additional environmental concerns. The endangered condition of plants does not call for you to dump out your synthetic oils, lock sandalwood in a box, or torch your spice rack. Frankincense and myrrh have always been rare. Treat your treasures as precious, and keep looking for sustainable sources.

The following chart addresses rarities and their substitutes. First, it's an example of combining plant energies—the scents may not match, but if you are working with herbs for their energetic signatures, you can directly replace some and combine others to get close to the emotive feeling you want. Second, especially for practitioners just starting out, most suggested substitutes are available at any grocery store, which is easier on a typical beginner's budget.

The listings in the chart were pulled from two sources: Cropwatch, an independent watchdog on the chemical industry, and the Red List, the most complete index of endangered species. The plants were selected for their combination of popularity and endangerment. For medical substitutions, a high-quality medical herbal such as the *Physician's Desk Reference of Herbal Medicine* or Dr. John Lust's *The Herb Book* will help you find alternative herbs for different maladies. You would also do well to consult a physician before making any drastic changes to your inner chemistry.

How to Support Long-Term Sustainability

When deciding what to use in your practices, consider the following basic rules to support long-term sustainability and justice.

If it is something that comes from a tree that does not typically come off of a tree on its own (such as nuts or fruit),

Overharvested Herb (listed as an endangered plant/species)	Substitute Herb (listed as of "lowest concern" for species protection)
Frankincense *(Boswellia sacra)*	Bay leaf *(Laurus Nobilis)*
Myrrh *(Commiphora myrrha)*	Lemon peel (multiple species)
Rosewood *(Dalbergia abrahamii)*	Actual roses, if possible (Rosaceae family)
Asafoetida *(Ferula assafoetida)*	Garlic *(Allium pendulinum)** and ground eggshell, combined
Dragon's blood *(Dracaena cinnabari)*	Damiana *(Turnera diffusa)* with horseradish *(Armoracia rusticana)*
Goldenseal *(Hydrastis canadensis)*	Wormwood *(Artemisia absinthium)*** with sorrel *(Clepticus parrae)*
Elemi *(Canarium luzonicum)*	Cedar *(Thuja plicata)****
Ginger lily *(Hedychium coronarium)*	Coriander *(Coriandrum sativum)* with ginger root *(Zingiber officinale)*

* There are some endangered members of the garlic (Allium) family. The chart refers to garlic available at a grocery store or at your local farmer's market.

** Wormwood is not a poisonous hallucinogen. According to the *Physician's Desk Reference*, not only is it actually a beneficial if harsh way to clean out the human liver, pet owners give it to their furry friends daily to prevent heartworms.

*** There are multiple endangered members of the cedar family. This refers to North American cedars, commonly available at the edge of Midwestern parking lots. Just pick the berries—no need to strip the tree.

Table continued on next page.

Overharvested Herb (listed as an endangered plant/species)	Substitute Herb (listed as of "lowest concern" for species protection)
Lady's slipper (*Cypripedium, Mexipedium, Paphiopedilum, Phragmipedium,* and *Selenipedium*)	Pansy (Junonia family)
Ginseng (*Panax* genus)	Chicory (*Cichorium intybus*) and/or rice
Adam and Eve root (*Orchis sitiaca*)	Aloe leaf (*Aloe babatiensis*) with an avocado pit (*Persea americana*)
Sweetgrass (*Hierochloe odorata* or *Anthoxanthum nitens*)	White sage (*Salvia officinalis*) possibly combined with sunflower seeds (*Helianthus annuus*) and aloe leaf (*Aloe babatiensis*)
Spikenard (*Nardostachys grandiflora* or *Nardostachys jatamansi*)	Mullein (*Verbascum nigrum*) with pomegranate seed (*Punica granatum*)
Hyssop (*Hyssopus officinalis*)	Clove (*Caryophyllus aromaticus*)
Saint John's wort (*Hypericum perforatum*)	Catnip (*Nepeta cataria*)
Eyebright (*Euphrasia aequalis*)	Lemongrass (*Cymbopogon citratus*)—while not the same planetary association, has a similar clarifying effect
Benzoin (Styrax family)	Hazelnut (*Corylus genus*) with sunflower seed and lime peel

Table, continued.

Overharvested Herb (listed as an endangered plant/species)	Substitute Herb (listed as of "lowest concern" for species protection)
Dittany of Crete (*Origanum dictamnus*)	Oregano (*Origanum vulgare*) with thyme (*Thymus* genus) and cucumber peel (*Cucumis sativus*)
Ravensara (*Ravensara anisata*)	Clove (*Caryophyllus aromaticus*)
Solomon's seal (*Maianthemum bifolium*)	Mullein (*Verbascum nigrum*)
Acacia (Acacia family, including gum arabic)	Gum mastic (*Pistacia lentiscus*)
Copal (*Hymenaea verrucosa*)	Chamomile (*Matricaria recutita*) with lime peel (*Sphaenorhynchus* genus)
Gentian (*Gentianella anglica*)	Turmeric (*Curcuma longa*) with licorice root (*Glycyrrhiza glabra*)

then it is likely something that might be endangered or over-harvested.

If you can grow it yourself, consider doing so, or at least buy it from someone who raises the plant in a cultivated environment.

Seriously consider more common, more easily replaceable herbs as potential substitutes for precious resins like frankincense and myrrh.

If you encounter an herb not on this list that appears on the endangered species list, you can find your own substitute.

Refer to an herbal that lists the planetary associations of a plant, and choose another plant with the same associations.

There are plants on the endangered species list that you can grow at home. In some cases, urban areas even offer incentives for people to install prairie gardens and similar spaces as a way of reintroducing plants back into the ecosphere. This gives you the added benefit of always having a supply of the plants you really want.

For Further Study

Cropwatch. http://cropwatch.org/unethical.htm and http://cropwatch.org/cwfiles.htm.

Cunningham, Scott. *Cunningham's Encyclopedia of Magical Herbs*. Saint Paul, MN: Llewellyn Publications, 1985.

Earth's Endangered Creatures. "Worldwide Endangered Plants List." http://www.earthsendangered.com/plant_list.asp.

The IUCN Red List of Threatened Species. http://www.iucnred list.org.

Lust, Dr. John. *The Herb Book: The Complete and Authoritative Guide to More Than 500 Herbs*. New York: B. Lust Publications, 1974.

Physician's Desk Reference for Herbal Medicines. 4th ed. Montvale, NJ: Thomson Healthcare, 2007.

USDA Plants Database. http://plants.usda.gov.

Herbal Trees

❧ by Suzanne Ress ❧

A bee or a butterfly cannot survive without flowering plants and trees, just as most flowering plants and trees cannot make it without the bees and butterflies. The former need the plants' pollen, nectar, and greenery to live and raise their young, and the latter need the insects' pollination services to procreate.

It's more difficult to see the roles plants and trees play in human life. The vital oxygen we breathe in is the same that they breathe out, and the carbon dioxide we exhale is just as vital for them. Plus there's the fact that we must eat plants (or eat other animals that have eaten plants) for our bodies to form the glucose necessary for life, and the plants and trees need our nitrogenous waste to nourish their roots. Amazingly, many plants and trees give us even more than this.

Sometimes, when I watch my dogs and horses wandering around at liberty in the fields in front of my house, I notice them sniffing at and then eating particular grasses, leaves, or plants rather than others. Further research has informed me that dogs instinctively know that couch grass helps prevent worms, and coarse grass stays a cough and settles the stomach. Horses somehow understand that willow leaves relieve mild stomach upset, and bamboo leaves clear a scratchy throat. How do animals know this?

For millennia, humans have used certain plants to cure or treat various conditions, illnesses, and discomforts. Only in the last hundred years or so has science proven that ancient tried-and-true herbal cures do work, and now we know why.

But how did our ancestors know? My belief is that they knew it intuitively, just as other animals still do now.

In our modern, money-centered world, we sometimes tend to think of trees as ornaments. Usually the word *herb* conjures the idea of a botanical herb plant—an annual or perennial small, scented leafy plant such as basil, horehound, or oregano. While the old definition of *botanical herb* excluded plants with woody stems, the broader meaning of the word herb includes any plant used for its aromatic or medicinal properties, in flavoring food, in medicines, or in perfumes.

Included among herbal plants are many trees, including the following: alder, ash, bay, birch, chestnut, elder, elm, fig, fir, hawthorn, hazelnut, linden, maple, mulberry, oak, pine, plum, pomegranate, poplar, quince, styrax, sycamore, tea tree, walnut, and willow.

Styrax

Perhaps one of the most anciently recognized herbal trees is the styrax *(Styrax officinalis)*, sometimes mistakenly confused with the sweet gum tree because of its similar appearance. Of all herbal trees, the styrax is the only one whose Latin name includes, as species name, *officinalis*. This means that it was a medicinal staple in the apothecary office of, most likely, the medieval Benedictine monks who gave it its name. It shares this honored position with such well-known botanical herbs as borage *(Borago officinalis)*, rosemary *(Rosmarinus officinalis)*, sage *(Salvia officinalis)*, valerian *(Valeriana officinalis)*, melissa *(Melissa officinalis)*, and marshmallow *(Althaea officinalis)*.

Styrax officinalis grows in warm, temperate or tropical regions, and can reach a height of about forty feet. The tree has evergreen, ovate leaves, something like rhododendron leaves, and produces pendulous white flowers, which then transform into the oblong drupes of fruit.

The resin from the styrax tree's bark is dried to create benzoin, considered one of the most ancient incenses, along with frankincense and myrrh. Bezoin incense is still used as an air freshener, and, amazingly, it is considered to be far safer than other natural incenses because, while burning, it gives off only minute amounts of benzene and formaldehyde, less than any other incense.

Benzoin has been used in perfumes since antiquity, and still is used in the perfume industry as a fixative. It has a mild cinnamon-vanilla scent, but, more than its own scent, it helps stabilize the scents of a perfume's other ingredients. Benzoin is also used as a common flavoring additive in foods such as ice cream, and chocolate products, because it contains the essential oil cinnamate, which improves the flavor of chocolate confections.

Tincture of benzoin dissolved in alcohol acts as an effective disinfectant and local anesthetic, and promotes healing of minor wounds and skin lesions.

From the styrax tree comes the name of the polystyrene plastic Styrofoam, which originally contained styrene from the styrax tree. Now it is industrially produced.

Bay Laurel

Another, maybe more familiar, herbal tree is the bay laurel *(Laurus nobilis)*. Who has never enjoyed the complex aroma of a fresh or dried bay leaf broken in half before being tossed into a stew or sauce? Bay leaves' wonderful transporting odor is due to their essential oil cineol. Cineol, also known as eucalyptol, is widely used in very small amounts in perfumes, mouthwash, cough syrups, beverages, and insect repellent. In larger amounts it is toxic! It is also naturally present in tea tree, basil, mugwort, wormwood, rosemary, and sage.

The bay tree is an aromatic evergreen, native to the Mediterranean region, with glossy, oblong, sharply pointed leaves. It can reach a height of up to fifty feet, but grows slowly. Its fruit is a small, shiny black berry.

The leaves, as everyone knows, are used in cooking, whether fresh, dried, whole, or crumbled. Contrary to popular belief, they are not poisonous and can be eaten, but, because they are so very pointy, they can be dangerous if swallowed whole. Their unique aroma is caused by a blend of cineol, terpenes, sesquiterpenes, methyleugonol, and other pinenes.

Bay laurel berries, which contain many of these same natural phytochemicals, are used to spice food.

Essential oil of bay is used to relieve arthritis and rheumatism. A poultice made by soaking a clean white rag in boiled bay leaf tea is an effective remedy against the sting of poison ivy and stinging nettle rash.

Hawthorn

Another fascinating herbal tree is the hawthorn *(Crataegus monogyna)*. The hawthorn has been called the "bread and cheese tree," because eating of its leaves gives one a feeling of satiety, and the "May tree," because its clusters of pretty white flowers typically bloom around May first.

Hawthorn leaves and berries can be dried and used to make herbal tea. Nowadays this tea is commonly used to treat cardiac problems, as it helps strengthen the heart and regulate blood pressure, arrhythmic heartbeat, and circulatory problems. The hawthorn's red berries, which ripen in September, can be added to apple pies, jams, and other fruit concoctions. Their bright color and high antioxidant flavanoid content combine with their healthy heart benefits to make for a sweet eating experience.

Tea Tree

A well-loved herbal tree is the Australian tea tree *(Melaleuca alternifolia)*. It is a relatively small tree with long, thin leaves. It produces spiky white flowers, which then transform into small cup-shaped fruits.

Since antiquity, aboriginal Australian people have used the leaves of the tea tree to treat wounds, heal skin ailments, and quell coughs. It was only in the 1920s that the anti-microbial properties of the essential oil contained in the tea tree's leaves were scientifically proven.

Camphor-scented tea tree oil is a topical antibacterial and antifungal very widely used in antiseptic solutions, deodorant, shampoo, soap, and lotions.

Ash

Another herbal tree is the ash (*Fraxinus excelsior* in Europe, *Fraxinus Americana* in North America). Ash trees can grow upward of one hundred feet and are common throughout Europe and North America. In olden times, a decoction and poultice of ash leaves and ash flower heads was used as protection against snakebite. Who knows if there is any truth to that, but nowadays an herbal tea is made of the dried leaves, which offers effective relief from the pains of rheumatism and gout. The tea is also useful as a mild laxative.

Birch

Birch (*Betula pendula* in Europe, *Betula papyrifera* in North America) is the lovely white-barked tree often seen in the woods, but used frequently as an ornamental tree in parks and yards as well. Its unique silvery white bark only appears after the tree is about six years old.

In natural habitats, birches usually grow together in communities, groves, or groupings. They do not live very long, usually only about fifty years or less, as they are prone to fungal diseases. During its lifetime, a birch tree may grow to a height of sixty feet.

Ancient people used the juice of birch leaves to relieve sores in their mouths. More recently, the tar oil from birch bark, which contains up to 20 percent betulin, has been put to use as an astringent ingredient in ointments prescribed for the treatment of eczema and psoriasis and other skin diseases and irritations.

Birch beer, the soft drink, contains oil extract of birch bark, and birch syrup, made the same way as maple syrup, is used as a sweetener.

Elder

The elder tree *(Sambucus nigra)* is a small scraggly tree whose wood gives off a strangely repellent odor when cut in the spring. On the other hand, its umbels of tiny white flowers perfume the air with their sweet, fruity scent when they bloom in early June. The tree's juicy, dark purplish-black berries are added to yogurt, fruit desserts, and jams, or used to make an antioxidant-rich juice, wine, or liquor.

The elder tree is one of the most valuable herbal trees around. Nearly all parts of this tree have a culinary or medicinal use. Its berries are antioxidants, with their high content of vitamin C (87 percent RDA from one cup raw). Elder flowers are used to make strong tea that relieves flu symptoms. A tincture made from eight drops elderflower essential oil added to two cups distilled water, used as a skin tonic, keeps the face free of blemishes. A poultice of crushed elder leaves helps soothe and speed healing of bruises and sprains. An infusion of the elder tree's bark has laxative properties.

Linden

The regal linden tree *(Tilia × vulgaris)* grows to a towering height of over one hundred feet. The linden tree is found growing wild in the woods, but is probably best known as the tree that borders avenues and entry roads, because it is majestic and stately, and its canopy of wide, heart-shaped leaves creates welcome shade in the summer. In the late spring, the linden tree's white flowers blossom, emanating a sweet honey-like scent and acting as a major honeybee attractant. The flowers then transform into tiny reddish berries, and by October the linden's foliage turns bright golden yellow before it falls.

Green linden leaves are dried and used to make a relaxing tea. Combined with chamomile flowers, it becomes a knockout sleeping potion.

An infusion of linden tree bark soothes a cough, and is also good to take after too large a meal, as a digestive. Because of its relaxant properties, linden tea is often recommended for high blood pressure.

Fir

The evergreen fir tree *(Picea abies)*, with its many needle-like leaves and pretty cones, is a familiar sight during the winter holiday season when it is used as an ornamented indoor tree or to make wreaths or other greenery decorations.

The pleasantly scented fir tree's resin is the font of oil of turpentine, pine oil, pine tar, and oil of tar.

Oil of turpentine is antiseptic and is widely used in muscle-ache ointments for its warming and anti-irritant effects. Pine tar is the active ingredient in special shampoos that combat eczema and psoriasis. Pine oil is used in cleaning products.

The scent of the fir tree's leaves is attributed to the terpene linalool, also found in mint and bay laurel.

Plum

The plum tree *(Prunus domestica)*, aside from being the subject of much poetry and Japanese haiku due to the beautiful delicacy of its white blossoms, is also valued in herbal medicine for its succulent fruit, its leaves, and its resin.

Plum trees do not grow very tall, nor, in most cases, do they live very long. Their fruits can vary in size from that of a walnut to that of a small apple, and in color from yellow, to red, to violet, to purplish blue. Plum juice and dried plums are reliable laxatives, suitable for all. Prunes are high in antioxidants (ORAC rating 8,000). They are also packed with vitamins K and A, potassium, manganese, copper, and magnesium, and make a perfect restorative snack after very strenuous exercise.

The dried leaves of the plum tree made into a decoction are also a laxative, and help in reducing fever. A small amount of the plum tree's sap, boiled in vinegar with the tree's leaves, and applied to the skin, is said to kill ringworm.

Pomegranate

The pomegranate *(Punica granatum)* is a small tree, usually no taller than fifteen feet, and often shorter, used as a shrubby hedge. Its small narrow leaves and the scraggly delicacy of its fine branches have an oriental look to them, and, in fact, this tree is originally from Persia. It will grow in any reasonably temperate climate if planted in a protected place away from wind and chill zones, and in full sun. In June, it produces amazingly bright red-orange flowers that are truly gorgeous, but scentless. The most incredible part of this tree is its peculiar fruit: leathery and reddish brown outside, with a funny little beard at one end. Cut into it and it's like finding a treasure trove of garnets. These juicy red fruit seeds are what gave the tree its name, *granatum*, which means "seeded" in Latin.

The fruit's juice, or a decoction made from pomegranate tree bark, expels tapeworms in human or beast, and a decoction of the fruit's rind can be employed as a gargle for sore throat. Pomegranate fruit or juice is indicated in cases of high blood pressure and in arthritis. It is high in vitamins C and K and the mineral folate.

Willow

Perhaps the herbal tree with the biggest medicinal claim to fame is the willow *(Salix alba)*. The beautiful gray-green color of its narrow foliage, its fuzzy yellow catkin flowers in early spring, its choice of waterside habitat, and its frequently imposing dimensions make this tree truly distinctive.

Baskets are made from its fine, flexible branches. Its very name is used in adjective form, "willowy," to describe someone tall, slender, and graceful. And last, but not least, its bark contains the origin of aspirin, salicin.

A decoction of willow bark is highly effective as a treatment for arthritis, any other muscular aches and pains, and simple headache. An infusion made from the willow's leaves is used as a digestive tonic.

It's easy to forget that human beings live in symbiosis with plants and trees. The faraway Amazonian forest trees are necessary for our survival, but so is that scruffy black locust in the neighbor's side yard, the magnificent elm in the park nearby, the tiny dogwood purchased recently from a garden center, and, of course, the many wonderful herbal trees. They all contribute to our lives, and we to theirs.

Culinary
Herbs

The Sweet Taste of Vinegar

❧ by Charlie Rainbow Wolf ❧

Summer is ending, and with it the fresh taste of the herbs from the garden may end, too, unless there is a way to save them to enjoy at a later time. Herbal vinegars are a wonderful way to keep the fresh taste of your summer herbs for use in the colder months. They can capture the flavors right from the garden by breaking down the natural oils from the herbs and preserving them.

Making herbal vinegars is fun and easy. It is possible to replicate the expensive gourmet vinegars that delicatessens and other shops sell. The preparations are wonderful additions to the kitchen and make great gifts, but there are some basics that have to be understood if the end product is going to be a success.

Choosing Your Vinegar and Herbs

The first thing that has to be understood is the vinegar itself. There are several types of vinegar. Most of them are equally suitable for making herbal preparations, but each vinegar does have its own personality. Like any good relationship, the partnership has to be compatible.

White distilled vinegar can usually be found on most supermarket shelves. This is made from fermented grains (often corn), to which a vinegar start is added. It has a sharp and intense flavor, and does not really blend with the flavors of the herbal additions very well. Don't discard this completely, though. It makes a great rinse for your hair!

Cider vinegar, sometimes called apple cider vinegar, is probably what comes to mind when first thinking about making herbal vinegars. Many people take it on a daily basis as a dietary supplement. This is the vinegar that is most often used when the flavor of the herbs is strong. Think garlic, rosemary, and other pungent additions. Cider vinegar is available from most grocers or health food stores and is fairly inexpensive.

Pasteurized cider vinegar is probably the best choice for those who are new to making herbal vinegars. It is possible to obtain an organic version, but this has a tendency to "mother." This is a layer of bacteria that grows on the top of the preparation, and while it will not harm the vinegar, it doesn't look very appetizing. There is nothing wrong with pasteurized vinegar; this just means the liquid has been heat-treated to neutralize any bacteria that might be present. Some people consider the live bacteria to be a healthy inclusion.

Use apple cider vinegar for its amber color and when using strong flavors of herbs. Dill, garlic, and bay are a good starter combination. I also like one that I call "Scarborough Fair," because it contains parsley, sage, rosemary, and thyme! Tarragon, basil, and lemon are another favorite combination that uses apple cider vinegar as a carrier.

Red wine vinegar is more of a specialty vinegar, and—as its name suggests—it is made from red wine that has turned to vinegar. Wine makers will be familiar with this! It is made commercially by adding a vinegar starter to wine, which causes it to "turn." It has a deep color and flavor, and is wonderful when used with fruits such as raspberries and other berries. It also takes the stronger herbs well.

White wine vinegar is similar to red wine vinegar, apart from the obvious difference. It has a subtle taste that does not overpower the flavor of the herbs. I like using white wine vinegar with my mints. It also works well with ginger and lemon balm.

Malt vinegar will be familiar to all who enjoy traditional fish 'n' chips. It is made from sprouted barley (or sometimes wheat). This is then fermented and turned into vinegar. It is dark and flavorful. It's not a particularly popular carrier for herbal vinegars, but it does take the intense flavors of herbs like dill, juniper, cloves, or garlic very well.

The outcome of the vinegar will depend on the type of carrier used, the herbs included, and also the time of harvest. Pick herbs when they are young and at their prime, and in the morning. Catch them before the sunlight has a chance to warm them, but after the dew is gone. Rinse them thoroughly to remove any garden debris or insects that may be among them, then dry slightly. A salad spinner is a good tool for this.

Methods of Making Herbal Vinegars

There are many methods of making herbal vinegars, and as usual, cooks and chefs disagree as to which is the best. Some advocate allowing the vinegar to come to a boil and then pouring it over the herbs, as one would pour boiling water over tea leaves. I'm not a fan of this, for I feel it is too harsh on the herbs. Gentler methods will be easier on the herbs, and will result in more aroma staying in the bottle.

When I lived on the farm, my mother-in-law taught me how to make raspberry vinegar (she used it as a cold remedy) by filling a quart jar with raspberries and pouring warm—not hot—cider vinegar over them. She added a couple of spoonfuls of honey, and covered the jar. This was stored in the larder, which was cool and dark. Every few days she would turn the jar upside down. After a two-week period, she strained out the fruit and put the vinegar into a smaller jar, ready for use.

It is possible to make herbal vinegars the same way as sun tea. While the results may not be as predictable as those of more modern and accurate methods, I like the natural process this entails, and I have had great success with it.

Fill a jar with a selection of herbs and the appropriate vinegar, and set it in the sun for several days. Next, strain out the herbs and place the vinegar in a noncorrosive container (with a noncorrosive lid). At this stage, a sprig of fresh herb or a couple of fresh leaves can be added for visual impact. They will continue to flavor the vinegar, but only subtly. Don't forget to label your bottle so you know what you've got! Decorative labels can be obtained from many places, or even perhaps created and printed using a home computer.

How to Use Herbal Vinegars

Today, I still make raspberry vinegar as my mother-in-law did, and I make an elderberry one in the same manner. Blackberries could also be used. I don't use these vinegars just for colds and flu, though. They make great salad dressings, particularly when used in a vinaigrette.

A vinaigrette is an emulsion of the fruit or herbal vinegar and oil. The laws of nature tell us that oil and vinegar simply don't mix. Shake the oil and vinegar, and within minutes they will have separated again. The trick to getting the mixture to emulsify, as opposed to just temporarily blend, is in the ratio of oil to vinegar.

A true vinaigrette usually takes more oil than vinegar. Choose a good-quality salad oil, such as extra virgin olive oil. More flavors can be added by using a specialty oil, such as walnut oil or—my favorite—roasted sesame oil. Take into consideration the flavor of the oil, and be sure that it is not going to overpower the flavor of the vinegar. Don't be afraid to blend different oils to get a specific flavor. Experimenting is half the fun!

Place the vinegar into a blender and start adding the oil drop by drop. Keep the blender running and keep adding the oil until the mixture begins to thicken. Some recipes say two parts oil to one part vinegar, some say more. I don't always want to use that much oil. If not used straight away, the vinaigrette may separate. That risk might be preferable to a heavily oil-laden dressing.

Remember, these preparations are not just for salads. They make lovely additions drizzled over steamed vegetables, sprinkled onto pasta, or used to baste roasting meat. Some of them can even be added to a beauty routine as a bath soak, hair rinse, or facial tonic. It is easy to get totally immersed in making herbal vinegars, for they are delightful preserves, make wonderful gifts, and are so simple to create. Use clean, noncorrosive containers, and let the herbs and the vinegars do the rest. Explore some tried and tested combinations, and then enjoy experimenting with some of your own medleys. You might just create the heirloom recipe of the future!

Tasty Tomato Treats

by Alice DeVille

Nothing inspires taste buds as much as the tomatoes that spice up your life when you incorporate them into meals. Tomatoes are the most versatile fruit on the planet—they go with just about everything and grow in red, green, yellow, orange, and purple hues. Use them fresh from the farm, homegrown, sun-dried, roasted, or canned to create a tasty dish. Dry sliced fresh tomatoes sprinkled with herbs in a slow oven, and freeze them for use in winter meals. Keep a tube of tomato paste handy in the refrigerator to add color and zip to soups, stews, and roasts.

The recipes featured here maximize the use of several tomato varieties and present options in every menu category to give the juicy tomato a taste-bud test. Treat your palate to one of these succulent recipes at your next meal.

A Colorful Starter

In party-giving circles, I'm known for creating appetizers and sandwiches that look like fancy cakes or desserts. Guests have said they look too pretty to eat and won't touch them until I cut servings that reveal the inner delicacies. This recipe combines savory Southwestern-style ingredients for a special appetizer cheesecake that looks and tastes fantastic and serves up to 20 guests.

Southwestern-Style Cheesecake

    1 cup crushed tortilla chips

    3 tablespoons butter, melted

    2 8-ounce packages cream cheese, softened

    2 eggs, lightly beaten

    2 cups (8 ounces) Monterey Jack cheese, grated

    1 4-ounce can chopped green chilies, drained

    1 cup sour cream

    ½ cup chopped sweet yellow pepper

    ½ cup chopped sweet orange pepper

    ½ cup chopped green onions (white and green parts)

    ⅓–½ cup chopped tomatoes (for extra color, use red and yellow tomatoes)

In a small bowl, combine tortilla chips and melted butter; press onto the bottom of a greased 9-inch springform pan.

Place on a baking sheet. Bake at 325°F. for 15 minutes or until lightly browned.

In a large bowl, beat the cream cheese and eggs on low speed just until combined. Stir in the Monterey Jack cheese and chilies; pour over crust. Bake for 30–35 minutes or until center is almost set.

Remove pan from oven and place on wire rack. Spread the sour cream over the cheesecake; carefully run a knife around edge of pan to loosen from sides; cool for 1 hour. Refrigerate overnight.

Remove sides of pan just before serving. Garnish with yellow and orange pepper, green onions, and tomatoes; garnish with a whole red chili pepper and serve. Refrigerate any leftovers.

Do-Ahead Salad

If you love a salad with great texture and deep flavors, this one hits the mark with ingredients complemented by fresh lemon and cumin. This creation is a variation of a Stephanie Witt Sedgwick submission to the *Washington Post*. You can make this salad ahead of time, keeping it covered and refrigerated for up to 8 hours. Makes 8–10 servings.

Avocado, Chickpea, Cucumber, and Tomato Salad

1½ tablespoons extra virgin olive oil

¾ teaspoon ground cumin (or to taste)

¾ teaspoon salt

¼ teaspoon black pepper

¼ teaspoon sugar

Zest and juice from 1 freshly squeezed large lemon

1 can chickpeas, rinsed and drained

1 English cucumber, peeled, seeded, and cut into ½-inch pieces

2–3 medium tomatoes, peeled, seeded, and cut into ½-inch dice (1½ cups); save time peeling tomatoes by dropping them into boiling water for half a minute—the skin will slip right off

3 scallions or spring onions, white and light green parts finely chopped (½ cup)

Flat leaf Italian parsley leaves, finely chopped, about ⅓ cup

1½ ripe avocados, cut into ½-inch dice

Freshly ground black pepper to taste

Whisk olive oil, cumin, salt, pepper, sugar, lemon juice, and zest in a large bowl.

Add the chickpeas, cucumber, tomatoes, scallions, parsley, and avocados; toss to combine. Season with black pepper. Don't be surprised if guests ask you for the recipe—it happens every time I serve this salad.

Italian Specialties

A tossed salad and crusty bread are perfect accompaniments for this recipe, a hearty dish that makes use of flavorful sun-dried tomatoes. I experimented with the ingredients over the years and developed this easy one that satisfies most pasta lovers.

Pasta with Sun-Dried Tomatoes and Artichokes

1 jar sun-dried tomatoes, at least 8 ounces

2 cans artichoke hearts, drained well and chopped

2 cloves garlic, finely chopped

1 pound bulk sweet Italian pork sausage (can substitute
  chicken or turkey sausage)

¾ cup white wine

1 can chicken broth

¼ cup fresh basil, chopped in short ribbon style

¼ cup fresh parsley leaves, chopped

Salt and pepper to taste

1 pound fusilli pasta, cooked according to package
  directions and salted generously

½ cup or more fresh mozzarella, finely diced

½ cup grated cheese (Asiago, Parmesan, or Romano);
  I prefer a combination of any two

Heat two tablespoons of oil from jar of sun-dried tomatoes.

When hot, add the chopped artichoke hearts and garlic.

When they start to brown, push them to the sides of skillet
and add the sausage.

Keep breaking up the sausage as it browns.

Add diced sun-dried tomatoes, then wine, then chicken
broth.

Add chopped herbs, then salt and pepper (at least ½ teaspoon each of salt and pepper).

Add drained fusilli pasta and then diced mozzarella.

Serve in bowls and sprinkle with grated cheese(s) of your
choice.

Most of my Italian relatives make homemade gnocchi, a
potato-based pasta that tastes best when the final cooked product is of light consistency. (I have tasted versions that were
either hard as rocks or gummy.) The secret lies in how well

you incorporate the flour. Don't be discouraged if your first attempt at this dish does not give you the desired results—it is an acquired skill but so worth the effort. Once you start working with the dough, you cannot leave it until you finish making the pasta. Your sauce of choice enhances the flavor. The gnocchi practically melt in your mouth. Most recipes start with boiled potatoes, but I prefer to bake them and work with them as fast as possible after they come out of the oven.

I serve this recipe with three different sauces as one of the festive entrées at our family gathering on Christmas Eve. The guests have diverse preferences, and this is the perfect season to spoil them! Options for making use of the dish's versatility include serving it with one of the following: a rich San Marzano tomato–meat sauce, a light cream Alfredo sauce, a broth-based herb sauce, or just plain butter. Some cooks serve gnocchi with basil pesto. It is hard to resist a second helping no matter which sauce you use, including the Tomato Vodka Sauce recipe given here, which has become a family favorite.

Gnocchi with Tomato Vodka Sauce

    6 large baking potatoes, scrubbed (Idaho or Russet)

    1¼ teaspoons salt

    Ground black pepper to taste

    1–1½ cups all-purpose or unbleached white flour, as needed

    1 egg (optional)

Pierce the potatoes several times so that moisture escapes during baking.

    Bake potatoes in a preheated 400°F. oven for 1 hour or until fork-tender.

Peel the potatoes while they are still hot and mash them, adding salt and pepper. Be sure you use enough salt to avoid a bland taste.

If using an egg, beat and knead into dough.

Add flour in ¼-cup increments, incorporating well after each addition until mixture forms a ball; do not overwork the dough.

Transfer the dough to a well-floured surface; gently knead the dough for two to three minutes, adding a little more flour to keep it from sticking.

Push the dough together in the shape of a loaf.

Flour your hands and slice one piece of the dough about an inch wide. Cover remaining dough to prevent drying.

Roll the dough back and forth into a rope about the thickness of your index finger; add a bit more flour to the board if the dough is sticky.

Cut the rope into 1-inch pieces, and gently roll the cut pieces in flour. Form the gnocchi by pressing over the back of a fork or your middle three fingers. Gnocchi should be slightly curved and marked with ridges to allow them to hold sauce when served. Repeat process with remaining dough.

Place the gnocchi in a single layer on baking sheets lined with wax paper and dusted with flour until ready to cook. Cover with plastic wrap and refrigerate for up to 12 hours or freeze until hard, then separate them into meal-size portions in freezer bags.

When ready to cook, bring a large pot of well-salted water to a boil. Drop gnocchi in batches in the water; they will sink to the bottom and rise to the surface after a few minutes.

Cook for 3 minutes or so from the time they float to the surface. Do not overcook. Remove with a slotted spoon or skimmer and place in a large serving dish; repeat the process until all gnocchi have been removed from the pot.

Serve with Tomato Vodka Sauce or your favorite sauce, and top with grated Parmesan or Romano cheese. Buon appetito!

Tomato Vodka Sauce

This sauce is creamy and delicious. It's also good with rigatoni, penne, and bowtie pasta.

¼ cup butter

1 tablespoon olive oil

1 chopped onion

1 28-ounce can of tomato sauce

1 28-ounce can of diced tomatoes

1 cup heavy whipping cream

¼ cup vodka

¼ teaspoon crushed red pepper flakes—or more if you prefer a spicier sauce

1 teaspoon salt

¼ teaspoon freshly ground black pepper

In a large skillet over medium-low heat, melt butter with oil. Add onion and sauté for 8 minutes or until transparent.

Add tomatoes and cook for 25–30 minutes on low heat until cooked down and not watery, stirring frequently.

Increase heat and add whipping cream, vodka, and red pepper flakes. Boil for 2 minutes or until thickened to sauce consistency; add salt and pepper to taste. Bring to a simmer.

Serve over gnocchi and pass the Parmesan cheese.

Perfect Summer Beverage

My family enjoys tomato-based drinks all year round, from bottled tomato juice with lemon to the spicy type or juice rendered from gazpacho ingredients served over ice. Yet fruity drinks reign in the summer, so it has been fun to experiment with ripe fruits, such as this combination of tomato and watermelon, to develop a new twist on an adult beverage. Since watermelons are at their sweetest in the summer, it makes sense to use them as the base ingredient for this cool, refreshing drink. This recipe, adapted from an Ina Garten mojito recipe, makes a big pitcher of mint and lime juice–accented mojitos for 8 thirsty guests.

Tomato/Watermelon Mojitos

> 1 large bunch of mint; tear off 20–25 small leaves and reserve remaining sprigs
>
> 4 thick slices of fresh watermelon
>
> 2 large tomatoes, skin removed, seeded, and diced (plunge into boiling water first to quickly remove the skin)
>
> ½ cup tomato juice
>
> 14 ounces light rum
>
> ¾ cup simple syrup (see note)
>
> 8 tablespoons freshly squeezed lime juice (4–5 limes)
>
> Mint sprigs and watermelon spears for garnish

Mash the mint leaves in a shallow soup bowl using a potato masher or mortar. Remove and discard the seeds and rind of the watermelon. Put watermelon and diced tomatoes into food processor and purée.

Put mashed mint into bottom of large pitcher, and add 3 cups of the pureed tomato/watermelon mix, the tomato juice, rum, simple syrup, and lime juice; stir to combine. Pour the mixture into a serving pitcher.

Place ice cubes in 8 old-fashioned glasses, and pour mojito mixture into each. Garnish with fresh mint sprigs and 3-inch watermelon spears. Serve ice cold.

NOTE: For the simple syrup recipe, combine 1 cup sugar and 1 cup water in a small pan; simmer until the sugar dissolves. Chill before adding to mixture.

Dessert

Every tomato pie recipe in my file is a main dish, but this "tomato cake" option satisfies a sweet tooth and is a tasty dessert made with canned tomato soup. Most people living south of the Mason-Dixon line have probably sampled a version of this moist cake. The ingredients are staples right from your kitchen pantry. I tried columnist Heloise's recipe years ago and prepared other versions made with a chocolate cake mix base. Many recipes suggest adding a coating of mini-marshmallows to the top of the cake as soon as it comes out of the oven. This made-from-scratch cake has a cream cheese frosting, with the option of adding dried cherries, raisins, or walnuts to the batter for more density.

Frosted Chocolate Tomato Soup Cake

½ cup butter

1⅓ cups sugar

2 eggs

2 cups all-purpose flour

½ cup powdered cocoa

1 tablespoon baking powder

1 teaspoon baking soda

¼ cup warm water

1 can (10¾ ounces) condensed Harvest Tomato soup

½ cup dried cherries, raisins, or walnuts (optional)

Preheat oven to 350°F. Grease and flour a 9 x 13-inch cake pan.

Cream butter and sugar together in a large mixing bowl; add eggs and beat until fluffy. Mix dry ingredients, including cocoa, together in a small bowl.

Mix water and tomato soup together.

Alternate the addition of wet and dry ingredients to the butter-sugar mix until incorporated.

Add optional ½ cup of dried cherries, raisins, or walnuts to batter.

Pour into prepared baking dish and bake for 30 minutes.

Let cool thoroughly before frosting.

Cream Cheese Frosting

8-ounce package of cream cheese, softened to room temperature

1 stick butter, softened

4 cups powdered sugar

1 teaspoon vanilla

1 tablespoon milk, cream, or half-and-half

Cream butter and cream cheese together, then beat in pow-dered sugar.

Add vanilla, and thin frosting out with a little milk.

Spread frosting over top of cake. Enjoy!

Herbs as Preservatives

⤞ by Elizabeth Barrette ⤝

A key challenge with food lies in preserving it, so that an abundant harvest lasts through times when a given item is not in season. People have long used herbs to help keep food safe, as well as adding to the flavor. Herbs can also preserve other things besides food, keeping clothes fresh and repelling pests. Different herbs have different qualities that aid in these purposes.

Natural Preservatives

Traditional preservation methods for food often use herbs. Pickles, herbal bread, and blended meat products such as sausage may be moderately to heavily spiced to extend their shelf life. People also deploy herbs in sachets and other combinations to repel pests that might ruin food or clothing. It helps to combine herbs with multiple preservation modes.

Acids preserve food by pickling. Some of them, such as vinegar, form a base for pickling, while others, such as lemon juice, are usually diluted with other liquids. Additional spices are then added for flavor and extra preservation effects.

Antioxidants retard decay by interfering with the oxidation process in food products. Synthetic antioxidants like butylhydroxyanisole (BHA) and butylhydroxytoluene (BHT) appear in many commercial foods, but customers are becoming more reluctant to buy products with artificial preservatives.

Antimicrobial herbs suppress the growth of both gram-positive and gram-negative bacteria, molds, and undesirable yeasts in food. They are particularly useful for foods stored at room temperature, such as some cheeses and sausages.

Repellents discourage pests such as ants, bedbugs, cockroaches, fleas, flies, mites, mosquitoes, moths, ticks, weevils, and mice. These spoil a variety of foods and household goods if not prevented from doing so.

Herbs with Preservative Qualities

Many different herbs and spices have features that help preserve foods and household items. They may have antioxidant, antimicrobial, or repellent effects. Here are some of the stronger and more popular ones.

Allspice *(Pimenta dioica)* is a large tropical tree. Its unripe fruit is picked and dried in the sun to produce the familiar brown allspice berries. The aromatic wood is also favored for smoking meat to flavor and preserve it. Allspice has medium antimicrobial effects. It harmonizes the flavors of sweet spices, so it appears in many blends. Cooking applications include Caribbean jerk seasoning, Cincinnati-style chili, curry powder, barbecue sauce, mole sauce, pickles, and sausage.

Amaranth (*Amaranthus paniculatus*) is an erect annual herb with oval leaves that grows from three to six feet tall. It shows a striking reddish-purple color throughout. It has edible leaves, roots, and seeds rich in beta-carotene, ascorbic acid, and folate. The purple to black seeds are used as a spice, and they have antioxidant properties.

Apple trees (*Malus domestica*) now come in many sizes, but originally grew thirty to forty feet tall. Apple wood delivers a distinctive sweet note to smoke for preserving and flavoring meat. Apples make excellent jelly, which is often used as a carrier for other fruits that don't make good jelly by themselves (or are too expensive to use plain), thus allowing them to be preserved. Cider apples produce a splendid fruity, slightly sweet vinegar that makes an excellent base for pickles and sauces. The high acid content preserves food very well; added to sliced fruit, vinegar prevents browning.

Caraway (*Carum carvi*) is a feathery biennial plant reaching about two feet high. It produces umbels of tiny white flowers. These yield curved brown seeds that are used as a spice with pungent, anise-like flavor. Caraway seasons bread, sauerkraut, and many other foods. It has medium antimicrobial qualities.

Chaya (*Aerva lanata*) is a woody perennial herb with succulent leaves and a prostrate growth pattern. It has edible leaves, and the dried flowers are used as a spice with antioxidant effects.

Cinnamon (*Cinnamomum verum*) comes from the bark of a tropical tree. Cinnamon sticks are whole rolled bark strips; you can also get cinnamon chips or powdered cinnamon. The essential oil is quite potent and can burn skin; it makes a good insect repellent when diluted, though, especially for ants. Cinnamon has strong antimicrobial qualities.

Cloves (*Syzygium aromaticum*) are the dried flower buds of a tropical tree. As a spice, they are sold whole and powdered. Whole cloves are used in making clove oranges, both for fragrance and for repelling pests. Cloves have strong antimicrobial effects as well. As a mulling spice, this helps keep beverages fresh and tasty. It combines well with other preservative spices such as allspice, cinnamon, cumin, and ginger.

Coriander (*Coriandrum sativum*) produces large round seeds with spicy floral flavor. The fresh leaves are called cilantro; they have a green, faintly citrus taste and are used as a topping or in salads. Coriander seed has antioxidant effects and medium-strength antimicrobial properties. It is favored as a pickling spice and is also used for flavoring some types of beer. Medicinally, it's boiled in water as a treatment for colds.

Cumin (*Cuminum cyminum*) is an airy plant with thread-like leaves. It reaches about twelve to eighteen inches high. The tiny seeds may be used whole or ground. Cumin lends an earthy, warming quality to foods. It appears heavily in South Asian, North African, and Latin American cuisine, along with certain cheeses and breads. Cumin has medium antimicrobial qualities.

Feverfew (*Tanacetum parthenium*) is a fluffy plant bearing ruffled green leaves with a citrus scent. Many tiny daisylike flowers appear later in the season. Feverfew grows about eighteen inches high. It repels ants, bedbugs, cockroaches, flies, mites, mosquitoes, moths, and mice. Feverfew is also used for treating insect bites to relieve symptoms and prevent infection. Medicinally, it reduces fever and headache.

Garlic (*Allium sativum*) produces large pungent bulbs comprising smaller divisible cloves. The leaves are narrow and long, and clusters of white flowers appear on stalks. The plant grows to about two feet tall. Garlic has very strong antimicrobial and antiseptic effects; in addition to flavoring and preserving food, it is also used to treat colds, flu, and many other complaints. It is a staple of Mediterranean cuisine and a common seasoning in Africa, Asia, and Europe. Garlic cloves are the main product, but the leaves are also edible, with a milder flavor. The intense pungent, spicy flavor of garlic mellows and sweetens with cooking. It repels biting insects if eaten or applied to the skin. In the ground, it repels rabbits and moles.

Ginger (*Zingiber officinale*) is a low-growing herb with narrow dark green leaves and a large knobbly root. The root may be used fresh, candied in sugar, or dried and powdered (in order of decreasing heat). It has a sweet, hot flavor and mild antimicrobial qualities. Ginger soothes an upset stomach and helps the body fight off illness, so it often appears in herbal remedies. In small amounts, ginger is good for blending both sweet and savory flavors of other spices.

Ivy gourd (*Coccinia indica*) is a large creeping vine related to pumpkin. It spreads rapidly over a wide area, producing beautiful white flowers and small round to oblong fruit. The fruit tends to be bitter when fresh and is usually cooked. In India, people eat the fruit, often in curries. In Southeast Asia, both the fruit and leaves are eaten. Ivy gourd contains riboflavin and thiamin, with strong antioxidant properties.

Juniper (*Juniperus communis*) is an evergreen bush or tree with a strong spicy scent. Its dried berries make a spice with meaty citrus notes and some preservative tendencies.

Lavender (*Lavandula*) is a bushy herb with narrow gray-green leaves and purple flowers. The dried flowers are often used, and whole flower stalks may be woven into lavender wands. Lavender oil is also available. This herb repels fleas, flies, moths, and silverfish. It makes excellent potpourri and sachets. It keeps clothes fresh and helps them last longer.

Lavender cotton (*Santolina chamaecyparissus*) is a low mounding plant with silver-green foliage and small yellow flowers. It has strong insect repellent qualities and makes a good ingredient for sachets.

Lemon (*Citrus × limon*) is a small evergreen tree that produces sour yellow fruit. Lemon juice is a very strong preservative that pickles food with acid. Added to sliced fruit, it prevents discoloration. Lemon peel retains its citrus fragrance when dried, due to the essential oils in the peel. It appears in potpourri and repels pests from closets or clothing. Lemon oil has both cleansing and preservative properties, making it a common ingredient in furniture polish.

Mustard includes three different plants: black mustard (*Brassica nigra*), brown Indian mustard (*Brassica juncea*), and white mustard (*Brassica hirta/Sinapis alba*). The plants are airy, with jagged leaves. Mustard has strong antimicrobial effects and also repels some insects. The seeds and oil are used to make pickles in India.

Oregano (*Origanum vulgare*) is a perennial herb growing one to two feet tall. It has rounded, fuzzy leaves. Tiny purple flowers appear in clusters on upright spikes. Oregano may be used fresh in salads or other recipes; it is more often dried and crumbled as a savory herb. It gives a warm, aromatic, slightly bitter flavor. Oregano is a staple herb of Italian cuisine and also appears in Egyptian, Greek, Latino, Turkish, and Philippine cooking. It has medium antimicrobial and antiseptic effects. Essential oil of oregano prohibits fungi on stored grain.

Peppercorns (*Piper nigrum*) come from a flowering vine, the fruit of which is dried to form a spice. They have mild antimicrobial effects, and most herbivores avoid them. Peppercorns strengthen the flavors of other savory spices.

Peppers (*Capsicum*) are the hot fruit of a small bushy plant; many kinds exist. Capsaicin in peppers is a strong preservative that also repels some pests such as mice and biting insects. The hotter the pepper, the more capsaicin, and the stronger the effects. Some pepper varieties dry very well and are strung for hanging. Others are dried and powdered. They are especially good in stew, chili, and meat products such as sausage. Peppers also aid in clearing sinuses and killing germs, which makes them popular in certain cold remedies and cough drops—if you can take the heat.

Rosemary (*Rosmarinus officinalis*) is a woody perennial herb with evergreen, needlelike leaves. The tiny flowers are white to purple. The leaves are dried as a spice, with a sharp resinous flavor. Rosemary has medium antimicrobial qualities. It preserves the fresh taste of foods and prevents off-flavors from developing.

Sage (*Salvia officinalis*) is a perennial, evergreen subshrub about two feet tall and wide. It has leathery, oval leaves and blue to purple flowers. The leaves are dried and used whole or ground in cooking. Sage has medium antimicrobial properties. Bundles or wands of sage sprigs discourage a variety of insects.

Sweet bay *(Laurus nobilis)* is an aromatic evergreen tree that reaches forty to sixty feet tall. Pale yellow-green flowers appear on separate trees for the male and female flowers, later producing a small, shiny black berry. These berries are pressed to extract essential and fatty oils. Dried berries are used as a robust spice. The wood yields a strong smoke for flavoring and preserving meat. The leathery oval leaves are dried for use in cooking. They are added to soups and stews, and are used to make stock or broth and to cook large pieces of meat in liquid. A bay leaf in a canister of flour, rice, beans, etc., discourages insect pests. It also has medium antimicrobial qualities. Bay leaf blends the flavors of savory herbs and spices.

Thyme *(Thymus vulgaris)* is a bushy herb with tiny oval leaves that grows six to twelve inches high. It bears clusters of minute white to pink flowers. Romans spread it throughout Europe, using it to purify their homes, as well as to flavor and preserve cheeses and liqueurs. Thyme has medium antimicrobial effects. The essential oil prohibits fungi on stored grain. It can also kill fungi that infect toenails. Thyme deters insects and prevents musty odors. Ancient Egyptians used this herb for embalming.

Wormwood *(Artemisia absinthium)* is an herbaceous perennial plant with silvery-green leaves and fibrous roots. It bears clusters of tubular yellow flowers. It grows two to three feet tall. Wormwood is used in bitters for flavoring and preserving beverages, especially absinthe. It repels moths, intestinal worms, slugs, and flies. It has strong antiseptic and antimicrobial effects, particularly against gram-positive bacteria.

Preservative Projects

For best results, combine several preservative herbs that have complementary fragrances, flavors, and/or properties. If you look at food recipes and craft projects, you will see that most of them feature a list of herbs working together. Here are a few sample projects to get you started.

Bouquet Garni

A *bouquet garni* is a savory herb bundle cooked in soups, stews, or other wet dishes but removed before eating. It may be made from sprigs of fresh or dried herbs tied together, dried herb sprigs and leaves in a muslin pouch, or loose dried herbs in a tea ball.

    1 bay leaf

    3 sage leaves

    1 clove of garlic

    1 sprig of rosemary

    8 sprigs of thyme

Pickling Blend

Pickling blend has two components: the spice mix and the liquid mix. The spice mix usually consists of whole seeds and leaves, or coarse pieces. It may be added loose or kept in a cheesecloth bundle. Pickling spices also work nicely for flavoring soups, stocks, or the cooking liquid for large roasts. The basic mix suits a wide variety of single and mixed vegetables. For dill pickles, add 1 tablespoon dill seeds. For fruit or other sweet pickles, add 2 or 3 cinnamon sticks (or 1 tablespoon cinnamon bark chips). Combine using about 1 tablespoon of spice mix per 6 cups of liquid. Bring to a boil, then lower the heat and simmer for 5–10 minutes.

Spice mix:

> 1 bay leaf (or ¼ teaspoon bay leaf flakes)
>
> ¼ teaspoon allspice
>
> ½ teaspoon cardamom seeds
>
> 6 juniper berries
>
> 1 teaspoon peppercorns
>
> 1 tablespoon coriander seeds
>
> 1 tablespoon mustard seeds

Liquid mix:

> 4 cups apple cider vinegar
>
> 2 cups water
>
> 1 tablespoon lemon juice
>
> 1 cup sugar
>
> ⅛ cup sea salt

Sweet Spice Blend

Sweet spice blend works with most fruits and also bread or pastry. To make fruit salad, it can be moistened with lemon or apple juice and tossed into cut fruit, or mixed with whipped cream or sour cream and folded into the fruit. Sprinkle sweet spice blend over pie filling before putting the top crust in place. You can poke half a cinnamon stick through the center of the pie to act as a fragrant and flavorful vent. Add sweet spice blend to bread dough. You can also mix it with brown sugar and use it as a filling in rolled or layered pastries, or pinwheel cookies.

Candied ginger, whether in slices or chunks or chips, makes an excellent garnish. Mix a batch of sweet spice blend and keep it in a spice jar with a shaker lid.

¼ teaspoon powdered clove

½ teaspoon powdered coriander

1 teaspoon powdered ginger

1 tablespoon powdered allspice

2 tablespoons powdered cinnamon

Closet Sachets

Closet sachets are small cloth bags stuffed with dried herbs and flowers. They may be placed in closets, drawers, chests, or other storage areas. They keep fabric and other household goods smelling fresh and clean. They repel pests such as insects and mice; they also discourage mold and mildew. Sachets make nice gifts if you use pretty cloth, such as calico cotton, for the bags.

1 cup dried lavender flowers

1 cup dried lavender cotton

½ cup dried feverfew

½ cup orris root chips

¼ cup chopped dried lemon peel

¼ cup dried sage

⅛ cup dried wormwood

Herbs for Beer, Wine, Mead, and Liqueurs

✿ by Suzanne Ress ✿

Human beings have known how to control the fermentation process that makes alcoholic beverages since around 7000 B.C.E., about the same time the first agricultural communities started using clay pots for storage.

Fermentation is a natural chemical process that occurs when a bacteria or yeast converts a carbohydrate such as sugar or starch into an alcohol. This can only happen in moist, anaerobic conditions. If someone were to leave a few bunches of grapes—or honey with a tad too much moisture content, or mashed barley sprouts—in a closed ceramic pot for several days or more, it would inevitably begin to ferment, making the base for wine, mead, or beer.

Even before humans started cultivating selected plants and animals for food, when they still roamed the earth as hunter-gatherers, they were already collecting certain wild leaves, flowers, berries, and bark for their high nutritional, aromatic, or medicinal value.

Although the first known written record of the existence of the occupation "herb digger" is attributed to the early Greek biologist/physicist Theophrastus in about 300 B.C.E., traces of herbal essences have been found in clay jars that Egyptians used for wine storage about 5,000 years ago. I think it is logical to assume that Neolithic humans were experimenting with adding various herbs to fermented beverages right from the start.

Recipes for beer that date back to before the sixteenth century often called for alehoof *(Glechoma hederacea)*, mugwort *(Artemesia vulgaris)*, yarrow *(Achillea millefolium)*, horehound *(Marrubium vulgare)*, heather *(Calluna vulgaris)*, sweet gale *(Myrica gale)*, or wormwood *(Artemesia absinthium)* for their flavoring or other properties. Not until some time after this did hops *(Humulus lupulus)* become the dominant herb used in beer making. To this day, hops are a key ingredient in brewing, because, in addition to the smooth, bitter flavor and aroma they add to the beer, they also act as a natural preservative.

Wine can and has been made from just about any fruit, herb, or flower, but the standard remains grapes, whether white or red.

The Egyptian wine jars from about 3000 B.C.E. contained wine made from grapes with the addition of lemon balm *(Melissa officinalis)*, coriander *(Coriandrum sativum)*, mint *(Metha)*, savory *(Satureja hortensis)*, a fresh fig, wormwood *(Artemesia absinthium)*, tansy *(Tanacetum vulgare)*, senna *(Senna alexandrina)*, thyme *(Thymus vulgaris)*, germander *(Teucrium)*, rosemary *(Rosmarinus officinalis)*, yarrow *(Achillea millefolium)*, wild fennel *(Foeniculum vulgare)*, marjoram *(Origanum majorana)*, oregano *(Origanum vulgare)*, and pine resin. This royal mixture is believed to have been used as medicine.

With the advent of agriculture, humans also quickly discovered that by adding water to honey and leaving it in a closed pot for a while, it fermented into mead. With the addition of herbs, mead's flavor becomes much more complex, and is called by the beautiful medieval name "metheglin."

Distillation is the process of transforming a liquid into its vapor form and then transforming the vapor back into liquid. This happens in nature when, for example, a sudden rainfall on hot pavement creates steam. If you walk through this steam after the rainfall, beads of water will appear on your skin. Those beads are distilled water. They are made of the evaporated H_2O that left the rainwater's heavier minerals behind on the pavement.

As early as 150 C.E., alchemists were experimenting with distillation of water and other liquids. It is believed that the distillation of alcohol was not successfully practiced (although it may have been tried!) until the twelfth century, at the medical school in Salerno, Italy.

Distilling fermented beverages makes a stronger alcoholic drink because much of the water is left behind. Distilled alcohol was called the "spirit" of the fermented liquid, by medieval alchemists, and we still call liquor spirits. It was considered strong medicine, and the process of making it was kept a guarded secret by the alchemists and physicians who knew how to do it until about the middle of the fourteenth century, when it was widely used throughout Europe as a remedy for the Black Death.

Shortly thereafter, easier methods for making distilled spirits from grains were developed, and people began drinking these as beverages. It was during the fifteenth century that many experiments using herbs in spirits were tried, particularly by alchemists and monks, who were looking for an elixir of long life.

One of these liqueurs, Chartreuse, has been made by French Carthusian monks since the 1740s. It contains extracts from more than 130 different herbs, and was originally adapted from an elixir recipe and intended to be used as medicine. People developed a taste for it, and it soon became a popular drink. Nearly three hundred years later, the recipe remains the same.

Herbal Liqueurs

Herbal liqueurs are made by macerating or infusing one or more types of herbs in distilled alcohol for any time between a few days and a few months, depending on the herbs used and the strength desired. The alcohol is then filtered and mixed with simple syrup at a ratio of 50/50, or more, or less, depending on what final product is being made.

Any relatively bland-tasting spirit can be used to make liqueur. The best are grain alcohol, clear grappa, or vodka. Whiskey, rum, bourbon, and tequila can also be used, but because each of these has such a distinctive flavor of its own, you will end up making a flavored whiskey, rum, bourbon, or tequila rather than a liqueur with a dominant herbal flavor.

Any edible herb can be used to make liqueur. I have made straight basil, sage, rosemary, mint, and horehound liqueurs, which were all successful after-dinner drinks at holidays and dinner parties. Combinations of certain herbs with flowers, nuts, or fruit can work well, as in lemon rosemary liqueur, or rose petal and lemon balm, or walnut and horehound. Combinations of two or more herbs make a more complex, intriguing liqueur. Royal liqueur and absinthe are two many-herbed combinations I've tried my hand at. Be creative and invent your own special blend. Here is one of my favorite recipes.

Walnut and Horehound Liqueur

On June 24, pluck 3–4 green walnuts from the tree (they must be unripe green ones!). Cut each into 4 pieces. Put them into a quart-sized Mason jar with 2–3 sprigs of fresh horehound. Cover all with half a quart of grain alcohol, put the lid on, and leave to macerate for 2 months in a dark, cool place.

On August 24, strain the alcohol, which will have turned dark brown, through a clean dish towel over a funnel, into a large glass recipient.

Prepare simple syrup by mixing 2 cups white sugar with 2 cups water in a heavy-bottomed stainless steel pot. Bring slowly almost to the simmering point, stirring frequently. It should turn perfectly clear before it simmers. Take it off the heat and let cool completely.

When cool, add all of the syrup to the alcohol and blend thoroughly. Using the cleaned funnel, decant the liqueur into bottles, and cork or otherwise close them. Store in a cool, dark place until December 24. This makes a smoothly complex bittersweet and nutty digestif for the holiday season.

Herbal Beer

For beer making, you will need some basic equipment (which can also be used in wine and mead making): an air lock, an air-lockable container, and a siphon. You must use brewing yeast, not wine yeast, and not bread or Brewer's yeast. Brewing yeast is available at beer-making supply stores and sites. You will also need malt syrup. Beer has always contained some form of bitter herb for a smoother flavor, which can be horehound, alehoof, costmary, nettle, yarrow, or dandelion, as well as hops. Other herbs can be added for flavor, including lavender, thyme, mint, borage, marjoram, chamomile, woodruff, melissa, and whatever else your imagination comes up with!

Making beer, from start to finish, takes much less time than mead or wine, so for many people it is the ideal fermented beverage to start experimenting with.

Melissa, Yarrow, and Nettle Beer

10-ounce jar of malt syrup

¾ cup brown sugar

3 ounces fresh herbs (melissa leaves, yarrow flowers, nettle tops—handle carefully!)

1 gallon water

1 teaspoon brewing yeast

Boil together the malt syrup, brown sugar, herbs, and water for half an hour. Cool to 100°F. (touchable, but warm), then strain out the herbs and add the yeast. Funnel into a large air-locked container and ferment for 7–10 days. Funnel into sterile bottles, cap, and leave for 10–14 days before drinking.

Herbal Mead, or Metheglin

Fermented honey beverages are ancient. Although mead was once very popular, nowadays many people only encounter it in historical fiction or at medieval fairs. In medieval times, mead, like beer, was usually homemade, and safer than water, when drinking-water sources doubled as sewers. While beer, with its alcohol content of 4–5 percent, was drunk by both children and adults throughout the day, mead, with an alcohol content sometimes as high as 18 percent, was usually reserved as an adults-only beverage for special occasions.

Straight mead's ingredients are only honey, water, acid, and yeast. Recipes for the much more complexly flavored metheglin may call for the addition of one, two, or as many as ten different herbs.

Metheglins were originally developed for their health and medicinal properties, but soon enough came to be enjoyed for their flavors.

When making your own metheglin it is best to use fresh raw honey from a local beekeeper. Light, mild-flavored honey makes the finest metheglin, as the tannins naturally present in dark honeys compete too much with the flavors of herbs.

Metheglin is not difficult to make, although you will need two air-locked containers and a siphon. You should use special wine or champagne yeast, available in beer and wine makers' shops, from beekeeping suppliers, and online.

Basil and Fennel Metheglin
½ cup fresh basil leaves

3 blooming fennel flower umbels

3 pounds honey

3 quarts water

2 cups lemon juice, plus the finely grated rind of 1 lemon

1 packet champagne yeast

1½ cups fresh orange juice, at room temperature

A handful of raisins

A clean potato peel (a decent-sized piece, about 2–3 inches long and ¾ inch wide)

3–4 acorns

Put the clean fresh herbs in a large bowl or container.

Boil the honey in 3 quarts of water for 10 minutes. Let cool, then pour over the herbs.

Add the lemon juice and rind, cover, and let sit for 24 hours.

Next, combine the yeast, orange juice, raisins, and potato peel in a Mason jar. Put the lid on, shake well, and let sit for about 2 hours or until bubbly. Add it to the honey mixture. Add the acorns, and let the mixture ferment. This will take 5–10 days.

Siphon the metheglin into an air-locked container, leaving all of the solids and dregs behind. Leave for 3 months.

Siphon into a second air-locked container. Leave for 6 months.

Repeat once more before bottling.

Store the metheglin upright in a cool, dark place for at least 6 months before opening.

Herbal Wine

Herbal wines are made in much the same way as meads, except that sugar is employed in place of honey, so the finished wine will taste more purely of the aromatic herb or herbs used. Be aware that making a pure herbal wine requires a lot of fresh herbs!

Parsley, Sage, Rosemary, and Thyme Wine

  1 pound coarsely chopped fresh herb mix (parsley, sage, rosemary, and thyme, or other, as desired)

  2 orange rinds, finely grated

  2 lemon rinds, finely grated

  4 quarts water

  3 pounds sugar

  4 acorns

  1 packet wine yeast

  A small handful of raisins

  A clean potato peel (a decent-sized piece, about 2–3 inches long and ¾ inch wide)

  1½ cups orange juice

Simmer the herbs and citrus zests in 4 quarts water for 20 minutes.

Strain this liquid into a large container. Add the sugar. Let sit for 24 hours.

Add the acorns.

Put the orange juice, yeast, raisins, and potato peel in a Mason jar and shake well. Let stand about 2 hours until bubbly, then add this to the large container.

Cover with a clean dish towel and let ferment about 10 days.

Transfer to an air-locked container, re-racking as necessary to clarify.

After the final rack, leave it in the air-locked container at least 6 months before bottling.

Store the bottles in a cool, dark place for 6 months before opening.

Sláinte!

Healthier Vegetarian Dishes with Herbs

❧ by Laurel Reufner ❧

My family members and I are not vegetarians, but we do enjoy a good meatless meal on a regular basis. We've also got some close friends who are vegetarian and who like to join us for dinner occasionally.

There are some amazingly tasty vegetarian dishes out there offering a great variety—if you're willing to poke around some—but most of the dishes in my cookbooks, while yummy-looking, seem heavy on the pasta, or offer endless variations on eggs or cheese (and more pasta). I'm a diabetic, so we try to avoid having lots of pasta dishes. And eggs don't always sit well with me. Besides, they get boring after a while, and we all know that a ton of cheese isn't healthy.

And what's the deal with so many vegetarian dishes making up for lack of flavor by going heavy on the hot and spicy? Not everyone likes that much heat in their food, my kids included. And I don't consider it an excusable means for covering up otherwise bland flavor. Spices should enhance your dish's other flavors, as well as each other, rather than hiding the lack thereof.

All of those considerations led to the idea for this article. I wanted to either adapt or come up with some healthier vegetarian options for my family. The following recipes have been tested on them, with at least three of the four of us giving each dish a thumbs-up. Often, I'd make the recipe and they would pipe in with suggestions for how to tweak it. And just so you know, my younger daughter is a picky eater. She's great about tasting new things, but she is very particular about what passes her "keep it" test.

There are some tricks to making a dish healthier or adapting it for your own tastes. Try using light or low-fat products. Check the labels, though. Low-fat often means higher sugar, especially in salad dressings and such. I tend to go for the regular options in those cases, but that's because of the diabetes. If you aren't diabetic, you don't have to worry about it as much.

We also try to substitute whole wheat pasta for regular, although it can take some trial and error to find a brand you like. And brown rice has a much heartier taste than white. If you just don't see yourself enjoying it, mix the two, like we do.

Another thing you might want to check for is sodium. It's amazing how much salt is in our food. In recipes calling for canned beans, you'll notice that I always start by rinsing the beans. This will remove a lot of the sodium, making them healthier.

Herbs and spices are your friends, as they can add a lot of flavor to your dishes. Start with a light hand and adjust them to taste. We love garlic around here, which I buy minced by the jarful nearly every payday. I also keep a good soup stock base on hand, which adds tons of flavor to your soups, stews, and some other dishes.

Kick can be added with chili oil, white and black pepper, garlic, cayenne, and even curry. Once again, have fun experimenting and don't be afraid to try new things.

Fiesta Taco Casserole

This recipe was adapted from a non-vegetarian recipe to be meatless. It has become quite the family favorite.

Filling:

1 15½-ounce can black beans, drained and rinsed well

1 can refried beans

16 ounces salsa

2 tablespoons taco seasoning (see recipe that follows)

1–2 cups coarsely broken tortilla chips

¾ cup chopped bell pepper, more or less

4 green onions, sliced

1 cup chopped tomato

1½–2 cups shredded cheddar cheese

¼ cup sliced black olives

Topping:

1 cup shredded lettuce

½ cup chopped tomato

½ cup crushed tortilla chips

In a large skillet, combine the black beans, refried beans, salsa, and taco seasoning mix. Heat thoroughly by bringing to a boil.

Place the crushed tortilla chips in a 2-quart casserole. On top of this, spoon in the skillet mixture, and top with layers of bell pepper, chopped tomato, green onions, sliced olives, and cheese. Bake at 350°F. for about 25 minutes.

Top with the remaining lettuce, tomato, and tortilla chips.

This is really tasty when served with sour cream and additional cheese and salsa. We sometimes also eat it out of bowls with whole tortilla chips.

Taco Seasoning

- 2 teaspoons chili powder
- 2 teaspoons chopped dried onion
- 1 teaspoon garlic powder
- ½ teaspoon cumin seed
- ½ teaspoon salt
- ½ teaspoon pepper

Combine all the ingredients. Store any leftovers in an airtight container for future use.

Garbanzo Salad

This was the second recipe I made for my family, shortly after the Fiesta Taco Casserole. We all liked it—even my husband, who very much dislikes mint. He thought it made the salad better. So if you dislike a strong mint flavor, you might want to try it anyway, or substitute some chopped parsley instead.

- 2 cans garbanzo beans
- ½ of a small container of grape or cherry tomatoes

2–4 ounces feta cheese, according to your taste

¼ cup fresh mint or parsley leaves, chopped

⅓ cup white or red wine vinegar

¼ cup olive oil

1 tablespoon sugar

¼ teaspoon black pepper

Make sure you rinse the garbanzo beans really well. Wash and halve the tomatoes. If they're still a little large, quarter them.

Toss the beans, tomatoes, feta, and mint together in a large bowl. Combine the rest of the ingredients in a screw-top jar and shake to combine. Pour the dressing over the contents in the bowl and gently stir to coat.

These are really great served with toasted or grilled pita. Something about the warmed bread offsets the taste of the chickpeas nicely. Also, if you're a diabetic, go easy on the chickpeas. I learned the hard way that they can really boost your blood sugar.

Lucky Seven Soup

The whole family signed off on this soup. It was so tasty that a few of us went back for seconds, even though the first bowl was plenty filling. If you want some to freeze for later, simply double the ingredients.

½ cup baby lima beans

½ cup black beans

½ cup chickpeas

½ cup great northern beans

½ cup kidney beans

½ cup pinto beans

½ cup lentils

1 cup chopped carrots

¼ cup chopped celery

1 14.7-ounce can chopped tomatoes (use a seasoned variety if you want the extra flavor)

2 bay leaves

1–3 teaspoons savory

1–3 teaspoons basil

Vegetable stock base

Place all the beans, except the lentils, in a large bowl or suitably sized stock pot, and cover the beans with water, plus a few inches. Allow them to soak for several hours or overnight.* Discard the water and rinse the beans.

In a large pot, place the beans, including the chickpeas, plus the carrots, celery, tomatoes, and seasonings. Add 7 cups of water plus enough of the stock base for the amount of water used. (I like to use a little extra base for extra flavor.) Bring to a boil and allow to simmer until the carrots and beans are tender. I usually cook for about an hour. Also, you can add some chopped potato or sweet potato if you'd like.

*I'll admit, I rarely plan my meals that far ahead. Fortunately, there's an easy alternative to soaking your beans overnight. Simply put them in the pot, cover with plenty of water, and bring to a simmer on the stovetop. Allow to cook for about an hour, then drain, rinse, and continue as you normally would.

Veggie Pita Pockets

These make a delightfully simple lunch. The crunch is wonderful, and if you choose your pita carefully, they can be really filling. For 1 sandwich, you'll need the following:

One whole-grain pita

Cream cheese

Slices of red, orange, or yellow bell pepper

Cucumber slices

Cut the pita in half, giving yourself two pockets to fill. Slather cream cheese on the inside of each pocket and pile in the veggies.

If you want to take these with you for lunch, I'd make them the day they're going to be eaten instead of the night before. Otherwise you run the risk of your pita getting soggy.

I found a heart-healthy, omega-rich variety of pita that's amazingly low in carbs and high in fiber. The net carb load is something like 4 grams! And they taste good!

Black Bean Veggie Soup

As you can tell from this article, I make a lot of soups. And this particular recipe makes a good bit. We tend to eat it as leftovers during the week. It's great heated up with some cheese added to your bowl and then scooped up with tortilla chips. As to the amount, you might want to consider halving it or freezing some for later use.

5 cans black beans, rinsed and drained

2 cans chopped tomatoes

3–4 cups potatoes, chopped

2 cups shredded carrots

1 cup portobello mushrooms, chopped

2 tablespoons savory

1 bulb of garlic

1 teaspoon salt

1 jar roasted red peppers, chopped

1 cup chopped parsley, reserved for end

This one is pretty easy to make—just put everything except the parsley in a pan and bring to a boil. Reduce to a simmer and allow to cook for 45 minutes to an hour. Add the parsley before serving and stir it in. We like to serve this soup with sour cream (light) and cheese, as well as some tortilla chips on the side. If you strain off the broth, it also makes a tasty tortilla filling.

Hot and Sour Soup

My husband and I particularly enjoy this soup. We especially like it during cold and flu season when we're both all stuffy-headed or suffering from a sore throat. Recently both of our daughters have also started enjoying Mom's Hot and Sour Soup. Even the youngest gave it a thumbs-up, having tried a little bit from our last batch. You can go easy on the white pepper and chili oil, letting diners add more at the table if they want to heat it up a bit.

I realize some of these ingredients will probably be hard to find in some areas, but the soup is so good, I just had to include it. If you're lucky, your local supermarket will have dried mushrooms, and most stores carry bamboo shoots nowadays. The hardest thing to find might be the lily buds, which you could probably leave out if necessary.

⅓ cup wood ear, black, cloud, straw, or shitake mushrooms (you can also use a small bunch of fresh enoki mushrooms)

⅓ cup dried lily buds

Boiling water (to cover the dried mushrooms and lily buds)

6 cups vegetable stock (I use a powdered stock base in water)

2 tablespoons cornstarch

1 can bamboo shoots, matchstick-cut if possible

4 tablespoons red wine vinegar

2 tablespoons white vinegar or rice vinegar

3 tablespoons soy sauce

12 ounces extra firm tofu, cut into small cubes

3 eggs, beaten

1 teaspoon sesame oil

1 small bunch of green onions, sliced small

1 can sliced water chestnuts (optional)

½ teaspoon salt (optional)

2–3 teaspoons ground white pepper

½–1 teaspoon chili oil

Place the dried mushrooms and lily buds in a bowl and cover with boiling water. You can use separate bowls if you'd like, but I just toss them all together and let them soak for about 20 minutes. Meanwhile, start either 6 cups of water or vegetable stock to boiling in a large pan. If using water, add enough stock base for 7–8 cups.

At the end of 20 minutes, begin removing the mushrooms from the hot water, and slice or chop them for the soup pot. Reserve a cup of the mushrooms' soaking water, and add the cornstarch. Stir to combine before adding it to the pan of stock. When done with the mushrooms, you can add those as well. The lily buds should be cut crosswise into halves or thirds and then sort of fluffed or torn with your fingers before adding them to the pot.

Add the bamboo shoots next. I like the matchstick-cut ones when I can find them, but my husband prefers the sliced ones. It's totally up to you. Mix the vinegars and soy sauce in a small bowl and add to the soup.

The tofu I usually buy comes in a solid block. I start by cutting it in half lengthwise. I then cube it into smallish squares. We prefer smaller pieces of tofu in our soup as opposed to something an inch or so bigger. Cube your tofu according to your own tastes. Add it to the pot and return everything to a boil if it's not already there.

In a small bowl or measuring cup, beat 3 eggs. Once the soup is boiling again, remove the pot from the heat and slowly pour in the eggs, stirring the soup the entire time. You want the egg to feather out in the soup, hence the stirring. The eggs will quickly cook in the heat.

Add the sesame oil, green onions, water chestnuts, salt, white pepper, and chili oil. Enjoy!

Cilantro: An Ancient Herb That Still Tops the Charts

❧ by Anne Sala ❧

Cilantro's world domination was inevitable. While its seemingly recent emergence in mainstream American cuisine makes it appear that cilantro's popularity is a brief trend, this herb has been known to humans for thousands of years. During that time, it has been chopped, crushed, preserved, and eaten fresh by millions of people. From street food in the Middle East to national dishes in Brazil, this herb's cheerful, feathery green leaves have sparked the imagination of an entire planet's worth of cooks.

Coriandrum sativum has the rare distinction of being an herb, a spice, and a vegetable. The leaves have a fresh green scent and a bittersweet

taste, and the root provides a more robust dose of that flavor. The seeds, however, have a distinctly different scent—more lemony—and a warmer, earthier flavor.

Cilantro is the Spanish word for this vibrant herb, and we know it as such in the United States because of the herb's use in Mexican cuisine. It is also known as coriander and Chinese parsley. Cilantro is actually part of the Apiaceae plant family, along with parsley (and carrots, cumin, fennel, Queen Anne's lace, and celery, to name a few), so that last name is only partially a misnomer, and, like parsley, is best used fresh, not dried.

The seeds, known simply as coriander, are utilized to season drinks, including the Scandinavian beverage aquavit, to make sausage and baked goods, and to preserve meat. Coriander is also used to make perfumes and is mentioned as a potent aphrodisiac in the book *One Thousand and One Nights* (often known in English as the *Arabian Nights*).

The roots look like thin, hairy parsnips, and are a popular ingredient in Thai cuisine, especially when shredded and used as a base for curries and soups. Furthermore, since the root is hardy, it is a good addition to dishes that have a long cooking time, but need the flavor of the herb's leaves to carry on.

A finicky annual, cilantro grows best in the spring and fall, when the weather is not too hot. Give it fertile, well-draining soil. When the seeds germinate, they shoot up ragged-edged, paddle-like leaves. These can be harvested about a month after they appear. In the warmth of July and August, the plant will begin to produce long, spindly leaves and pale white or pink flowers in umbels at the top. These blossoms will turn into the small, round, segmented coriander seeds. Harvest the seeds when they turn brown, and allow them to dry thoroughly before use.

There are few herbs in the world with a history as long and varied as cilantro. Since almost the beginning of time, it has shared its life with humans. With a sharp green scent to its leaves and the preservative powers of its seeds, the herb must have quickly caught the attention of early travelers through its native habitat around the Mediterranean Sea and Middle East.

The oldest known example of the plant's cohabitation with humans is the 8,000-year old remnants of coriander seeds found in the Nahal Hemar cave in Israel. They date to the Neolithic period—which was before humans discovered how to make pottery. Seeds were also found in King Tutankhamun's tomb in Egypt. Coriander seeds are also mentioned in the Book of Exodus, and the fresh leaves are used as a bitter herb in the Jewish observance of Passover.

The Romans, as usual, are attributed with spreading the use of cilantro through Europe and into England, where it was particularly popular up through Elizabethan times. When the Colonists came to America, they carried cilantro with them. Simultaneously, the Spanish conquistadors brought the herb to Mexico and South America, where it was quickly assimilated into the native cuisines. As cilantro's influence was making its way west to the New World, it was also heading east into Asia, where its vibrant flavor married well with the salty, spicy dishes popular in the region.

Medicinally, cilantro and its seeds have been used as a digestive aid and to treat stomach problems. It is interesting to note that in Europe, China, and India, healers combined coriander seeds with other seeds in a similar fashion—using cardamom, caraway, and fennel—in their remedies for dyspepsia. Some cultures use it as a sleep aid. In China, it was believed that the seeds would bring immortality to those who consumed them.

Even though cilantro is popular all around the world, there are a number of people, particularly in Europe, who find the smell and taste of its leaves to be offensive. The name coriander comes from the Greek word *koris*, which means "bedbug." The smell of its leaves is thought to be similar to the smell of that small parasite. Furthermore, while many find coriander's flavor to be pleasingly fresh, some say it has a soapy or "lotiony" taste.

For many years, it was thought that a person's dislike of the herb was culturally learned—that if they lived in a place where bedbugs were a problem, they might grow up finding the smell repulsive. But if the person was determined to get to the point where they could eat and actually enjoy cilantro, all they had to do was recondition themselves to associate the smell with tasty foods rather than bugs. That might work for some people, but recent scientific studies indicate that this aversion may have a genetic cause.

According to a 2010 article in the *New York Times*, flavor chemists pinpointed the source of cilantro's scent to "modified fragments of fat molecules called aldehydes." These molecules are similar to the ones found in certain bugs, lotions, and soap.

The reason why particular people fixate on these aldehydes when they smell cilantro might lie in a group of olfactory-receptor genes. A 2012 article about cilantro in the science journal *Nature* details how several researchers have only just identified genes that encode certain olfactory and bitter taste receptors. These particular genes could affect a person of European descent's reaction to cilantro.

No matter a person's genetics, as the world's cuisines begin to blend, it will be fascinating to see how cilantro continues to shape the way we eat.

Cilantro Recipes

Here is a collection of recipes that exemplify cilantro's importance in food cultures around the globe. I invite you to explore them with the same inquisitiveness that spurred on the prehistoric cooks who first held the herb's tender leaves to their nose, imagining its potential.

Roasted Vietnamese Chicken Salad and Cilantro Dressing/Dipping Sauce

Cilantro is an important herb in Vietnamese cuisine, where it is known as rau ngó. This recipe really plays up the herb's vibrant flavor, as you get to taste it in three different ways. With the addition of rice paper wrappers, you could easily turn this recipe into excellent spring rolls. Serves 6.

For chicken and marinade:

   1 3–4-pound chicken, cut up

   1 cup cilantro leaves and stems, chopped

   ⅓ cup green onions, chopped

   1 tablespoon garlic, minced

   ½ cup soy sauce

   2 teaspoons garlic pepper sauce, such as Sriracha, or to taste

   3 tablespoons fish sauce

   Zest and ⅓ cup juice from 1 lime (zest the lime before juicing it)

   2 tablespoons brown sugar

   2 tablespoons honey

   1½ teaspoons ground black pepper

½ teaspoon Chinese five spice powder

3 tablespoons neutral-tasting oil, such as peanut or grapeseed

For salad:

1-pound package rice noodles

1–2 heads oak leaf lettuce, washed and torn

2 large carrots, peeled and shredded

1 large English cucumber, peeled and sliced thin

½ bunch cilantro, washed and dried

½ bunch fresh mint (spearmint, preferably), washed and dried

1 lime, cut into wedges

Dipping sauce (recipe follows)

Place all the chicken pieces into a gallon-size zip-seal bag. Prop the bag so the mouth stays open, and add the rest of the marinade ingredients. Seal the bag and squeeze the contents to mix. Refrigerate overnight, turning chicken over occasionally. You can also place all ingredients in a nonreactive pan and cover.

Remove chicken from marinade and pour marinade into a small saucepan. Use paper towels to dry the chicken pieces and place in a roasting pan. At the same time, bring the reserved marinade to a boil for at least 1 minute.

Bake the chicken in a 400°F. oven. Turn and baste the pieces with marinade every 15 minutes, until the juices run clear—about 45 minutes. Or, use an instant-read thermometer to make sure the chicken's internal temperature reads 165°F. at its thickest part. Remove from oven and allow to rest for at least 10 minutes. Then use two forks to shred the meat from the bones.

Prepare the rice noodles according to the package directions while chicken cooks. Allow the noodles to cool.

To serve, place a portion of the lettuce into the bottom of each person's bowl. Top with rice noodles, shredded chicken, carrot, cucumber, cilantro, mint, lime juice, and dipping sauce.

Cilantro Dressing / Dipping Sauce

⅔ cup fish sauce

2 teaspoons garlic, minced

4 tablespoons sugar

¼ cup fresh lime juice

1 cup warm water

2 tablespoons cilantro, chopped fine

1 teaspoon Sriracha or other pepper garlic sauce

Stir together all ingredients until sugar dissolves.

Salmon Moqueca Baiana

Moqueca is a traditional fish stew from Brazil that has a history going back at least three hundred years. This version is adapted from the Moqueca made in the northeastern state of Bahia. Another version, made without coconut milk, is called Moqueca Capixaba and comes from the southeastern state of Espirito Santo. To make the Moqueca Baiana even more authentic, add 1 tablespoon dark red palm oil, or Azeite de Dende, along with the coconut milk. If you use frozen sweet potatoes, or cook the potato in the microwave first, it will significantly speed up the construction of this easy and flavorful soup. Serves 6–8.

For the marinade:

1½ pounds salmon fillets

1 28-ounce can diced tomatoes

1 cup cilantro, chopped

1 yellow onion, chopped

2 garlic cloves, peeled and crushed

¼ cup lime juice

1 tablespoon olive oil

1 teaspoon salt

Place all ingredients, except for fish, in a food processor or blender and process until smooth. Pour over fish in a nonreactive bowl. Cover and place in refrigerator to marinate for 30–60 minutes.

For the stew:

1 large sweet potato, peeled and diced

2 tablespoons olive oil

1 zucchini, chopped

1 green pepper, chopped

1 red pepper, chopped

½ cup water, or more if necessary

¾ cup whole coconut milk

1 tablespoon dark red palm oil (optional)

½ cup green onion, bottom parts only, minced (garnish)

½ cup cilantro, chopped (garnish)

Sauté the sweet potatoes in olive oil over medium heat for 10–15 minutes in a large skillet until they become soft. Add splashes of water to the pan to prevent burning.

Add zucchini and peppers and continue to cook until tender, about 5 minutes. Continue to add water if necessary.

Stir in the ½ cup water and coconut milk. Add the dark red palm oil, if desired. Bring to a boil and then simmer for 2–3 minutes.

Add fish and marinade. Simmer for 10–15 minutes, or until fish flakes.

Serve the soup with the green onion and cilantro as garnishes.

Pork in Green Sauce

Pork loves cilantro, and this tomatillo-based green sauce brings out the herb's vibrancy in a very straightforward way. This is a rather simple recipe. It can easily take in more ingredients, such as spices like cumin or allspice, hot peppers, or tomatoes. Serves 4.

6 medium tomatillos, husked and rinsed

Cold water (to cover tomatillos)

2 pounds pork shoulder, cut into 1-inch chunks

2 tablespoons vegetable oil

1 teaspoon salt

3 garlic cloves, peeled

½ cup cilantro, coarse stems removed

Soft tortillas, lettuce, tomatoes, onion, sour cream or crema, and fresh cilantro (garnish)

Place the tomatillos in a saucepan large enough to hold them in one layer. Cover them with cold water and place over high heat. Bring to a boil, then reduce heat. Simmer uncovered for 15 minutes or until they are tender but still intact.

Meanwhile, brown the pork on all sides with the oil and salt in a large, heavy pot, over medium-high heat. Work in batches so the meat is not crowded.

When the tomatillos are finished cooking, remove them from the pot and place in a blender with 1 cup of their cooking water, the garlic, and cilantro. Blend until smooth.

Return all the pork to the pot and pour over the tomatillo sauce. Stir to coat the meat and bring to a boil. Reduce the heat, cover, and simmer the meat until it begins to fall apart, about 1½–2 hours.

Serve with soft tortillas, lettuce, tomatoes, onion, sour cream or crema, and fresh cilantro.

Classic Mexican Salsa

When friends drop by, there is no better way to keep their tummies happy than with fresh salsa. This recipe can be increased to suit the size of your gathering or the number of tomatoes you have available. Serves 4.

   3 medium tomatoes, diced, juices reserved

   1 fresh jalapeño pepper, diced (remove seeds and veins to reduce the heat, if you like)

   ½ medium onion, diced

   ½ bunch cilantro leaves and stems, chopped

   ½ tablespoon extra virgin olive oil

   Juice from half a lime, or to taste

Salt and pepper

Corn tortilla chips

Combine the first five ingredients and tomato juice in a small bowl. Squeeze the lime over the contents and add salt and pepper to taste. Toss to distribute evenly. Serve with corn tortilla chips.

Chicken Shawarma Pita Pockets

A fast-food staple around the Middle East, shawarma meat is similar to gyro meat. It can be chicken, beef, veal, lamb, or goat. The meats are layered on a spit and rotated before a heat source. To serve, the meat is sliced off with a long knife and stuffed into a pita or piled on lavash. This chicken version is easy to make at home. The spices are also great to toss with green beans and potatoes before roasting. Serves 4.

2 tablespoons fresh ginger, peeled and grated

2 teaspoons ground cinnamon

1½ teaspoons salt, divided

1 teaspoon ground allspice

1½ teaspoons ground coriander

1 teaspoon ground cumin

1 teaspoon ground cayenne pepper

2 teaspoons olive oil

8 boneless, skin-on chicken thighs

1 large cucumber, peeled and sliced thin

½ cup plain yogurt

2 tablespoons red onion, diced

2 tablespoons fresh mint, chopped

½ teaspoon ground pepper

¼ teaspoon sugar (optional)

4 loaves pita bread, split in half

1 medium tomato, sliced

½ head oak leaf lettuce, washed and shredded

In a small bowl, stir together the ginger, cinnamon, 1 teaspoon salt, allspice, coriander, cumin, cayenne, and olive oil to make a paste.

Preheat oven to 400°F.

With your fingers, massage a bit of the spice mixture onto both sides of each chicken thigh. Place on a shallow roasting pan, skin side up.

Cook, turning occasionally, for about 35 minutes, or until the chicken's internal temperature reads 165°F. Remove from the oven and allow to rest for at least 10 minutes.

While the chicken cooks, combine the remaining ½ teaspoon salt with the rest of the ingredients, except for the pita bread, lettuce, and tomato, to make a creamy tzatziki dressing.

Slice each chicken thigh into ½-inch strips before placing in a serving bowl.

Allow diners to build their own pita pockets, layering the chicken, lettuce, tomatoes, and tzatziki to their liking. Serve with hot sauce on the table.

Further Reading

Callaway, Ewen. "Soapy Taste of Coriander Linked to Genetic Variants." *Nature: International Weekly Journal of Science.* September 12, 2012. http://www.nature.com/news/soapy-taste-of-coriander-linked-to-genetic-variants-1.11398.

Hollis, Sarah. *The Country Diary Herbal.* New York: Henry Holt & Company, 1990.

Kruger, Anna. *An Illustrated Guide to Herbs: Their Medicine and Magic.* Great Britain: Dragon's World, 1993.

McGee, Harold. "Cilantro Haters, It's Not Your Fault." *New York Times.* April 13, 2010. http://www.nytimes.com/2010/04/14/dining/14curious.html?_r=0.

Natural Standard. "Medicinal Uses for Coriander." August 2011. http://www.naturalstandard.com/news/news201108030.asp.

Not Your Mother's Tea:
An Herbal Brunch Menu

❧ by Jill Henderson ❧

Depending on where you live, it might surprise you to learn that tea is the most popular prepared beverage in the world today. Although no one knows precisely when tea began to be used as a pleasant beverage, there can be no doubt that the leaves of the common tea plant *(Camellia sinensis)* were first used for medicinal purposes. Even today, tea is favored for its ability to reduce inflammation, nausea, and pain and to stimulate blood flow and increase energy while still having a calming and soothing effect on the body. Researchers have confirmed green tea's ability to help reduce the incidence of diabetes, stroke, and certain types of cancer.

The History of Tea

The first humans to gather and use the leaves of the tea plant were no strangers to the use of wild plants as medicine. When they happened upon *Camellia sinenses*, they quickly realized that a decoction of the leaves was not only safe and healthful, but that it tasted good, too.

Tea was first introduced to Europe by Dutch traders who imported leaves from China in 1606. Almost sixty years later, tea was brought to Britain by the Portuguese wife of King Charles II. Being rare and unusual at the time, tea was tentatively embraced by members of the British aristocracy, but it wasn't until the 1800s, when the East India Company was given exclusive rights to import Indian tea to the British Isles, that drinking tea became much more popular.

For the British elite, "low tea" was a formal social event that often took place in a comfortable parlor where fine, delicate sweets and tea were served on low tables. As tea became more affordable and popular among the working class, they renamed their tea time "afternoon tea."

As with any trend, tea time took on many roles and names. "Cream tea" consisted of scones with jam or clotted cream. "Light tea" included finger sandwiches and delicate sweets. "Full tea" was more of a meal than a snack and included heartier fare such as quiches, tarts, and meat pies. If a special occasion arose, full tea would fill all of the above roles, with the addition of refreshing cider drinks, light wine, or champagne. The ever-evolving nature of tea time eventually led to "high tea," a moniker that referred to the time of day. This particular tea was the equivalent of dinner, and common fare included meat pies, potato cakes, and filling casseroles, with a few sweets on the side.

As the British Empire colonized far-flung parts of the world, the custom of taking tea followed. In America, where early British customs pervaded the common culture, tea would become an important symbol of American independence. The rebellious and independent attitude of the inhabitants of the New World pervaded and changed many of the customs associated with the British. What once was afternoon tea became a coffee break, and high tea, an elegant Sunday brunch. For the Western working class, meat tea became known simply as dinner. Yet despite the changes and associations with British colonization, tea as a refreshing drink never lost its appeal in the West, and a resurgence of interest in formal tea parties is again on the rise.

Types of Tea

Of course, a tea party just isn't a tea party without the tea, and these days, Americans are lusting for that perfect cup. To the uninitiated, the dizzying hierarchy of tea types, flavors, and classifications can be quite confusing, but in reality, there are only a few specific types of tea under which all teas fall, including black, green, mate, rooibos, and herbal.

It goes without argument that most common teas are the black and green types. These teas, along with their subtypes, are made specifically from the leaves of the woody shrub *Camellia sinensis*. The varying darkness of tea comes from an exacting process known as fermentation, which is actually the simple process of natural oxidation. A tea's caffeine content, flavor, and color depend on how long the tea leaves are allowed to dry before enzymatic action is halted through steaming or heat drying. Dark teas such as Ceylon, Assam, Earl Grey, and Darjeeling are produced through a more thorough fermentation process, while lighter white, green, and oolong teas are either lightly fermented or not fermented at all. While all *Camellia* teas have nutritive and medicinal value, green and white teas are often considered to be the most healthful.

Mate (mah-tay) is tea made from the leaves and twigs of the yerba mate tree, a relative of the common holly. A regional favorite, mate is found primarily in the South American countries of Brazil, Argentina, Uruguay, Paraguay, and Chile, where it has attained a sort of cult status. Where mate is popular, you will find people walking around with their favorite mate cup (a specialized tisane cup with built-in straw) in hand and a thermos of hot water tucked beneath their arm. With a practiced elegance, the mate cup is quickly and repeatedly filled with hot water for an endless cup of tea.

Another unusual form of tea is rooibos (roy-bos). This tea is derived from the needlelike leaves and twigs of the shrub *Aspalathus linearis*. Commonly referred to as red bush, this unusual evergreen is a member of the legume family of plants native to the dry, mountainous region of the Western Cape of South Africa. Like black and green teas, rooibos is fermented to varying degrees through enzymatic oxidation. This is what gives African red tea its distinctive color. Unlike mate, rooibos is often taken British-style, with milk and sugar or a wedge of lemon for sweetness. Totally caffeine-free, rooibos is also thought to be both nutritive and medicinal, helping improve digestion and strengthen the immune system.

Although herbal tea is the last form of tea on our list, it is anything but last in popularity, healthfulness, and flavor. In fact, one could argue that all of the teas mentioned here are in fact "herbal" in nature. That being said, a true herb consists only of the airy parts of herbaceous plants. Over the last decade, the consumption of herbal teas around the world has skyrocketed. Sometimes referred to as a tisane, herbal teas are incredibly diverse and can be made up of one to many dried herbs, fruits, flowers, and spices or blended together with more traditional green and black teas. Unadulterated herbal teas are naturally caffeine-free and have numerous medicinal and nutritive qualities, but what those benefits are depends entirely on the herbs being used. Some of the more traditional tea herbs include peppermint, chamomile, and lemon balm. Whether taken hot or iced, plain or sweetened, when it comes to herbal tea, the sky truly is the limit.

Not Your Mother's Tea

If you have not dared to throw a tea party for fear of going about it all wrong, or if a formal party is not your cup of tea, by all means let your hair down! Gone are the days of the rigid protocols of Miss Manners, and what's in are fun, festive gatherings filled with color and flair. To start things off on the right foot, begin by leaving dainty bone china in the cupboard. Instead, go for the shabby-chic look of colorful, even mismatched plates and cups. The whimsy of the bright colors will immediately convey to your guests that this is definitely not your mother's tea.

Our herbal brunch menu follows the classic lines of a traditional tea time with a fresh herbal twist. When throwing an herbal brunch tea, keep in mind that the food and drinks served should complement one another. If you hold your herbal brunch tea in the summer, focus on using herbs, spices, and edible flowers that are light and fresh to the palate, such as lemon balm, mint, rose, and lavender. The same can be said for the types of food you serve. Spring and summer herbal brunches should include fresh seasonal fruits and vegetables and lighter entrées made with chicken, fish, and tuna. Equally, fall or winter brunch teas should reflect the bounty of the season by using rich, warming herbs and spices such as sage, tarragon, horseradish, and bay and seasonal favorites such as buttery squash, ham, and hearty cheeses.

Plates of tea treats can be passed around a table or sitting area, with condiments and tea within everyone's reach, or you can let your guests serve themselves buffet-style. Either way, the keys to a successful herbal brunch are good food, good friends, and lively conversation.

The Menu

Icy Mint Lemonade

Orange Liqueur–Infused Chocolate Strawberries

Basil Pesto Roll-Ups with Onion and Tomato

Basil Salad with Watermelon and Blueberries

Rosemary Cheddar Biscuits with Garlic Butter

Classic Cheese and Herb Quiche

Brownie Mint Trifle with Strawberries

Hot Tea

Icy Mint Lemonade
   2 cups water
   1½ cups sugar
   1 cup fresh mint leaves, lightly bruised

4 teaspoons grated lemon rind

2 cups freshly squeezed lemon juice (approximately 10 lemons)

Fresh lemon slices

2 cups ginger ale

2 cups cubed ice

Crushed ice

Fresh mint sprigs

In a small saucepan, boil 2 cups of water. Add sugar and stir until dissolved. Cool for 15 minutes. To the sugar syrup add bruised mint leaves and lemon rind. Cover and steep for 1 hour. Strain syrup into a large pitcher, and add the fresh lemon juice and several lemon slices. Refrigerate until needed. When ready to serve, add the ginger ale, ice cubes, and enough cold water to fill the pitcher. Serve over crushed ice in tall glasses, and garnish with a lemon slice and fresh mint sprigs. Yield: about 3 quarts.

Orange Liqueur–Infused Chocolate Strawberries

1 pint medium-large strawberries

1 cup Hershey's milk chocolate chips

1 tablespoon shortening

¼ cup orange liqueur or orange brandy

Toothpicks

Foam block

Marinade injector

Wash and dry strawberries. In a small double boiler, slowly melt chocolate chips and shortening over a gentle boil. Stir until smooth. Insert a toothpick into the leafy end of each strawberry and dip bottom third into melted chocolate. Allow excess to run back into the pan. Push the toothpick into the foam block and allow chocolate to cool. Do not store in the refrigerator. Before serving, fill the marinade injector with orange liqueur or brandy and insert the needle at the leafy end and push down into the center of the berry. Inject a very small amount of liqueur, taking care not to overfill. Place on a decorative plate and serve within the hour. Yield: 1 pint.

Basil Pesto Roll-Ups with Onion and Tomato

6 8–10" plain, whole wheat, or tomato-flavored flour tortillas

1 8-ounce jar basil pesto

1 large Vidalia or red onion, thinly sliced

2–3 Roma tomatoes, thinly sliced

2 cups horseradish Jack cheese, grated

Fresh basil sprigs (garnish)

Cover each tortilla with 2 tablespoons of pesto and top with 2–3 slices each of onion and tomato. Sprinkle with grated cheese. Roll tortilla into a tube, taking care to roll firmly and evenly. Cut off uneven ends and slice the roll into three equal pieces. Insert a toothpick into the loose edge to hold the roll closed. Cover with plastic wrap and refrigerate until ready to serve. These roll-ups can be made several hours ahead of time. Serve on a platter with fresh sprigs of basil as garnish. Yield: about 18 roll-ups.

Basil Salad with Watermelon and Blueberries

- 2–3 cups fresh basil, torn (not cut)
- 1 medium seedless watermelon, cut in 1-inch cubes (about 4 cups)
- 1 cup fresh blueberries
- ⅓ cup olive oil
- 2 tablespoons balsamic vinegar
- Salt to taste
- Sugar to taste

Place all ingredients in a large bowl and toss gently until blended. Cover and chill 1 hour or until ready to serve. Serve the same day to avoid a watery salad.

Suggestions: This salad is all about the fresh basil, so don't be afraid to use lots of it! To prevent blackening of fresh basil, tear it into piece with your hands. Cutting fresh basil with a knife will make it turn black.

Rosemary Cheddar Biscuits with Garlic Butter

- 2 cups all-purpose flour
- 2¼ teaspoons baking powder
- 1 teaspoon salt
- 2 tablespoons fresh rosemary, minced
- ½ cup butter
- 1 cup sharp cheddar cheese, coarsely chopped
- 1 cup buttermilk
- Parchment paper
- Garlic butter (recipe follows)

In a medium bowl, blend together the flour, baking powder, salt, and rosemary. Cut in butter until crumbly. Stir in the cheese until evenly distributed. Using a gentle folding motion, work in just enough of the buttermilk to moisten the flour mix evenly and bring the dough together. The dough should be light and moist. Measure out each biscuit with a regular soup spoon, dropping each 2 inches apart onto a parchment paper–lined baking sheet. Bake at 350°F. for 10–13 minutes or until a toothpick inserted in the center comes out clean. Do not overcook. Serve with cold garlic butter. Yield: 24-30 biscuits.

Garlic Butter

    1 stick of salted butter, softened

    ¼ teaspoon salt

    4–6 garlic cloves, minced

Blend butter, salt, and garlic in a small bowl until combined. Transfer to a clean serving bowl or press into a butter mold. Cover and refrigerate at least 3 hours before serving.

Classic Cheese and Herb Quiche

    1 package 12-inch deep dish pie shells (2 shells)

    1 cup sharp cheddar cheese, grated

    1 cup Swiss or Jack cheese, grated

    ½ cup Vidalia or red onion, minced

    4 large mushrooms, sliced

    2 tablespoon butter

    ½ pound baby spinach, chopped

    6 large eggs

    ½ cup Ricotta cheese

1 cup half-and-half

1 tablespoon fresh parsley

½ teaspoon dried dill leaf

½ teaspoon dried marjoram

½ teaspoon dried thyme

Fresh white cheese and parsley (garnish)

Place one pie crust in a 12-inch deep-dish pie plate, and sprinkle evenly with the grated cheeses. In a large pan, sauté the onion and mushrooms in butter until almost tender. Add the spinach and toss until wilted. Let cool. In a large bowl or food processor, blend all of the remaining ingredients until smooth. Stir in the onion mixture and pour slowly over the grated cheese. Do not overfill. Bake quiche at 400°F. for 40–45 minutes or until the top is golden brown and the quiche is firm to the touch. Allow to cool for at least 10 minutes. Quiche can be served hot or cold. Garnish with a light sprinkle of fresh white cheese and parsley. Yield: 8 servings.

Suggestion: This recipe can be used to make mini-quiches in a muffin tin or a sheet quiche in a baking pan. For individual quiches, roll out both pie crusts and cut into 12 rounds with a 3½-inch cookie cutter. Press the rounds into the muffin tins; fill and bake at 400°F. for 10–15 minutes or until set. For a sheet quiche, layer both pie crusts in a 9 x 13-inch baking pan so they overlap in the center. Trim to fit, and use trimmings to fill any holes. Fill and bake at 400°F. for 30–35 minutes.

Brownie Mint Trifle with Strawberries

¼ cup water

½ cup sugar

4 cups fresh mint leaves, chopped

1 package brownie mix, prepared (1 lb. 2.4 oz.)

2 quarts strawberries

3 tablespoons sugar

2 cups heavy cream

Fresh strawberry slices and fresh mint sprigs (garnish)

In a medium saucepan, bring water and sugar to a boil, stirring until sugar is dissolved. Remove from heat and stir in the mint leaves. Cover and steep for 15–20 minutes, then strain. Refrigerate until cold.

Prepare the brownies in the largest pan allowed by the instructions on the package (a 9-inch square pan should yield 16 brownies). Allow to cool completely. Cut brownies into rounds using a 2½-inch cookie cutter. Set aside.

Hull the strawberries and slice into a large bowl. Sprinkle with 3 tablespoons of sugar and stir. Set aside.

In a large bowl, whip the heavy cream until very firm. Gently fold in the cold mint syrup mixture. If the cream softens, whip it again until stiff peaks form.

When ready, layer the ingredients into one large trifle bowl or individual parfait cups in this order: brownie, whipped cream, strawberries (with juice). Repeat layers and finish with whipped cream. Garnish with a few strawberry slices and a sprig of mint. Refrigerate until ready to serve. Yield: 8 servings.

Tea

Dessert should be served with one or two hot herbal teas, such as fresh mint or raspberry, and one black dessert tea, such as Darjeeling, with optional milk and sugar.

Herbs for Health and Beauty

Using Herbs at Home: A Do-It-Yourself Spa Night

≫ by Susan Pesznecker ≪

M ost of us live busy, stress-filled lives, and we often spend our hours seeing to the care and needs of others. Every now and then, when the weight of the world bears down, you may feel the need to withdraw from the hectic pace, look inward, and reenergize. A wonderful way to accomplish this is with your own home herbal spa night. With some of your favorite herbs and a few inexpensive supplies, you can craft a spa "retreat" to nourish mind, body, and soul.

Making Plans

Start by setting the date and time for your spa night. Allow at least two or three hours for the most fun, although if time is an issue, allowing even an hour to soak in the tub and pamper yourself will feel incredibly special. If you're lucky enough to have the time, you might even make a weekend out of it!

Next, make a simple plan for your spa night. What is it you'd like to include or accomplish? Do you want to work with your hair? Include a facial? Work in a manicure or pedicure? Will your spa be for you alone, or will you include a friend or partner? Make plans and gather the supplies and materials you'll need well in advance.

Consider the setting and ambience. Native American drums and flute music provide a melodious backdrop, as does soft Celtic music. Candles and natural oil lamps are wonderful for local atmosphere, and their herbal scents add another sensory layer to the surroundings. "Dress" candles by rubbing them with a few drops of essential oil, adding another drop or two to the "well" at the top of pillar candles.

Speaking of ambience... For the best experience, let your family and friends know that you need to be unbothered throughout your spa night experience. And please, turn off your smart phone and other electronics, and put them far enough away that you won't be tempted to look at them. Remember, this time is for you, and you don't want to be distracted.

Getting Started

Every good spa night has a starting point. If you went to a commercial spa, you'd first be taken to a private room and asked to slip into a robe and perhaps handed a glass of mineral water. In the same vein, start your spa night with your own opening preparations. This will set the tone for the evening, help you leave the stress and fatigue of your daily life behind, and guide you into a kinder, more nurturing place. Here are a few ideas to get you started:

Warmth

Crank up the thermostat to a slightly warmer-than-usual setting, allowing you to feel comfy even if lightly dressed and sitting still.

Garb

Remove your everyday clothes and slip into something loose, comfortable, and relaxing. Don't forget comfy slippers or soft, clean socks for your feet. As you undress, visualize peeling away the layers of care and stress that encumber you. As you don your spa night clothing, be aware of feeling nurtured and protected.

Meditation

Sit in a quiet space, dim the lights, and light a scented candle. Spend 5–10 minutes sitting quietly and watching the flame. As you do, be aware of the silence within and without. Breathe slowly and evenly, feeling your body relax as a sense of peace slips over you. Imagine your cares drifting away. (Note: you may wish to burn incense instead of a candle.)

Ablutions

Wash your hands and face using warm water scented with a drop or two of essential oil. As you wash, imagine that stress and negative energies are being washed away, leaving you clean—a blank slate ready for rejuvenation.

Refreshments

Serve yourself a glass of wine, a cup of tea, or whatever else feels "treat-ful."

And now, you're ready to begin! I'm going to give you some general ideas here, and I'll follow this with recipes and suggestions.

Spa Night Treatments

The Bath

Human history contains innumerable references to the luxurious, soothing, even sacred powers of the bath, and you can't go wrong in starting your spa night with a nice long soak in the tub. The hotter the water, the greater the relaxation: I'm convinced it's impossible to remain tense or worried in a steaming hot bathtub. But be aware that hot water is drying to the skin. This shouldn't be a problem, as you'll be able to slather yourself with your favorite herbal lotion after you finish. You can also add bath oil to the water if you're worried about dryness.

For your bath, draw a tub of hot water and stir in a handful of sea salt or kosher salt, one or two cups of herbal infusion (recipes to follow), or several drops of your favorite essential oil. Light some candles, dressed with your favorite essential oil, and set them around the room to create a tranquil setting. Ease into the tub and soak; be aware of your muscles unwinding and your cares drifting away. Enjoy your soak, perhaps as you read a favorite book or sip a cup of herbal tea. Use a bar of herbal soap and a scrubby bath pouf to cleanse your skin and wash away impurities. Choose the soap carefully based on what you're trying to accomplish: some herbal soaps are rich in oils and lubricate the skin, while others may be more drying. Herbal soaps impregnated with large bits of herbs will help rub away dry or dead skin, leaving you soft and refreshed.

You may wish to shower quickly after soaking to remove soap traces. When done, towel lightly and, while your skin is still moist, apply lotion or cream over your damp skin to seal in the moisture. Pay special attention to knees, ankles, and elbows. For an extra zap of moisture, pour a bit of infused oil on a clean cloth and rub this over the freshly lotioned areas. Slip your softened self into a soft bathrobe or pajamas that you've washed and dried in advance (having added a few drops of essential oil to the laundry rinse water). Don't forget to moisturize your feet as well, donning slippers or socks afterward.

If you're sharing your spa with another person, an after-bath massage is incredibly relaxing as well as being a great way to work more moisture into the skin. Ditto for hand and foot massages, which can feel wonderfully luxurious.

Your Hair

Spa night is a great time to pamper your hair. Begin with a shampoo and conditioning treatment. You might then choose to apply a moisturizing or nourishing deep conditioning treatment, an herbal rinse, or a color or tint. You could even trim your bangs or try out a new hairstyle. Have some fun!

Your Face

You might devote your spa night to pampering your face. Begin by washing your face deeply, using a clean nubby cloth and the soap of your choice. Rinse well, then splash your face with witch hazel to tighten the pores. (Witch hazel is a natural astringent and can be purchased at pharmacies and in most stores' skin care sections.) Pat dry with a clean towel and apply your favorite herbal masque. Once the masque is finished, remove all traces, rinse with clean warm water, and apply moisturizing cream. With your skin soft and supple, it's an excellent time to pluck and shape eyebrows or remove facial hair.

Your Hands

Want to dedicate spa night to improving the condition of your hands? Start by removing any old fingernail polish, then wash your hands with soapy, warm water and a fingernail brush. Rinse well and pat dry, then trim the nails and take care of cuticles. Slather on your favorite hand cream, apply a bit of infused oil over the cream, and slip your hands into clean cotton gloves. If possible, leave the gloves on overnight while you sleep: a gorgeous set of softened hands will emerge in the morning!

Your Tootsies

It seems like our feet always need attention, and spa night is a perfect time to tend to your tootsies. Begin with a foot bath: a basin of hot water (big enough for your feet) to which you've added a handful of Epsom salt and a few drops of essential oil. Pat your feet dry, trim the nails, and use a pumice stone or pedicure file to remove dead skin. If your feet tend to be dry and calloused, apply lotion followed by oil and slip into clean cotton socks, leaving them on overnight for best results. Apply new polish if you wish.

Finishing Your Spa Night

Once you've soaked, bathed, lathered, trimmed, and luxuriated, spend time relaxing and savoring the experience. Wrap yourself in a soft blanket and read, enjoy a movie, or sip a cup of tea or a glass of wine. Relax as completely as you can, holding yourself apart from schedules and worries for as long as possible before returning to the real world.

The Recipes

You can certainly purchase ready-made herbal preparations for your spa experience, but it's easy to create your own.

The simplest approach is to purchase high-quality unscented lotions, creams, shampoos, etc., and then stir in essential oil—a couple drops at a time—until you're satisfied with the fragrance. Plant-based carrier oils (sunflower, olive, almond, etc.) can likewise be perfumed this way and are a wonderful natural base for skin care preparations. Use baby oil if you like the scent, but be aware that baby oils are scented mineral—rather than plant-based—oils.

Herbal Infusions

It's easy to make herbal infusions, a fancy term for herbs that have been soaked or gently simmered in near-boiling water, extracting the herbs' properties and scents. To make an herbal tea, use 1 teaspoon dried or 2 teaspoons fresh, chopped herb per cup of near-boiling water. Pour the water over the herbs, allow to steep for 3–5 minutes, strain, and drink. Try a combination of chamomile and mint for relaxation.

To make a large quantity of strong infusion for a bath or hair rinse, use 1–2 cups fresh or dried herb per quart of water. Simmer for 20–30 minutes, then strain, cool slightly, and use. Juniper and rosemary are stimulating additions to the bath, while chamomile, mint, and lavender are more soothing. Rosemary and chamomile make excellent hair rinses for brunettes and blondes, respectively. Ginger, calendula, and sage work especially well in footbaths.

To make an infused oil, heat 1 cup carrier oil with 2 teaspoons fresh or dried herbs very gently in a double boiler. Don't exceed bath water temperature. Simmer for 15–20 minutes, allow to cool, and strain before using.

Interested in going a step further? Here are some base recipes. Experiment by varying the herbs and oils used.

Lotions

For a simple lotion, combine equal parts of water-based herbal infusion and carrier oil. Simmer over low heat until the mixture reduces slightly in volume and thickens. Cool slightly and whip with a whisk until the mixture thickens and becomes opaque.

Creams

For a simple cream, heat 3 parts infused carrier oil with 1 part grated beeswax over very low heat until melted. Blend well and cool. Both cream and lotion store up to a few months in a cool place or longer in the refrigerator.

Lemon Cleansing Cream

Here is the recipe for my favorite lemon cleansing cream (a bit more complex, but worth it!). Melt 1 tablespoon beeswax and 1½ tablespoons petroleum jelly in a small saucepan over low heat. Warm 3 tablespoons carrier oil plus 1 teaspoon grated lemon peel in a separate container; remove from heat and allow to sit for 30–60 minutes. Strain the oil and add to the beeswax mixture. Beat with a whisk for 3–5 minutes. Combine 1 tablespoon witch hazel, 1 tablespoon fresh lemon juice, and ⅛ teaspoon borax; slowly add this to the beeswax mixture, beating until cool and creamy. Stir in 6 drops lemon essential oil.

Soaps and Bath Salts Dressed with Essential Oil

Soap making is a process beyond the limits of this article. It's easy, however, to dress soaps with essential oil by spreading the oil over the soap and allowing it to sit overnight. Coarse kosher salt can be dressed with oils as well, making your own custom bath salts.

Facials

And what about facials? Try mixing crushed or chopped herbs with your favorite cream or oil, mashed avocado, or beaten egg white. Apply, allow to sit 30 minutes, remove with a paper towel, and rinse well.

Enjoy your herbal spa night—may it renew and inspire you!

Recommended Sources

Gladstar, Rosemary. *Rosemary Gladstar's Herbal Recipes for Vibrant Health: 175 Teas, Tonics, Oils, Salves, Tinctures, and Other Natural Remedies for the Entire Family.* North Adams, MA: Storey, 2008.

Pesznecker, Susan. *The Magickal Retreat: Making Time for Solitude, Intention & Rejuvenation.* Woodbury, MN: Llewellyn Publications, 2012.

Vibrational Healing with Flowers

⇾ by Tess Whitehurst ⇽

There's a good chance you're familiar with flower essences: you know, those homeopathic stress remedies—in cute little dropper bottles—derived from flowers. You may have even purchased a few at your local health food store, or created your own. As such, you may already know that flower essences are not made from the actual flowers themselves, but from the vibration of the blossom, or what you might call the flower's unique healing wisdom. What you may not know, however, is that you can receive similar healing benefits directly from the blossoms themselves: no dropper bottle required.

Writing my latest book, *The Magic of Flowers*, provided me with an excellent excuse to spend hours and hours at my local botanical garden, tuning in to, and documenting, the distinctive healing frequencies of a whole variety of flowers. Over and over again, I directly experienced something similar to what Dr. Edward Bach (the originator of flower essence healing) must have experienced on the English countryside as he assembled his thirty-eight core essences. As I sat with the flowers, relaxed, and got into a meditative state, I began to feel that I was receiving an energy healing, or a counseling session, from the blossom with which I sat. And you can do the same! Just as flower essences can impart their healing vibration to anyone who imbibes them, simply spending time in the same vicinity as a blossom can help heal your emotions and psyche. And, of course, consciously relaxing and tuning in can increase the effect. It's actually quite easy, and you need not even leave your own garden.

There are a number of ways to receive vibrational healing from a flower. The most basic way is to begin by sitting comfortably, with your spine straight, near the blossom (or blossoms), while it is still a part of a living, growing plant. (Standing is okay, too, if the ground is wet.) It might help to be aware of your intention, or your present healing needs, as you begin the process, so you can program your personal energy to receive exactly the type of healing it needs most from the flower. Then, gaze softly at the blossom as you relax your body and take some deep breaths. As much as you can, really be present in the moment. Feel the sunlight and breeze on your skin, and the ground beneath you. Relax your consciousness into what you imagine the flower's consciousness might be like. This might take a little while, or it might happen immediately. Don't rush it or overthink it. For the purpose of getting into this type of awareness, it might help to simply imagine that you're having a picnic or a date with the flower: you know, just spending time in order to spend time.

At some point, just as the energy behind human thoughts and feelings naturally bounces back and forth between two friends, you will begin to receive healing from the flower. You might just feel relaxed and pleasant as you receive healing, or you might be conscious of the process in some way. If you're conscious of the process, you might receive wisdom and guidance that your mind translates into words, or you might see a picture in your mind's eye that is meaningful in some way for your healing, such as a vacation spot (if you need to take a vacation) or a particular allergen that the flower's vibration is signaling you to avoid. Or you might feel literal physical healing going on, such as warmth or tingles in a particular area of your body.

Other ways to receive healing from flowers (other than taking flower essences) include:

- Bringing a bouquet or a single cut flower into your home, or sleeping with it near your bed.

- Placing (non-irritating/nontoxic) flowers in your bath water.

- Drinking tea made with dried (edible) blossoms, or eating (edible) blossoms.

- Decorating your clothes or hair with one or more flowers.

- Cultivating and/or caring for a living, blossoming plant on a regular basis.

Every single variety of blossom has its own unique healing vibration, and there are no adverse affects working with them in these ways. So, provided you have no allergies or sensitivities, you can sit near any blossom and spend some quality healing time, or work with any of the previous ideas.

In order to choose a flower that will best serve your present healing needs, you have two choices. First, you can let your intuition choose. Any flower you feel particularly drawn to (coming from a feeling place rather than a thinking one) will definitely be a great flower to choose, since your vibration will naturally seek out what it needs, just as you crave certain foods when you need the nutrients they contain. Second, you can do some research to find a flower that suits the type of healing you're looking for. Seek out one of the many wonderful books on the subject (such as mine!), or just do a Web search.

To get you started, here is a small sampling of flowers and an overview of their vibrational healing properties.

Rose

Roses are believed by many flower essence healers to possess the purest and most positive vibration of any living thing, and (similarly) to resonate at the frequency of love. Indeed, spending quality time with a rose can reap considerable benefits, including detoxification of the mind/body/spirit, strengthening of the vitality and energetic field, opening and fortifying the heart (on both physical and spiritual levels), clearing and purifying the skin, and reducing the effects of stress.

Jasmine

Jasmine's vibrational medicine is very sensual and luxurious. Jasmine brings us into our bodies and helps us heal any negative patterns surrounding self-love, body image, and sexuality. It's also excellent for helping us to realize that luxury and wealth are our natural state: in other words, it can help us reprogram limiting beliefs pertaining to finances and material resources.

Poppy

Like the poppy field in *The Wizard of Oz*, poppies specialize in issues related to sleep and relaxation. They also support us while we are grieving by helping relieve stress and aiding in the process of acceptance. Additionally, poppies can be employed while working to heal from drug or alcohol addiction, as they help connect us with that natural feeling of transcendent oneness that is naturally available to us all.

Marigold (Calendula)

For a general immune system boost and potent vitality tonic, hang out with some calendula blossoms (or float a few in your bath water). Similar to the pure white light of the nourishing, life-giving sun, the vibration of calendula can help strengthen your physical body and energy field, lighten your spirit and reduce stress, and recalibrate your physical and mental systems in ideal ways.

Daisy

If you feel overwhelmed and like the complexities of modern life are taking their toll on your stress level and health, daisy might be the flower guru for you. Bringing us back to the basics by simplifying and streamlining our mental environment, daisy's stress-relieving wisdom can provide a wonderful immune and vitality boost. Relax with a daisy and allow its cleansing vibration to clear clutter from your mind, body, and spirit.

Water Lily

If you've been going through some serious issues, or if you're working on consciously healing from past events, gazing at a water lily and allowing its unique vibrational signature to permeate your consciousness would be a very wise move. Water lily's alignment with water makes it a natural match for helping to heal emotional wounds, as water and emotions are related. The way that water lilies are grounded in the mud and reach upward through water and then air to reach toward the light mirrors the way we successfully transmute our old challenges and injuries into wisdom and strength.

Crab Apple

One of the thirty-eight Bach remedies, crab apple is especially adept at helping us to feel emotionally and spiritually clean and pure. This can be helpful for those of us who may feel as if we easily absorb pain or negativity from others or our environment, or for those of us who, for whatever reason, may sometimes find ourselves feeling intrinsically unclean, or overly concerned with cleanliness. Although the flower essence is more readily available than the blossom (which only comes around once every spring), if you're lucky enough to encounter a blossoming crab apple tree, I highly recommend taking a moment to bask in its purifying vibration. You'll feel cleansed, energized, and positive, and your skin will also get a boost, as crab apple's vibration is famously employed as a skin clarifier.

Herbs for Skin Healing

＊ by Darcey Blue French ＊

S kin problems are one of the most commonly experienced woes of life here on planet Earth; we fall down, we slip with a knife, we react to plants, we burn in the sun, and we get infections and splinters. They happen to everyone, young and old, on a semi-regular basis. Fortunately, the plant world has provided us with lots of help for all of our troubles.

Tips for Applying Herbal Remedies to the Skin

We can rely on a selection of plants that are useful for many kinds of skin problems, depending on how we prepare them. Here are a few things to remember about applying herbal remedies to the skin.

- Herbs can be infused into oil and applied as is, or used as a salve when combined with beeswax. These methods are best for dry, itchy, tender, open skin. Salves and oils soothe and moisturize, and seal the skin from the elements. It is best not to use a salve or oil when there is an infection that could potentially be spread by the substance.

- Herbal tinctures (in alcohol or vinegar) can be applied to the skin to dry up weepy rashes, to cool hot, red, inflamed skin (unbroken), or when fresh plant or oil is not available. If applied to an open wound, tinctures should be diluted by at least half with saline water. Tinctures are excellent for addressing infections in the skin, as both the alcohol and plant help with disinfecting.

- We can also use plants steeped or decocted into hot water for compresses, washes, and soaks. These are best for large areas of skin, for skin that is to tender for alcohol washes, for the sensitive skin of babies and elders, for rashes all over the body (try soaking in a bathtub of herbal tea!), or for when you do not have other preparations handy but can make tea from your dried herbs.

- Fresh plants can be chewed or mashed and applied directly to the skin as a poultice for wounds, bites, rashes, sores, etc. Dried plants can also be used as a poultice but must be rehydrated with water and often need a binder, like clay, flour, or flax seeds, to hold it together on the skin. Never underestimate the power of a spit poultice. Just chew a fresh plant leaf in your mouth to crush it, and then apply the crushed leaf and saliva to the area of the skin.

• If a wound or condition is serious, doesn't stop bleeding, or doesn't respond to your treatments after 24 to 48 hours, it is prudent to seek additional assistance from a skilled practitioner, herbalist, doctor, or nurse—especially if in combination with a fever, confusion, or head injury. These are serious signs for concern and must be addressed.

Plants

Alder *(Alnus rubra, A. incana, A. oblongifolia)*

Alder trees offer us a versatile medicine from both the leaf and bark. Alder is a superior antiseptic, disinfectant, astringent, and anodyne. It is cooling, drying, and anti-inflammatory. It can be used as a tea, a tincture, an oil/salve, or even a fresh poultice.

I find alder bark tincture or tea compress to be one of the very best herbs for infections of any kind of the skin—anything pussy and weepy, with blisters or pustules, or bleeding. It relieves the pain, itch, and inflammation and infection of bites and stings of vemonous insects almost instantly (mosquitos, chiggers, caterpillars, wasps, bees, kissing bugs, spiders, etc.). Alder bark and leaf salve is an excellent remedy to apply to herpes sores and shingles rash. It is particularly good for poison ivy/oak rash (as a compress or soak) and is a good all-purpose remedy for minor cuts, scrapes, and rashes of unknown origin.

I received a large and painful sting from a caterpillar (they have dangerous hairs here in the Southwest), and I chewed every leaf I could find until I got to the alder tree. As soon as I put that alder leaf on my sting, the pain disappeared.

Bee Balm *(Monarda punctata)*

Bee balm is a common garden perennial, though it does grow wild in some places in North America. It has a warming, drying, and very spicy, aromatic flavor—some varieties are hot like a super-powered oregano. Its large amounts of volatile oils are highly antiseptic and pain-relieving, and I often combine bee balm with alder for all sorts of skin infections, even quite serious ones. It is most appropriate as a tincture or tea compress for skin infections, but oil infused with bee balm is wonderful as an application to relieve the pain of burns. (With any burn, please cool the skin with vinegar or cool water before applying any oil-based product.) One of my favorite preparations with bee balm is the flowers and leaves infused in honey as a wound dressing to prevent infection and speed healing.

Calendula *(Calendula officinalis)*

Calendula is perhaps the most oft-cited herb for skin healing. It is a wonderful garden plant with sunny yellow flowers that are sticky and fragrant. The flowers are vulnerary and antiseptic, anti-inflammatory, and drying. Calendula is most often used infused in oil for rashes, cuts, scrapes, burns of all kinds, diaper rash, general skin tone, and beauty treatments. When in doubt, give calendula a try. It is just as effective used as a tincture or tea compress, and is gentle enough for baby skin. It can be used daily on the face or body to promote healthy skin tissue.

Comfrey *(Symphytum officinale)*

Almost everyone has heard of the wound-healing properties of comfrey. It is the best herb bar none for sealing up, healing, and closing wounds. It is moistening, emollient, and cooling, and can be used liberally for all kinds of skin itches, rashes, and burns. Most people find a salve of the root to be most effective, though I have used the leaf-infused oil just as often with good results. But fresh comfrey leaf and root make a wonderful poultice as well, when you have it available. The only caveat with external use of comfrey root is that it can seal up wounds so quickly, and stimulate skin-cell regeneration so fast, that it can seal in infections. If you are at all unsure if the wound is clean or is showing signs of infection, do not use comfrey. Wait until the wound has been thoroughly cleansed and all chance of infection has passed.

Mugwort *(Artemisia vulgaris, A. ludoviciana, etc.)*

Mugwort is found growing in abundance in the wild and is also cultivated in gardens for its fragrant and beautiful silvery-green foliage. It is less commonly known as a skin healer, but is easily found and very useful. It is cooling, drying, antiseptic, antifungal, and pain-relieving. A fresh leaf chewed and applied to mosquito bites is soothing, and a cool wash of mugwort tea or mugwort infused in apple cider vinegar calms a burn. It is a good remedy for weepy poison ivy rashes and is equally useful to calm the itching, burning, and pain of herpes and shingles outbreaks. The tincture is even useful as a bug repellent when sprayed on the skin.

Neem *(Azadirachta indica)*

Neem seed oil is one of the best antifungal herbal preparations I have used, and when nothing else seems to relieve the itch of a yeasty rash (thrush or candida), neem oil often works. It is a much quicker remedy for toenail fungus than tea tree oil, and reduces the duration of herpes and shingles outbreaks significantly. I use neem oil on athlete's foot, rubbed on the feet before bed and before putting shoes on for the day. Neem seed oil is a very smelly product, with an odor like cooked garlic and peanuts, but it is a remarkably good skin treatment for acne and infected pustules on the skin, and is one of the few things that really works to repel ticks, chiggers, and mosquitos when applied to the skin (if you don't mind smelling!).

Pine Resin *(Pinus spp.)*

Any species of pine resin can be used the same way, as one of the best herbal remedies for drawing out items lodged in the skin—including thorns, splinters, cactus spines, small pieces of glass, or even small pebbles. I usually melt pine resin collected from the bark of pine trees into olive oil (1 part resin to 2 parts oil, and strain well through a cheesecloth), and make that oil into a salve to apply to any area where there is an object I want to draw to the surface and out of the skin. But even if you are on the trail, and don't have any pine-resin salve, you can find some soft resin on a tree and use it to pack a small wound (much like a primitive bandaid) to prevent infection or further damage (until the wound can be tended to), or apply it directly to the skin to help dislodge splinters or thorns. It forms a protective barrier on the skin, and can also be helpful for chapped and windburned skin or lips that need protection from the elements. It doubles as a woodsy perfume when applied to the skin and pulse points.

Plantain *(Plantago major, P. lanceolata)*

Plantain is a common weed found all over the country, and is often called the herbal bandaid because it can be picked fresh, chewed, and applied as a poultice to any kind of cut, scrape, bite, sting, or thorn you might come across in your day outside.

Children love to learn about this plant! It is cooling and drying, emollient and soothing, and vulnerary. It speeds skin healing and cell regeneration, relieves itching, and draws out bug venom or thorns. Almost all herbalists like to have plantain-infused oil around for all-purpose skin-healing needs, and this can be combined with calendula, comfrey, alder, or any number of other plants for an all-purpose healing salve.

Rose *(Rosa spp.)*

Rose petals are a supreme anti-inflammatory and cooling remedy for all kinds of hot and inflamed skin troubles. Rose petals infused in apple cider vinegar are my favorite go-to for fresh burns. A bit of rose-infused vinegar mixed with cool water and applied with a cloth as a compress can relieve the pain and remove the heat from a sunburn or stove burn extra quickly. It is also soothing and calming to any inflamed, red, and rashy area of the skin. Women like to use rose water, rose tea, or rose-infused oil on their faces to restore moisture, reduce redness, and soothe daily stress on the skin. I have found rose to be a fantastic remedy to calm herpes sores as well. Rose is so gentle and soothing that it is good for every age, and smells sweet besides.

St. John's Wort *(Hypericum perforatum)*

Another favorite of all herbalists, St. John's wort is used for far more than depression! It has long been revered as a wound herb that is pain-relieving, astringent, cooling, anti-inflammatory, and nerve-regenerating. This is the herb to use whenever you have any sort of nerve damage or nerve pain associated with a wound, and is one of the top remedies for the pain of herpes and shingles. Both the oil and the tincture are effective, but open wounds will burn if alcohol is applied, so I prefer the oil for skin use. St. John's wort is wonderful for healing red rashes and burns, and I often use it in combination with other cooling remedies like alder or rose. It is also excellent for healing bruises and injuries when applied externally on the skin.

Yarrow *(Achillea millefolium)*
Achilles was said to use yarrow to dress his soldiers' wounds in battle. Yarrow is a first-aid remedy everyone should have handy. The freshly chewed leaf can stop the bleeding of a wound very quickly. It can even help stanch a nose bleed when placed in the nose. It grows as a weed in the fields, and grows easily in the garden as well. The fresh plant is most effective, but the fresh plant tincture or oil is also excellent. Yarrow is a styptic and an anodyne for all kinds of skin rashes, cuts, scrapes, and wounds, and can be used as a tea compress, tincture, or infused oil. The tincture or oil is also widely used as bug repellent.

Herbal and Natural Remedies for Women's Menstrual Health

⤜ by Sally Cragin ⤛

Have you ever noticed how common it is to see the word *menstrual* next to the word *problem*? For centuries, the medical profession has viewed women's reproductive health as a "situation" that needs to be "cured," "fixed," or "eased." However, as more and more women seek careers in the chemical and pharmacological professions, we can all hope there will be better products to assist and support women's menstrual health—but we're not there yet.

The first purveyor of products specifically designed for female health and reproductive cycles was the brilliant Lydia Pinkham. I created a presentation for libraries and historical societies some years ago on the topic of patent medicines, and the story of Lydia Pinkham, of Lynn, Massachusetts, takes center stage. Back in the 1800s, she began bottling a medication made of herbs and other natural substances to help women with what we now call PMS (premenstrual syndrome), as well as post-childbirth recovery. Her "Vegetable Compound" was widely advertised and widely purchased, but the revolutionary aspect of her story is that every bottle came with extremely detailed medical advice, as well as testimonials. This was the first opportunity women had to read information by another female about understanding their own bodies. Lydia advised women to "loosen their stays (corsets)" and "let doctors alone." She advised a diet heavy in vegetables, fruits, and grains versus meat, and she advocated for exercise in the open air.

Sound familiar? The ingredients in her Compound (still being made, by the way, by the Numark Corporation) include black cohosh, dandelion, raspberry leaf, gentian, and other herbs. These ingredients are still being marketed vigorously by a variety of purveyors as helpful for various female conditions. But I think the important takeaway from Lydia's story is that it's crucial that you have wisdom and observe your own health, as well as maintain good health practices. Understanding your own menstrual health and cycles is extremely helpful, yet few women take the time to observe their own cycles and energy levels. (I'd love to hear stories from readers about your own understanding of your own cycles.)

Understand this first: we are not machines. We don't necessarily run at full rev throughout the day. Most people have natural active tendencies that may vary throughout the calendar year. Don't ask a morning person (like my mom) to stay up really late, and don't expect a night owl (like me) to greet the dawn chorus with anything but dismay. Understanding your own daily rhythms is crucial. When I switched from caffeinated coffee to decaf a while ago, I found I was less likely to "crash" in the afternoon. (Plus, with decaf, you can drink lots of coffee without getting jittery!)

Observation and Record Keeping

Over the decades, as an astrology columnist and adviser, I have spoken to a lot of women who have challenging or difficult personal cycles. I always suggest to clients that it's helpful to keep a journal on how you're feeling or what you're experiencing on a daily basis. Since most women are on a 28-day cycle (more or less), you may find you're on a 14-day cycle—the days leading up to ovulation, and then the days leading up to bleeding. When I was younger, the concept of PMS didn't exist, but now, there's a much greater awareness of menstrual cycles. However, there are lot of other days to account for as well.

The ancient Greeks worshipped the goddess Diana, the huntress during the time of labor and childbirth. Even though she was a virgin, mothers in labor would pray to her to shoot an arrow to take away the pains of labor. Of course, no such arrow exists, but there are various herbs that have been used for generations to assist labor or help healing. Raspberry leaf tea is said to help "tone" the uterus for labor, and sipping cups throughout the day starting in the third trimester is one recommendation. You can let this tea steep for longer than the customary 3 to 5 minutes. I have found that letting the leaves steep for 20 minutes or even longer works fine. Now, I happen to like the taste of raspberry leaf tea, but if it's too "natural," feel free to add a chamomile tea bag or peppermint, or whatever strikes your fancy. I also find raspberry tea pleasant to drink when it's cold.

As I write, the moon is waning. The shadow on the right side is growing ever larger, and the brightly lit globe is slowly becoming a crescent—a Cheshire cat smile. For many women, the full and new moon are times to reflect on their menstrual cycle, which can also synch up to a 28-day calendar. (The words *menstrual* and *moon* share a Greek root.) Keeping track of the phase the moon is in is definitely "step one" as regards taking a natural view toward understanding your own menstrual health and cycles. Since most women ovulate approximately 14 days after the uterus sheds its lining, you may find that your body wants to harmonize with one of those two phases.

If you're menstruating when the moon is full and ovulating when the moon is new, you may find that you're tense and fragile, craving gallons of ice cream before you start to menstruate. If you find you're irritable and likely to speak harshly to others, and the moon is getting more and more full, you are also very much in tune with the moon! The time of the waning moon can be a period of letting go or losing interest or having less energy, whereas the time of the waxing and full moon brings more energy (manic or productive) and the urge to multitask.

Over the course of a year, you may find that your pattern of bleeding on or around the full moon will start to shift, so that later in the year, you're actually ovulating when the moon is full and menstruating when the moon is new. Understanding the 29-day lunar cycle (we have 13 full moons in a year) is an enormous help when it comes to getting a better understanding of how your body works.

PMS and Cramps

Menstrual cramps seem to go with the territory for just about every woman. Herbs that help with this include chamomile (in tea) or valerian (in the evening). A hot wet towel on the belly can also ease pain. I've also seen recommendations for white willow capsules, which have a similar effect to aspirin but are less harsh on the stomach. PMS can, for some, be far more difficult than the cramps—for many of us, starting to bleed comes as a relief (except when you're trying to get pregnant, of course). Symptoms of PMS include water retention, which makes for a bloated feeling, headaches, tender breasts, and mood swings that can go from weepy to snarly in a heartbeat. Dietary decisions should involve foods that are naturally diuretic; these include celery, onion, eggplant, asparagus, brussel sprouts, cabbage, carrots, cucumbers, tomatoes, watercress, artichokes, lettuce, garlic, and watermelon. In addition, the herbs hawthorn, corn silk, and parsley are used as diuretics in natural medicine. Of these, hawthorn *(Crataegus oxycanthus)* is the most powerful.

I've tried two herbal remedies, evening primrose oil and vitex (also known as chasteberry), and I feel the vitex is what works for me. The recommended dose for evening primrose oil is between 500 to 1,000 mg a day, which can also be added to 400 IU of natural vitamin E. Vitex usually comes in 20-mg pills, and what it does for your body is to help control levels of the hormone prolactin. It's called chasteberry because its folkloric backstory is that it suppresses the sex drive—and once was recommended for monastery residents!

Pregnancy

In my lifetime, the conception industry has expanded exponentially. It seems that more and more women are "postponing" having kids, compared to previous generations. There's plenty of information about how problematic pregnancy is after the age of 35. I put "postponing" childbirth in quotes because for most of written history, women have had one main job: getting pregnant, having babies, and raising children, along with keeping a house. More women are getting further education (yay!), and societal influence has relaxed for many people so that getting married young is not the only option. It's common for people to live with multiple partners over a period of years. Despite a high divorce rate (primarily the result of the ease of divorce), many of the women I know (who live in a western Europeanized culture) are choosy about life partners. And they're particular about whom they choose to help raise children.

In the late 1950s, my mother was told by her obstetrician (no "OB/GYN" back then) that she "better get going" if she wanted to have a family. So she did, and I was born shortly after her twenty-sixth birthday. This kind of thinking was prevalent for earlier generations, although if you want to go wa-a-ay back, you'll find most women continued having children deep into their forties (unless they died first). When the United States had primarily an agricultural economy, a large labor force was essential for the smooth operation of a farm. Plus, the only methods of birth control were withdrawal and the rhythm method. When I look back on my own family genealogy, there are female ancestors in the eighteenth and nineteenth centuries who had upwards of twelve children! That means they spent about nine years of their lives pregnant. This is astonishing to think of, but consider this: in the developing world—particularly in Africa, the Middle East, and the Far East—large families are still the norm. And with radically different cultural expectations (lack of education for females, lack of medical knowledge about avoiding pregnancy), it's definitely a harder life for millions of women overseas.

However, here in the post-industrial world, we have choices, options, and medical care, as well as widespread information about reproductive options and female health. I remember talking to my own gynecologist in my early thirties, as I wasn't ready to have kids and didn't have the right partner. I was anxious about waiting too long (whatever that means), and I remember her saying something along the lines of: "You know, it's not like you fall off a cliff statistically. What studies show is that around age thirty-five, there is a gradual drop in fertility, so there is still plenty of time."

Herbs for Reproductive Health

If you are in your thirties and anxious about having this blessed event happen for you, there are herbal and natural remedies and methods that can help prepare your body for getting (and staying) pregnant. Chasteberry can be a boon to many women, helping alleviate PMS and also helping make your cervical mucus more conducive to the passage of sperm. Other herbs include black cohosh (suggested during first half of your cycle, from bleeding to ovulating), dong quai (which I would recommend getting a naturopath's advice before taking, along with your doctor's), and evening primrose oil from menstruation to ovulation, then switch to flax seed oil from ovulation to menstruation. Red raspberry leaf (in a tea) can be used throughout your cycle, as it helps tone the uterus, but when you are pregnant, it's said that one should avoid this herb until the final trimester.

Natural Methods

Okay, here's a little autobiography: I had my son when I was nearly forty-three. The month we made a visit to the fertility doctor to see what we were doing wrong-wrong-wrong was the month I conceived. I had a typical pregnancy and stayed very active throughout, and when my son was ten days past his due date, I went in for a pitocyn drip–induced labor. I had a great doula to help me through this and had no pain meds at all.

I was delighted to be a parent in my early forties. My son was lovely, I knew exactly who I was, and my husband and I had emotional and financial stability. It was the right time for us, and I well remembered friends who'd had kids in their twenties and thirties and did so much juggling with jobs and childcare and financial anxiety. However, having a baby at my age definitely meant there was time pressure to have another. Every passing month in my early forties always had a little bit of hope—and a whole lot of disappointment as I didn't get pregnant. We finally resigned ourselves to having an only child.

However, when I was forty-six—a year past the absolute-dead-cut-off that one hears about—I started bringing my son, who was three, to a really lovely church-group program for kids in one of the rougher neighborhoods in our city. We went every Wednesday, and he liked playing with the little kids, and I liked doing arts and crafts with the older ones. The next year,

I ran for school committee, and about six months into my term (I won a seat), I found I was expecting. I was almost forty-eight years old, and again had a textbook pregnancy and, this time, a natural childbirth.

So here's my natural method: spend time with kids and babies. I was convinced that the amount of time I'd spent wiping other kids' noses, and having them on my lap, and helping guide their little hands while they bent pipe cleaners or painted, had made a difference I couldn't quantify. Think of the women you know who are close friends or roommates whose menstrual cycles synch up, or those who get pregnant within a couple months of each another. The natural method I recommend is the one that may strike some folks as callous or uncaring, but it's this: if you are yearning for a child, spend time with children who are craving stability and love. The kids I worked with were and are extremely needy kids who come from backgrounds of neglect, mental anguish, and financial uncertainty. Kids would disappear and then reappear months later, as their parent or grandparent moved from apartment to apartment. However, they were happy to see me again, and I was happy to see them, and I felt that on some microscopic endocrinological level, something got triggered in my forty-seven-year-old body!

Reflexology

The ancient craft of reflexology, in which parts of the hands and feet are manipulated, is completely non-invasive and is growing in popularity in this country. How it works is that every organ in your body has a corresponding "point" on your hands and feet. By gently massaging those areas, you can ease pain in those organs or parts of the body. There are many books on the subject, with helpful diagrams to assist, and if you live in a larger urban area, chances are there's a reflexologist in your neighborhood.

An easy hand workout that focuses on the reproductive organs goes like this: With your left thumb, gently find the point just below your right thumb. That corresponds to the uterus in women and the prostate in men. Gently press it two or three times. Do the same on the left hand. Next, take the middle finger of your left hand and find a point just below the wrist on the side of your hand with the pinkie. The point is just before the wrist bone. Press gently two or three times and repeat on the left side. Finally, you can use reflexology on the part of your hand that corresponds to the fallopian tubes for women and the vas deferens for men by using your left thumb or pointer finger to rub from the wrist bone below your thumb, to the wrist bone below your pinkie. This is the "bracelet" that corresponds to this part of the body.

Drinking Water and Some Final Thoughts

Women are blessed with a biological ability that really is miraculous: the ability to grow a living child in our own bodies. However, it is up to us to keep our bodies healthy, fit, nourished, and hydrated. So here's a really simple tip: be smart about when you drink water. If you drink two cups first thing in the morning, your internal organs will be lubricated, which means your body will operate more efficiently. If you drink a glass of water before a meal, you probably won't overeat. If you drink a glass of water before a shower or bath, your blood pressure will be better regulated. And if you drink a glass of water before bed, you reduce the risk of heart attack or stroke. I've noticed that if I don't drink at least one glass of water in the morning, before anything else goes in my body, I can feel lightheaded early in my day. Simple? Yes, but definitely something most of us need to be reminded about.

Keeping your body healthy is the most important task you have. And if you grew up in a family where female body processes weren't talked about or, worse, were regarded as unclean or "gross," you have my sympathies. Over the years, as an astrologer, I've talked to dozens of female clients about the importance of understanding their own personal cycles, as well as understanding the influences of planetary and lunar shifts. It's important to take pride in the amazing "machine" that is your body. Understand that the monthly rhythm of sloughing off menses is your body operating at top ability. We are all miracles and should embrace the sentiment in an ancient parable: the hand that rocks the cradle rules the world.

Sources Consulted

Andrew Weil, MD. http://www.drweil.com.

Mindell, Earl, RPh, PhD. *Earl Mindell's New Herb Bible*. New York: Fireside, 2002.

Valiani, Mahboubeh, Elaheh Babaei, Reza Heshmat, and Zahra Zare. "Comparing the Effects of Reflexology Methods and Ibuprofen Administration on Dysmenorrhea in Female Students of Isfahan University of Medical Sciences." *The Iranian Journal of Nursing and Midwifery Research* 15 (December 2010): 371–78.

Offsetting Indoor Air Pollution with Plants

❧ by Diana Rajchel ❧

Indoor air pollution comes from a host of common sources, many of which are necessary to create a clean, well-maintained home. While lead paint and asbestos still terrorize fans of the fixer-upper, modern paint chemicals emit toxins that can cause nausea and disorientation for months after they dry, dust can creep in from anywhere, and molds cling to the slightest moisture. Each one degrades the quality of indoor air.

Most homes require heating, and no fuel currently used is totally non-polluting. Oil, gas, kerosene, and wood all leave byproducts. These leftovers linger in the air, on our walls, and in our bodies. Combine this with

other sources of smoke, such as cigarettes and incense, and we can inadvertently create an indoor smog zone.

Sources of indoor air pollution besides smoke can slip past us simply because we do not see any physical residue. Personal care products such as oils, soaps, and lotions often come loaded with synthetic fragrances, phthalates, and other chemicals. While the amount of chemical per bar of soap or bottle of lotion alone is not dangerous, years of regular use can eventually cause harm to the body and leave byproducts in the air.

We already know that most of our cleaning materials are hazardous. We scrub with ammonia only when we can open windows, we keep poisons out of reach of children, and we ventilate as much as possible when we use any of these chemicals. The fumes are often dangerous for several hours after use.

Offsetting Indoor Air Pollution

There is no perfect system to completely avoid indoor pollution, but you can offset the pollution by taking certain measures with your home. Begin by auditing your home for pollution. Look at the Environmental Protection Agency's online article "Care for Your Air: A Guide to Indoor Air Quality" (epa.gov/iaq/pubs/careforyourair.html) to get guidelines of what to look for and where to look. Common items on these checklists include radon, mold, and highly flammable materials.

In terms of priorities, how you heat your home matters most, followed by the quality of your home's ventilation system. Adequate-size, well-placed windows provide great ventilation in good weather, but if you live in a place subject to climate extremes, the windows alone may not help. If you live in a rental property, you also do not have choices about your windows.

After examining heating and ventilation, examine your habits. Smoking indoors always increases air pollution. Not only is it dangerous to small children and pets, increasing their risk of cancer, asthma, and other bronchial diseases, but even the most powerful air filter on Earth will not prevent smoke byproduct from embedding itself in absolutely everything you own. Items such as candles, incense, and heated aromatherapy tools are other common offenders. The smoke they create, however, is easy to remediate. You do not actually need to let candles and incense burn all the way down in one session: you can snuff and relight both, burning them off in shorter periods and reducing the amount of soot and smoke collecting in the air.

Weatherizing or winterizing your home can reduce how much heat or cooling you need. Reduced heating not only saves you money, it also means that you reduce the amount of smoke byproduct your heating source releases into your home. Installing or fixing storm windows, caulking around windows and doors, and using blown-in wall insulation make your home both toastier during cold months and cooler during warm ones. These small actions build up over time—the less heating product you need, the less you must deal with the consequences of using it.

After making these physical changes to your home, you will need to make a plan to maintain that good air quality. The best way to do this is to clean regularly. For those prone to clutter, this is definitely daunting and is best prepared for with strategy and in some cases professional counseling. For those who have only cyclical clutter, however, it's possible to get your home to a state where a twenty-minute daily walkthrough will be enough to maintain low-stress cleanliness, boosted by weekly scrub-bings to the dustiest and dirtiest spots (usually the kitchen and the bathroom). When you do this, look carefully at what clean-ing products you use. The more caustic the product, the more likely it is to damage the air quality. Unless it's truly a "needs bleach" situation, save the hard stuff for the heavy-duty messes. Vinegar and baking soda really do work for the small stuff.

Using Indoor Plants as Natural Air Filters

You can do more than just clean and seal to improve your indoor air quality. Indoor plants create a natural air filter. All plants absorb carbon dioxide and release oxygen. They also absorb and sometimes alter other gases that enter your home and atmosphere.

While every plant brings the benefit of some filtration, some plants make more effective air filters than others. For ex-ample, a spider plant can actually filter out formaldehyde in an airtight laboratory environment—so in a typically not-airtight home, it can likely improve what you breathe a great deal.

Here are some common houseplants, all tested in labora-tory conditions for their filtration ability. Read carefully, be-cause some plants, while wonderful for the air, do horrible things to the pets that eat them.

Spider Plants *(Chlorophytum comosum)*

These plants can completely filter formaldehyde. An espe-cially fertile spider plant "gives birth" to smaller spider plants, making it a self-sustaining source of fresh filters. There is, however, a significant downside for pet owners: spider plants are, like antifreeze, both highly toxic and highly attractive to cats. If a cat eats a spider plant, it will have seizures or worse.

The Palm Family

Houseplants, like pets, often come in specifically domesticated breeds. While you can find palm trees growing wild, those common to houseplants have often been bred specifically for indoor use. This includes the areca palm *(Chrysalidocarpus lutescens)*, lady palm *(Rhapis excelsa)*, dwarf date palm *(Phoenix roebelenii)*, and bamboo palm *(Chamaedorea seifrizii)*. In laboratory testing, these plants rapidly filtered common chemical pollutants hexane and benzene.

The Fig Family

The fig family includes the famed houseplant, the ficus. This group grows well in poor conditions, making them excellent as indoor plants. Ficus alii *(Ficus maclellandii 'Alii')* was expressly bred for indoor use as a decorative accent, but it still filters indoor air effectively. Weeping fig *(Ficus benjamina)* is actually a tree, but it often looks like a simple mass of green leaves reaching upward. The rubber plant *(Ficus robusta* or *Ficus elastica)*, a relative of the ficus, differs in that its sap actually does turn into rubber when dried. This is not the same as *Hevea brasiliensis,* which grows the material necessary to make latex.

Dracaena 'Janet Craig' *(Dracaena deremensis 'Janet Craig')*

This flowering African shrub can flourish even in low lighting. It has also successfully filtered indoor pollutants such as formaldehyde, xylene, and toluene.

English Ivy *(Hedera helix)*

The ivy that climbs the walls of institutions is an invasive species—but domesticated or cultivated as an ornamental plant, it filters air quite well. People with allergies to carrots should avoid contact with this plant, as it contains high amounts of falcarinol.

Boston Fern *(Nephrolepis exaltata 'Bostoniensis')*
Also called the sword fern, this plant fits beautifully in a hanging basket. What makes the Boston fern even more remarkable is that it can filter arsenic.

Peace Lily *(Spathiphyllum sp.)*
These decorative plants flower with a hood over the stamen, creating a wand-like effect. These plants can filter formaldehyde and benzene.

Mums *(Chrysanthemum)*
Most people think of mums as outdoors plants, but they may do the most growing indoors. In Chinese tradition, mums have significant use as vegetables, in medicinal teas for influenza, and as a natural insecticide. In a NASA clean air study, mums received the highest marks for their ability to filter chemicals. Along with filtering the usual culprits of formaldehyde, benzene, and toluene, mums also clear trichloroethylene and ammonia. Unfortunately, they can poison cats, dogs, and horses, as well as insects.

Aloe Vera
The common household plant aloe vera was cultivated for indoor use. This indoor succulent often comes recommended by herbalists as a handy plant to have for treatment of sunburns and small kitchen accidents. As of 2012, however, the medical effectiveness of the aloe plant in treating burns is under dispute, with research suggesting it may be carcinogenic.

Research also demonstrates, however, that aloe not only significantly removes formaldehyde from the environment, but in the process of doing so, its own capacity to absorb and filter the air and water around it increases.

If you weatherproof your home, you will get that much more out of any plant that you put into place afterward. Taking the steps of weatherproofing your home, removing sources of radon, asbestos, and lead, and maintaining a cleaning schedule, as well as keeping air-filtering plants around, will go a long way toward helping you breathe easy indoors.

For Further Study

Cunningham, Scott. *Cunningham's Encyclopedia of Magical Herbs.* St. Paul, MN: Llewellyn Publications, 1985.

EPA.gov. An Introduction to Indoor Air Quality." http://www.epa.gov/iaq/ia-intro.html.

National Center for Complementary and Alternative Medicine. "Aloe Vera." http://nccam.nih.gov/health/aloevera.

Wikipedia. "List of Air-Filtering Plants." http://en.wikipedia.org/wiki/List_of_air-filtering_plants.

Wolverton, B. C., A. Johnson, and K. Bounds. NASA Clean Air Study Results, "Interior Landscape Plants for Indoor Air Pollution Abatement." http://www.scribd.com/doc/1837156/NASA-Indoor-Plants.

At the Intersection of Two Worlds: Modern and Holistic Medicine

⪧ by JD Hortwort ⪦

What does the term *traditional medicine* mean?

One hundred years ago, it meant the use of herbal and animal-derived solutions to treat disease. Now, due to the dominance of modern, human-made chemical and surgical solutions, traditional medicine has become synonymous with the American Medical Association (AMA). Herbal medicine has been relegated to the category of "alternative and complementary" medicine.

To be sure, those in the holistic community, which includes herbalists, still refer to their practice as "traditional." But ask the guy on the street where he traditionally goes for medical help, and he'll probably point to the nearest hospital or corner emergency care clinic, both of which will be staffed by people who have gone through many years of training in the skill and art of Western modern medicine.

Still, old-school healthcare has been making a comeback. A survey of 31,000 adults reported on by the University of Maryland Medical Center indicated that almost 70 percent had used some kind of complementary or alternative medicine in the past year. Twenty years ago, the Office of Alternative Medicine under the federal National Institutes of Health didn't exist. Its creation was followed shortly thereafter by the National Center for Complementary and Alternative Medicine (NCCAM), all to address the growing interest in the use of old forms of medicine.

A Matter of Philosophy

Two views of treatment could not be further apart than those of modern and holistic medicine. The American medical education system trains students for four years in general healthcare, followed by four years of internship and a period of residency. In this setting, students learn specifically to identify disorders and illnesses, treat the patient, and send the patient home. Some students go on to specialties that require more years of schooling.

Disease is a matter of chemistry and biology in conventional medicine. Bring these back in balance, and the patient can go about his normal routine. If the disease isn't "fixable," the conventional medical practitioner will usually offer advice on lifestyle adjustments and supplement with pharmaceuticals to make the patient's life as close to normal as possible.

Those trained in holistic medicine advocate prevention. When necessary, treatments take into account a review of the patient's entire life—from the stress of work, to eating habits, to exercise regimens. While the major reason for this is general philosophy, another reason is practicality. Alternative medicine isn't equipped to "fix" a patient overnight. You'll never hear an herbalist say, "Take two of these and call me in the morning." Herbs don't work that way. Neither do acupuncture, aromatherapy, tinctures, or any of the alternative medicinal practices. The patient can be brought back into balance, but it will take time and dedicated effort on the part of both the practitioner and the patient.

Benefits of Herbal Remedies

So why would anyone eschew the benefits of the latest research in lieu of a plant-based remedy suggested by a family friend or an anonymous website? Could it be simply a matter of latrophobia (fear of doctors)? As my mother said when we tried to get her to the doctor on numerous occasions, who wants to hear bad news? It may be a common joke, but we all know that when we go to the doctor, he or she will tell us something is wrong. Why else would we be there? And then he or she will give us something nasty to take and a healthcare regimen that includes eating better (bummer!) and getting more exercise (groan!).

No one would deny, as pointed out in a Tufts Managed Care Institute study, that part of the problem is high cost. Study authors noted that "the United States has the highest per capita spending on healthcare, as well as the highest percentage of Gross National Product dedicated to this sector."

The Kaiser Family Foundation reported that health expenditures in the U.S. were almost "$2.6 trillion in 2010, over ten times the $256 billion spent in 1980."

By comparison, a short drive to the nearest well-stocked discount store or nutritional outlet gives anyone access to a variety of commonly accepted treatments, usually for less than ten dollars.

The complexity of the U.S. healthcare system is also a factor. A visit to the average doctor's office will involve running a gauntlet of professionals. Will you see an LPN, a CNA, an RN, an NP, a PA, or all of these? Will you get to see the doctor or specialist at all? And how will you pay for your visit—with cash, a co-pay, insurance (with or without a deductible), a health savings account, Medicare, Medicaid, or an installment plan? How many forms will you have to fill out, track, forward to the appropriate source, duplicate, cross-reference, and archive (hopefully in a cloud network where you might be able to actually find it the next time you need it)?

Herbal remedies are so comfortable and easy when contrasted with the modern, miracle medicine experience. They don't judge. You can stay home while you take them. They are relatively inexpensive. They are available. Most of the time, they come in soothing flavors like honey, peppermint, and cherry. Who wouldn't rather head off a bout of the flu with a cup of warm sage tea than get stuck in the arm with a needle?

Drawbacks to Herbal Treatments

But there are problems with this growing, albeit positive, trend to choose herbal remedies over traditional ones. One major drawback is the issue of self-diagnosis. This is one time when we can literally be too close to the problem.

My older sister inspired my own study of herbs and their uses. As a young adult, she developed a reputation as an animal lover. Bring her any type of animal, domestic or wild, and she would nurse it back to health. She was a voracious reader (and this was in the days before the Internet). Her treatments of choice were almost always herbal.

It was only a matter of time before she began to be solicited for health advice for people. Again, her preference was for supplements and herbal cures. She also collected quite a lot of stories about the shortcomings of modern medicine, from bureaucratic horror stories of red tape to misdiagnoses by seemingly uncaring healthcare providers. Our experiences watching our mother die of ALS only intensified her distrust of conventional medicine.

When she began to feel out of sorts herself later in life, she did what she always did. She hit the books (and the Internet). Based on her general intestinal discomfort and the pain in the upper right side of her body, she determined her problem was in her gallbladder. After all, she was fair, fat, and over forty, the classic criteria for a patient with gallbladder problems.

She set about treating her problem with dietary changes, supplements, and herbs. Most of the time, these seemed to ease her symptoms, but the problem never fully went away. One day after a bout of intense pain in her abdomen, she finally agreed to be taken to the doctor. He put her in the hospital almost immediately. She had heart surgery the next day.

My sister's problem was heart disease. She had double bypass surgery. Like many women, she misdiagnosed the symptoms for heart disease in her gender. The typical heart-attack symptom—a radiating pain in the left shoulder and arm—is less likely in women. Women who suffer from heart disease are more likely to experience abdominal pain, nausea, dizziness, and fatigue.

Laypeople—those of us without direct education for or experience in treating medical conditions—don't have the skill sets to make diagnoses. It's one thing to treat the common cold or a simple cut. It's something else entirely to know when a respiratory illness has progressed to pneumonia or an infected cut has moved on to sepsis, a potentially deadly bacterial infection in the blood.

People tend to think that because herbs and supplements are readily available over the counter, anyone can determine their usage. Herbs can be drugs; we just don't call them that when they come in capsule form. People also don't realize that, just as in modern medicine, years of study are required to develop an understanding of herbs and their proper usage. A well-trained herbalist, naturopathic, homeopathic, or holistic healer then spends more years interning under an experienced professional to become qualified to treat others.

In a sense, people who hope to treat themselves with herbs fall into a paradox. On the one hand, they are inundated with information from self-help books and the Internet. On the other hand, they can't get the information they need to develop in-depth diagnostic skills just from reading about it.

The quality of the information available can be suspect as well. The Internet is filled with well-meaning testimonials from people who simply don't know what they are talking about. It is also filled with crooks who are perfectly happy to sell anyone a bottle of rainwater as a miracle cure for what ails them. As George Mason University economist Robin Hanson noted in a study examining medical outcomes, "Usually even untreated people get better eventually. " That snake oil treatment you bought over the Internet may not have killed you, but it certainly didn't cure you.

The quality of the product can be suspect as well. Just as you should never buy prescription medicines from an unreliable source, you should always be certain of your source for herbal supplements. You may know the difference between grass clippings and stinging nettle when you see them in their fresh, green state, but can you tell the difference when both are dried and minced?

Even when the correct herb is purchased, do you know if the dosage has been standardized to include the right amount of the active component in the herb? Gardeners know that growing conditions can make a big difference in the strength of a plant. Anyone who has grown herbs in a shady, damp location knows that the essential oils in those plants will not be as strong as in herbs grown in their proper setting in full sun.

Herbalists have to consider even thinner lines of demarcation. Gardeners are familiar with the popular perennial echinacea as the tall, purple, daisy-shaped flower. When purchased from the local garden center, this is most often *E. purpurea.* Herbalists are more inclined to speak of the native Midwestern flower *E. augustifolia.* Both have similar properties in herbal medicine. However, medicinally, *E. purpurea* may deplete the body's stores of vitamin E if used over a long period of time. Also, some herbalists may specify one type of echinacea over the other. Generics don't work in herbal medicines.

Potential Herb-Drug Interactions to Avoid

The National Center for Complementary and Alternative Medicine did a survey that indicates the most popularly used herbs are echinacea, garlic, gingko biloba, ginger, ginseng, peppermint, and St. John's wort. Echinacea is by far the most popular. Each of these herbs has been used for centuries. However, in our modern world, they have some dangerous interactions with commonly used humanmade drugs.

Echinacea is one of the first herbs we reach for in cold and flu season because it is an immune-system stimulant. As such, it can interact with medications used to treat HIV/AIDS. Women trying to get pregnant may want to avoid echinacea, as it can interfere with the release of eggs into the fallopian tubes. People who are allergic to flowers in the aster family of plants may also want to avoid echinacea.

Garlic, considered by herbalists to be a hot herb, not surprisingly can interfere with the use of Bifidus and Lactobacillus cultures to restore a proper balance of intestinal flora. Garlic should not be used medicinally with blood thinners like aspirin and warfarin (Coumadin).

Ginger, that spicy component of many Asian dishes, is another herb that can interact with blood thinners like aspirin, warfarin (Coumadin), and clopidogrel (Plavix). It may increase the effect of barbiturates in some patients. People scheduled for surgery are advised not to use ginger medicinally for two weeks prior to their operation.

Gingko biloba is considered by many to be a useful aid to improved brain function. Some studies have linked it to an interaction with some MAO (monamine oxidase) inhibitors like Wellbutrin and Zyban. There is also some evidence that large doses of gingko biloba used with blood thinners like aspirin can cause problems with bleeding.

Ginseng is a key ingredient in many energy drinks and stimulants due to its reputation for improving alertness and energy. Too much ginseng can raise blood pressure, so avoid ginseng without a professional's consent if you are on blood pressure medications or blood thinners.

Peppermint—what could possibly be dangerous about an ingredient that is pervasive in candy and teas? Peppermint is one of the safer herbs out there. Still, there are considerations such as for those with gallbladder disorders. Peppermint slows the passage of bile through the gallbladder and should only be used for a mild attack. Peppermint can also interfere with the heartburn medication cisapride (Propulsid).

St. John's wort is an herb that even laypeople know is used for depression. Fewer may know that it is also used to fight infections and has pain-relieving benefits. Its precautions are many. Although the dangers of photosensitivity are overstated, people taking angiotensin-converting enzyme (ACE) inhibitors for high blood pressure should not use St. John's wort due to a risk for sunburn. This herb should never be used in combination with any of the prescribed treatments for depression or psychosis. St. John's wort is also known to interact with blood pressure medications, birth control pills, and some chemotherapy drugs. Stop using St. John's wort well before surgery, as the herb is known to intensify the effect of anesthesia.

Blending Old-World Remedies and New-World Cures

We live in a precarious situation. Patients in the U.S. today stand between two worlds: one is a world of modern medicine, the other of alternative medicine. People who complain about the nature of modern medicine would probably agree they don't want to go back to a time when the treatment for insanity was to tie a bag of buttercups around the patient's neck and bloodletting was the cure-all for everything.

Those who argue that anything other than modern medicine is hokum haven't read the latest research into common herbal therapies. Yes, willow bark is an effective precursor to aspirin, without the stomach churning side effects. Astragalus does show beneficial effects on the immune system, and chamomile has been found to be effective in easing mild to moderate anxiety in adults. The rediscovery of herbal solutions for our aches and pains goes on. In other words, when speaking of herbs, today's researchers are less like to say, "There's no way that can work," and more likely to say, "Let's study this a little further."

Old-world remedies and new-world cures don't have to be at odds. These should be complementary worlds where a dialogue exists for the best outcomes for patients.

For additional information, or to locate an experienced herbalist in your area, contact the American Herbalists Guild at www.americanherbalistsguild.com. To locate a licensed naturopath in your area, contact the American Association of Naturopathic Physicians at www.naturopathic.org.

Sources

Balch, Phyllis A. *Prescription for Nutritional Healing.* New York: Avery Trade, 2010.

Hoffmann, David. *Medical Herbalism.* Rochester, VT: Healing Arts Press, 2003.

National Center for Complementary and Alternative Medicine. http://www.nccam.nih.gov.

Herb Crafts

Gifts That Grow: Making Plantable Botanical Paper

❧ by Jill Henderson ❧

Making paper is one of the easiest and most rewarding forms of arts and crafts, unparalleled in its unique beauty and functionality. When you add a few special flower or herb seeds to handcrafted paper, it becomes a plantable gift that keeps on giving.

Making seeded paper is easy and doesn't require fancy or expensive tools and supplies. In fact, most people can come up with everything they need to make their own seeded botanical paper right at home. All it takes is a few supplies and a little space in the kitchen or workshop.

Tools and Supplies

The basic tools for making plantable paper include:

- Mold (screen)
- Deckle
- Sponge
- Dedicated blender
- Recycled paper
- Bucket, plastic storage tub, or sink
- Wool felt, heavy brown paper, or newspaper
- Seeds
- Decorative additions

Molds and Deckles

One of the most important tools in papermaking is the mold, which is essentially a fine-meshed screening material stretched over a frame. Molds are used to capture paper pulp and allow excess water to drain away from the forming paper. By necessity, molds should have strong frames that don't wobble or bend and screening material that won't sag under the weight of wet paper. Because the papermaking process includes submerging the mold in water, make sure it will fit completely inside of a watertight sink, bucket, or storage tub.

If desired, molds can be purchased from specialty craft suppliers. These are good, but aren't always cheap. Another option is to buy a small, adjustable replacement window screen at the hardware store. These sliding screens are usually around fifteen inches long and have an aluminum outer frame. By removing the sliders that hold the screens together, you can have two excellent papermaking molds for around seven dollars. You could also recycle old or discarded window screens, although most will be too large to handle easily. If you do find a small screen, be sure that the material isn't saggy and is free of holes.

Another inexpensive mold option is to repurpose found objects such as picture and mirror frames. Begin preparing the frame by removing the glass, the paper backing, and any staples or nails that you find. Cut a piece of regular fiberglass window screening two to three inches longer and wider than the outer dimensions of the frame. Lay the screening evenly over the back of the frame. Working on one side at a time, fold the excess screen over the side and staple it securely. Move to the opposite side and pull the screening taut, and again secure it with staples. Do the other two sides the same way, and you will have a functional papermaking mold.

If you're feeling up to a little construction, you can easily build any size mold you like using 1 × 1 inch lumber. For the kids, use waterproof glue to join four jumbo craft sticks together in a square, rectangle, or triangle, and secure the screening with staples. If a round mold works for your project, embroidery hoops are easy to find and very economical.

Most molds are small—usually not much larger than a standard sheet of notebook paper. If you would like to make bigger sheets of paper, select or build a mold that will accommodate the desired size, plus two additional inches on all sides.

Once you have your mold ready, it's time to decide whether you will be using a deckle. Deckles are molds that are set on top of the other mold and are used to make uniformly sized paper with defined edges. They're also used to make fun shapes, such as stars, hearts, and flowers. Deckles can be any-thing with a smooth inside edge, including cookie cutters, egg or pancake molds, embroidery hoops, old picture frames, and more. If you need a custom-size sheet of square or rectangular paper, deckles can be custom-built using quarter-round floor trim or 1 × 1 inch pine.

Reduce, Reuse, Recycle

The great part about making your own seeded paper is that you get to reuse waste paper that would otherwise wind up in a landfill. Indeed, homemade paper can be made from just about any kind of nonglossy paper or paper product you can imagine, and each will lend its own character and strength to the finished product. Here are just a few of the types of paper you can recycle into the perfect seeded gift card:

- Cardboard
- Cardstock
- Construction paper
- Egg cartons
- Greeting cards and invitations
- Junk mail
- Manila envelopes
- Nonglossy magazines
- Napkins
- Newspaper
- Old book pages

- Paper grocery bags
- Paper towel and wrapping paper rolls
- Paper towels
- Phonebook pages
- Picture frame matting
- Recycled copy or printer paper
- Recycled envelopes
- Tissue paper

Although there are many kinds of paper to choose from, there are a few types that you should avoid when making home-made paper. These include paper that has a waxy or glossy surface, such as sale ads, cereal boxes, slick posterboard, and any other paper that has a waxy surface. The fibers in these kinds of paper don't break up well when blended with water and can leave big, unattractive lumps in the finished product. Very dense papers can be used, but they usually need longer soaking times to soften completely. Also, avoid commercial paper printed with intensely colored inks and raised or glossy inks, which often contain unpleasant chemicals that should not be used in the garden.

You might hear differently, but most newspaper, colored paper, and copy-machine paper—even those with colored ink—are safe to use. Most of the inks used in these printing processes are still soy-based and can be safely used in the garden. So go ahead and bring home that trash bag full of shredded documents and failed copies from the office and do your part to make the world a greener place.

Color and Texture

The type of scrap paper you choose will determine the final color and texture of your seeded paper. If you would like the finished surface to be relatively smooth, use smooth paper scraps, such as recycled printer or copy paper, tissue paper, envelopes, and invitations. Use a combination of smooth and rough papers to achieve rustic or artistic surfaces. Paper scraps from construction paper, egg cartons, and cardboard will all give your final paper an organic look and feel.

When making homemade paper, it is very important to realize that no matter how hard you try, your paper will not be perfect, super-smooth, or bright white. The good news is, it doesn't matter! Those little flaws and bumps are part of the beauty of homemade plantable paper. Plus, every sheet you make will be 100 percent original.

Obviously, using random paper scraps of various materials and colors can create some interesting—and some not so interesting—colors. But if you select your paper carefully, you can come pretty close to any color you choose, except pure white and jet black. These two colors cannot be created without the use of special pulping paper found at specialty papermaking outlets. However, that doesn't mean you can't create an off-white or ivory paper using only recycled paper. If you want something close to white, choose only white or ivory paper scraps. The same is true for black, although all-black paper is harder to find.

While mixing up a batch of white or purple paper seems pretty straightforward, choosing the papers to blend together to achieve a particular color is not always so obvious. What happens if you mix black and white newspaper with orange construction paper? How about cardboard and egg cartons with green tissue paper? No matter how hard you try, there are bound to be a few "everything but the kitchen sink" moments where your paper turns an icky gray or putrid purple color.

Thankfully, papermaking is a forgiving craft. Should you wind up with a color that reminds you of the Slug That Ate New York, adding a good dose of white paper will often save the day. Better yet, avoid the dreaded slug altogether by referring to the following tips on how to blend colors, and you'll be whipping up the perfect shades in no time.

Mixing the Perfect Color

It might surprise you to learn that every color known to humankind comes from three simple colors: red, blue, and yellow. These are known as primary colors. When primary colors are mixed together in various combinations, they create what are known as secondary colors. Secondary colors are violet, green, and orange.

Red + Blue = Violet

Blue + Yellow = Green

Yellow + Red = Orange

By mixing these six colors together in various combinations, twelve tertiary (or "in-between") colors can be made as follows:

Red + Violet = Red-Violet

Violet + Blue = Blue-Violet

Blue + Green = Blue-Green

Green + Yellow = Yellow-Green

Yellow + Orange = Yellow-Orange

Orange + Red = Red-Orange

These twelve colors alone can create hundreds of new colors, and with the addition of one or more of the three neutrals, black, white, and gray (which are not considered true colors), those colors can be endlessly toned and shaded. Of course, white lightens and brightens any color, while black darkens and deepens it. Gray is a combination of white and black and is used to mute and soften.

By following these simple guidelines and using scraps whose colors are complementary to one another, you will be able create an endless variety of tones and shades for your special seeded papers.

Decorating Your Paper

Now that you have given some thought to the desired color and texture of your paper, consider adding one or two additional items that will add a bit of drama and flair to the finished paper. Like all crafts, there are many kinds of products you can buy specifically for decorating paper. However, many decorative elements can be had for free if you just keep an open mind. Look to your kitchen and craft supply shelf for free, fun, and organic textural elements such as these:

- Confetti and paper punch-outs
- Cotton string or thread
- Crushed egg or sea shells
- Dried herbs and spices
- Hemp, thread, or sisal
- Mica
- Pressed flowers, petals, or leaves

Keep in mind that adding too many decorative items, especially large or very smooth ones, can leave holes in your finished paper and detract from the overall look you are trying to achieve. Some elements, such as paper punch-outs and dried herbs, should be stirred gently by hand into the prepared paper slurry just before it is poured into the mold. Doing so will blend the elements into the paper without distorting their shapes or colors.

Don't Forget the Seeds

Of course, seeded paper isn't any good without the seeds! While almost any type of seed can be added to your paper, larger seeds demand a thicker finished paper. The smaller the seeds, the thinner the paper can be.

One fun way to make your seeded paper into a special gift is by customizing it around a central theme. One of the easiest themes to use for any occasion is color. Is your best friend having a baby? Make shower name cards that have been embedded with pink flower seeds for a girl and blue flower seeds for a boy. Wedding favors can be tagged using seeded paper with several kinds of white flowers, such as baby's breath, Gerbera daisies, and white carnations. Here are a few more seed groupings that will help you get those creative juices flowing:

- Annual or perennial flowers
- Butterfly plants
- Kitchen herbs
- Medicinal herbs
- Native wildflowers
- Vegetables

Ready, Set, Make Paper

These instructions are written with the beginning papermaker in mind. At first glance, the process might look intimidatingly long, but it's as easy as pulping the paper scraps, pouring the pulp into a deckle on the mold, and drying the finished paper.

1. Tear or shred scrap paper into small chunks or pieces and put into a small bucket or large cooking pot. Cover the paper with just enough water to wet everything down, and let soak for an hour or so. This helps soften the paper.

2. Place a handful or two of softened paper in the blender with enough additional water to allow the paper to move freely. Blend until no paper chunks are left and the mixture is smooth. Add as much paper or water as needed to fill the blender.

3. If adding textural elements such as string, mica, herbs, leaves, spices, or whole flowers to your finished paper, remove the blender from the stand and gently stir them in.

4. Position the deckle(s) on the mold. Place the mold down into a bucket or tub so that it is secure. If needed, bricks or other objects can be set in the bottom of the container to support the mold. Fill the container with just enough water to immerse the deckles in water halfway up their sides.

5. Pour the paper slurry very slowly and evenly into the deckles. Because the deckles are immersed in water, the slurry will appear to "float." The amount of slurry needed for each deckle depends on how thick the paper will be. The idea is to have as thin a layer of slurry as possible without leaving any gaps or holes.

6. Use your finger or a craft stick to spread the slurry around to make it even and smooth. If needed, you can use

tweezers to pick out large clumps of paper or other unwanted elements. By keeping the deckles submerged in water, the slurry will stay liquid, making it easier to work with. If it doesn't, add a bit more water to the tub.

7. Once the slurry is smooth and even, sprinkle your chosen seeds across the surface in a random pattern. How much seed you spread depends entirely on what type and size of seed you are using and, of course, your personal preference. If needed, the seeds can be lightly pressed into the slurry.

8. Slowly and evenly lift the mold out of the water. You can balance the mold over the water tub, a kitchen sink, or some other bit of elevated support to allow it to drain for a few minutes. If a counter or bench is all you have, place the mold on top of one or two thick cotton towels that have been spread out evenly across the counter.

9. Allow the slurry to drain for a couple minutes before removing the deckles, but don't wait too long or the paper will stick to the sides. Begin the couching process by covering the wet paper with wool felt. Using a clean cellulose sponge, apply even and gentle pressure to the paper to remove as much excess water as possible, squeezing out the sponge as needed. Keep in mind that pressing down too hard will make the paper fibers spread out. This will result in the loss of the clean edge formed by the deckle and could possibly create thin spots, tears, or holes in the finished paper.

10. Once you see that most of the water has been sponged away, lift up one edge of the wool felt and see if the paper is sticking to it. If it is, continue lifting the felt from the mold. The paper should stick to the felt and come cleanly away from

the mold. If the paper does not stick to the felt, lay it back down and sponge off a bit more water before trying again.

11. Once the paper sticks to the felt, transfer it—paper side down—onto the drying surface. This can be a clean, dry piece of wool felt, several sheets of newspaper, heavy brown paper, or fabric interfacing that has been spread out on a cookie sheet or another screen.

12. Before trying to remove the felt from the paper, sponge it a few more times to force more water out of the paper. This last sponging also smoothes out any screen marks on the back of the paper. If needed, a very gentle application of a rolling pin can help smooth the paper as well.

13. Once the drying surface absorbs more water than the seeded paper, the latter will stick to it and the wool felt can be peeled away cleanly. If your paper still wants to stick to the felt, sponge it a few more times.

14. Peel the felt from the paper. At this point, the "front" of your paper is facing up, affording the perfect opportunity to remove air bubbles or to lightly emboss your paper with a rubber stamp, if desired.

15. Once the paper is free, simply allow it to air-dry. Do not place your paper in the sun or try to dry it with a blow dryer, as it will dry unevenly and curl.

16. When the paper is dry, gently peel it away from the drying material. It will probably be a little wavy and may curl at the edges a bit. To flatten your paper, simply cover one or more sheets with a piece of cardboard topped with heavy books. Press paper overnight for best results.

Seeded Paper Projects

Seeded paper is amazingly tough. It can be folded, cut, or torn into any shape or size and can be glued, taped, or stapled. Some of the heavier papers can even be stitched together by a sewing machine! In addition to being strong, homemade paper is versatile and can be used in many different ways. Turn large sheets into decorative wrapping paper, small gift boxes, book covers, picture matting, placemats, wall art, party favor cups, decoupage paper, and more. Seeded paper is used to best effect in sizes that are convenient for planting. Cards, bookmarks, and table place settings make lovely gifts that the recipients can use to grow their very own garden!

To allow the natural beauty of your seeded paper to shine through, keep additional adornments to a minimum. My favorite way to decorate small cards is to punch a hole in one corner and thread it with pretty ribbon, jute, or raffia. To let the recipient know exactly what it is they have just received, a short explanation, such as this, can be written on the back:

This handmade paper is embedded with the seeds of Genovese Basil. Simply tear the card into small pieces and plant ¼-inch deep in good garden soil spaced 15 inches apart. Seeds will germinate in 7–10 days.

Of course, you can write whatever you like on the front or the inside of the card. Most types of ballpoint, gel, roller, and calligraphy pens work well on seeded paper, but test it on a piece of scrap just to be sure. Should your paper not take well to the ink you want to use, brush the surface with diluted acrylic matte medium and allow it to dry completely. This will seal the paper, enabling you to use any kind of ink, or even watercolors, to make your seeded botanical paper even more special.

There are many methods and tools for making paper at home and even more ways to use them. By making these simple and simply beautiful seeded botanical papers, you can give a special, one-of-a-kind gift that is sure to grow.

Herbal Product Development

❧ by Dallas Jennifer Cobb ❧

Many people grow herbs in backyard and kitchen gardens or in big planters on decks and balconies. We grow what we need for cooking and baking and to use in the house and garden. Mid-summer, when everything is in abundance, we take time to dry and preserve some of our herbs for winter use, and give some to our friends and family. When the herbs are really abundant, many of us dream of selling fresh herbs and making some money.

Maybe you already have an herb business, and sell fresh herbs at the farm gate, in a farmers' market, or to local businesses. You might do this as a sideline, and dream of quitting your main job and making a living from your herb business, but have lots of questions about how to make it substantial enough to support yourself.

Or you might already be depending on your herb business as your primary source of income and feel the need to further develop the business and the potential for income from it.

Whether you are someone who dreams of a diversified herb business or someone who has the business already and needs to diversify it, this article is for you. It can help you to brainstorm and plan a new herb business, or move your existing business along to its next stage of growth. Even if you don't have any interest in operating an herb business, you might find the ideas for making homemade herbal products useful for making gifts.

A portion of my income comes from the products of my own herb business. Living in a rural area, I have seen many other agricultural-based businesses come and go. I have also seen a few businesses grow, develop, diversify, and stay. What follows is some of what I have learned from all of this.

Simple Economics

To understand how to grow your business, it's helpful to understand a little bit about economics. When describing economic activity and production, these common terms are used to indicate the different types of activity and production: primary, secondary, tertiary, and quarternary. While these terms are most often used in reference to a country's economy, they can also be applied to a smaller economy, such as your individual business. Herbs will still be your main business, but looking at the spin-off products that can be produced from herbs will enable you to grow your herbal business, branching out to produce and sell a variety of products that might appeal to the same people who are buying the herbs.

From an economic perspective, a primary product is what you harvest from the earth. In this case, it is herbs. You might grow lots of one herb, like lavender, or grow a wide variety of herbs. Whether you sell these herbs in pots as a plant or seedling, or as cut herbs, fresh or dried, they are still considered primary products. These primary products can be packaged or unpackaged.

Secondary production is manufacturing and includes the products that you can make from your primary product. So imagine things you can make by adding to, or mixing with, your herbs. This can also include processing that alters the primary product, such as cooking, rendering, bottling, or brewing.

Tertiary products are services. So if herbs are your primary product, your tertiary products could include herbal health consultations, workshops, lectures, massages, garden design, pest control, or even gardening assistance.

The quarternary sector of the economy consists of "intellectual activities." Related to an herb business, the quarternary products could include articles written about herbs, research done with herbs, websites set up with information on herbs, herb books written and published, or even business support as a consultant to herb businesses.

Know Your Business

Sometimes the best thing you can do for a business is sound planning in advance of any activity or investment. Even if your business is already operating successfully, you can benefit from an analysis of your current business and putting a plan in place for the expansion of it. Following a few simple steps can help to get your creative ideas about product diversification flowing.

With diversified products you have diversified income streams, and this means money flowing in different patterns and amounts at all times. When your primary products are out of season, you can still be selling secondary, tertiary, and quarternary products. Let's identify what products you currently have, and then brainstorm some more.

List Your Primary Products

Write "Primary Products" at the top of a sheet of paper and list all of your primary products down the left side. This is a list of all the herbs that you produce. It might be really long, or it might be just a few items. I grow a variety of versatile herbs, including lavender, chamomile, sage, lemon balm, thyme, sweet grass, mint, spearmint, rosemary, calendula, garlic, chives, and oregano. Early in the season I sell seedlings of several types of annual herbs in small pots for people to plant in their own gardens. These primary products can be sold as seedlings, fresh herbs and dried herbs, packaged or unpackaged.

With a list of primary products—those being the herbs grown—let's figure out a way to expand the number of products produced, because the more that is produced, the more there is to choose from, and the more that can be sold. With more items for sale, the products of the business appeal to more people, and sell more overall. The easiest way to expand the number of products you produce is to create secondary products: things made from the primary product that you grow.

List Your Secondary Products

On another sheet of paper, write the heading "Secondary Products," and down the left side identify everything that you make *from* your herbs, singularly or combined with other herbs. These are your secondary products.

I make herbal vinegars and oils; steep herbs and decant the oils to make moisturizer, lip balm, hand cream, and body lotion; process herbs into butters, sauces, pastes, dressings, and dips; combine herbs to produce therapeutic teas and savory seasoning combinations; process herbs to make tinctures; and bake a wide variety of goods containing herbs. While I regularly use herbs in what I cook and eat, I don't sell edible products beyond baked goods because the packaging and labeling requirements feel too onerous. If you are interested in producing food products, be sure to check into the food safety legislation in your area, and be certain of packaging and labeling requirements.

List Your Tertiary and Quarternary Products

Lots of herb businesses have only primary and secondary products, but I think the tertiary and quarternary sectors are natural places for business expansion. On a separate piece of paper write your headings, and if you already offer some sort of herbal services and intellectual products related to herbs—such as a newsletter, fact sheets, or an article in the local paper—list these too.

My tertiary products are few: I have provided garden design and set-up services for several themed herb gardens. My quarternary products are many: I write and publish articles, I have contributed research for food policy planning, and I've produced fact sheets and newsletters about herbs.

With all these lists in hand, you now have a clear idea, and a current record, of all the products of your herb business. Now you can plan for herbal product development and expansion, and successfully grow your herb business.

Diversify Your Primary Product

The simplest way to grow your herb business is to look at your potential: how you can do more of what you already do well, and where you can add other products. Start at the beginning of the year and work through the seasons, brainstorming ideas on how to grow the number and variety of herbal products that you can produce.

If you want to expand the number of herbs that you grow, then winter is the time to plan your garden. Consider adding more primary products, by growing either more types of herbs or more varieties of one particular herb. Diversification of your product offerings means that you will have something to satisfy the needs and desires of more customers, and more items to entice existing customers with. Look at your list of existing herbs and ask yourself what would complement them, combine well with them, and coexist peacefully in the garden with them.

Early in the spring when you start your own seedlings, consider starting a few extra rows. Transplant these to small pots and sell them to interested gardeners, capitalizing on the spring buying surge of garden-related items. In addition to offering singular seedlings, you could also design planters with three different herbs, marketing them as specialty kitchen herb pots with an Italian or Mediterranean theme, or even a "skin care herbs" theme. The possibilities are endless.

Late in the spring often feels like a period of pause while most cultivated herbs are growing madly, but while you wait for them to mature, there are lots of opportunities to expand your primary herbal product offerings. You might make a foray into nature and wildcraft early dandelion, lambsquarters, and chickweed greens, and sell them to upscale bistros. Tend to your own garden, pinching the scapes off the top of the garlic, a step necessary for the production of great garlic heads. Not only are the scapes edible, tasty, and attractive, but they are also versatile and easily used.

Early summer herbal offerings are gorgeous as edible flowers—such as calendula, pansy, nasturtium, and chive—bloom. Edible flowers are a trendy, gourmet-quality garnish. Sell them to restaurants catering to foodies.

Mid-summer, during the peak period of herb production, it is easy to sell fresh herbs bundled alone or with other complementary herbs. Make up combinations that you can attach a simple recipe to, inspiring the purchaser to try something different.

During this period of overproduction, consider drying a portion of the herbs and turning them into packaged products. While fresh herbs lose their peak condition quickly, dried herbs keep for a very long time. This can help stretch out your selling season, as you offer a wider variety of dried herbs all year long.

Herbal Product Development

Now that you have expanded your primary product line, it is time to look at increasing your secondary product list. Pull out the list of secondary products that you made, and let's brainstorm more ways to process herbs to produce something new.

Organize the items that you already make under a few broad headings, such as "Body Care," "Culinary," and "Gift Items." For each of these headings, brainstorm everything you could make from your herbs, and list these ideas down the right side of the paper. It should be a pretty long list. Think of all the things you have seen, bought, read about, or dreamed of.

Choose just a few of these ideas to try at first, focusing on what is easy to produce, won't take huge amounts of time to make, and will complement what you already offer. Try to meet a niche market need, making products that there is a demand or market for. It also makes sense to make only things that you will use if they don't happen to sell. Late summer and early fall are the time to go into full production mode with your secondary product line. The recipes for some of the secondary products suggested here are provided at the end of this article.

Culinary Products

Some secondary culinary products can be made quickly and sold right away. I love to make and sell baked goods, because they almost sell themselves. Paying a small amount of money at the farmers' market feels like a manageable financial risk, especially on a Saturday when there's a good amount of pedestrian traffic. I like to focus on items that sell well and complement what is already sold by other vendors. My favorites are focaccia bread in a variety of flavors (rosemary, olive and herbs, garlic, or herbes de Provence), herbed tea bisquits, savory scones, and herb cookies.

These are easy to prepare, and involve most of my day and evening on Friday in preparation for the Saturday market. In addition to the fresh baked goods, I take dips, sauces, and spreads that pair well with bread and buns. Offering small samples of garlicky pesto, fresh cilantro salsa, or garlic and chive butter gives the customer a taste of both products. When someone wants to buy just bread, it's easy to upsell them with a quick taste of a delicious dip or spread.

Other easy secondary culinary products include herbal sugars and salts. Add herbs to these simple baking and cooking ingredients for a gourmet taste. They are easy to make and sell, offer a great profit margin, and keep for a long time. Both sugar and salt easily absorb flavor and smell. Make lavender sugar to use in cookies, cakes, muffins, and tea, or thyme salt for rubbing chicken before roasting.

Other secondary products that take time to make can be produced at this time. I prepare a wide variety of herbal vinegars and oils that steep for a few months and get pulled out for late November and December sales. These can be sold on their own, or assembled into attractive gift packages or baskets featuring a variety of herb items.

Body Care Products

During the cold months, when I have more time, I undertake more laborious projects like body care products and gift items. Since Christmas is such a great time for selling quality handmade items, I produce a lot in October and November. Even if you don't make essential oils, you can focus on producing a wide variety of products with herbs.

Think of all the things you can produce from lavender: bath salts, bath bombs, and floral water spray; lavender dryer bags, sleep pillows, eye covers, and sachets; and the mystical lavender wand. Now, can you imagine the variety of secondary products you could make from all the other herbs you grow?

Gift Items

Think of any sort of item that you neither eat nor use on your body and that is a gift item. With an herb business, there are quite a few I can think of: herbal paper and envelopes, pressed herbs, lavender wands, sweet grass braids, dried sage for smudging, lavender braids, garlic braids for doors, herbed deep-sleep pillows, eye covers, potpourri, herb sachets, and even moth-repelling lavender bags to use with clothing.

Growing Your Business

You now have good lists and ideas for a wide variety of herb products to diversify your business and income streams. Next, brainstorm ideas for where and how to sell your products.

I am a fan of "start small and build." I like to minimize my financial risk and maximize my return. Maybe you start out by selling a few simple items at the gate. With a bit of money in hand, you could pay for a booth at a one-time event like a community fair or seasonal celebration. This is a great way to limit your overhead and motivate yourself to prepare a variety of products for that one day. You can test out the market, and gain wider recognition for your name and products.

If a one-day event is successful, the next logical progression would be to take a regular booth at a farmers' market. Even though it is one day a week, you can make tons of products and enjoy good sales from a focused clientele—people come to the market to buy good, fresh food.

You can plan for annual events, like spring seedling sales, and turn them into long-weekend, multipurpose events. Why not sell seedlings, offer samples, and sell marinades and sauces produced from last year's crop? You could also sell seeds for the do-it-yourselfers, offer workshops, sell how-to herb articles or fact sheets, sell a wide variety of diverse products, and celebrate your business.

Easy, Versatile Recipes

Focaccia Bread

2¾ cups whole wheat flour

1 teaspoon salt

1 teaspoon sugar

1 tablespoon yeast

1 tablespoon vegetable oil (plus more for greasing)

1 cup water

2 tablespoons olive oil

1 tablespoon grated Parmesan cheese

Preheat oven to 450°F. Mix flour, salt, sugar, and yeast in a large bowl. Add vegetable oil and water. Mix well. When the mixture is doughy, place on a lightly floured surface, and knead until smooth and elastic. Lightly oil a large bowl, put dough inside, and roll it around to coat with oil. Cover with damp cloth, and let rise in a warm place for 20 minutes.

Punch dough down. Place on an oiled cookie sheet, pressing it to ½-inch thickness. Brush with the olive oil. Sprinkle with Parmesan cheese and your choice of herbs: garlic, oregano, thyme, basil, or black pepper. Vegetable combinations are optional, such as tomato basil, garlic scape pesto, and roasted red repper and oregano. A decadent version can be made by adding 1 cup shredded mozzarella, spread evenly, with herbs scattered on top.

Bake for 15 minutes, or until golden brown. Serve warm.

Herb Sugar

In a large jar, combine 1 part herb and 7 parts sugar. (I prefer to use dried herbs because it cuts down on the possibility of mold growth.) Seal the jar and let sit for a month. Use a sieve to remove herbs from the sugar to maintain normal consistency in baking. Best herbs: lavender, calendula, mint, and lemon balm.

Herb Salt

In a large jar, combine 1 part herb and 4 parts salt. (I prefer to use dried herbs because it cuts down on the possibility of mold growth.) Seal the jar and let sit for a month. You can use a sieve to remove herbs from salt to maintain normal consistency, or leave herbs in if used for a meat or poultry rub. Best herbs: thyme, sage, oregano, and garlic.

Herb Butter

Cream butter with fresh herbs, and serve with warm bread. Best herbs: garlic, chive, and oregano.

Herb Bath Salts

½ cup herbs (I prefer to use dried herbs)

20 drops lavender essential oil

5 cups Epsom salt (magnesium sulfate)

2 cups Dead Sea salt

Mix together and place ½ cup in small mesh bag. Throw bag in running water. The salts and essential oils will disperse in water, and the herbs will remain. Best herbs: lavender, chamomile, and mint. If I am making these in large quantities, for sale, I mix everything in a large container, and measure out the appropriate amount into a resealable plastic bag that is labeled and sealed.

Ornamental Oregano

⋙ by Ember Grant ⋘

Like many casual gardeners, I purchase most plants at retail outlets and look mainly at the popular name rather than the Latin genus and species. The oregano that has been growing in my herb garden for the past several years came from one such store, its plant information card long discarded. I must confess that all I recall about the plant is that it is the herb oregano; I never took note of what specific variety I actually have. I used the leaves for cooking once or twice, but since the flowers are so pretty, I mainly use this plant for decoration. As it turns out, I have one of the many varieties of ornamental oregano. While not recommended for cooking, these types are best used as showpieces in the garden and for floral arrangements.

Oregano is known mainly as a culinary herb, and there are many varieties, but I'd like to introduce you to the ornamental called *Origanum laevigatum*, sometimes called Pilgrim.

This plant emerges in spring as dense clumps of bluish-green leaves. Throughout the summer, purplish-pink flowers appear on long stems and the plant becomes quite vigorous—great for the backs of borders and other large spaces. This variety is hardy to zone 7 and doesn't require any special accommodations—just lots of sun and well-drained soil.

Oregano originated in the Mediterranean and Eurasia; the name *Origanum* comes from the Greek *oreos* ("mountains") and *ganeos* ("brightness/joy/beauty"), meaning "joy of the mountain." The Egyptians also cultivated it more than 3,000 years ago. Oregano is sometimes confused with marjoram and is often called wild marjoram. Marjoram is *Origanum majorana* and is often called sweet marjoram. These plants are related, and both are members of the mint family. Because of its myriad uses, oregano has been called the "prince of herbs." The "classic" oregano, *Origanum vulgare*, has a stronger flavor than marjoram and is the oregano of choice for the kitchen.

With its origin in Greece, oregano naturally has a rich mythology and folklore. One legend surrounding oregano is that it grew only in Aphrodite's garden on Mount Olympus. In Crete, dittany (a type of *Origanum*) was dedicated to the moon and the goddess Diana. Legend says this herb was burned to aid contact with the spiritual realm. The Greeks and Romans used oregano to fashion wedding crowns for both the bride and groom, and it was commonly used in love spells and potions. In addition, oregano was used for protection against evil—it was hung in doorways and thrown over thresholds. It was also put on graves with the belief it would grant peace. Oregano was popular in nosegays during the Middle Ages and used in spells to attract wealth. In Egypt, marjoram was dedicated to the god Osiris—they also wove the herb into crowns for religious rites. In the language of flowers, oregano means "blushing," "innocence," "joy," "and happiness."

Practical uses throughout history include fragrance and cleaning, dyes, disinfecting, and preserving various foods. The oils have been used in soaps, perfumes, and lotions. Oregano has a long history of being used as a folk remedy for a variety of ailments, from coughing to upset stomach, as a tea or by adding it to the bath. It has also been used to treat various types of external wounds.

It's easy to imagine the flowers of *Origanum laevigatum* being used as a wedding crown, since the stems are flexible and easy to wrap. This is one reason this type of oregano is perfect for wreaths. Every summer I gather these flowers and tuck the stems around a grapevine wreath, adding other herbs and flowers to create many different styles. Making a wreath is easier than it sounds—you can use fresh or dried herbs and secure them with wire or hot glue where necessary. For a midsummer wreath, combine the mauve oregano flowers with lavender and yarrow. For a pretty combination in late summer, mix oregano blossoms with dried wheat sheaves and yarrow. These are all plants that hold their shape and color well when dried. You can allow your plants to dry on the wreath—just go ahead and hang it. Decorate your wreath with ribbons of colors that complement the flowers you use.

Add fresh or dried oregano flowers to arrangements and bouquets. They're a wonderful accent to use in place of baby's breath. Combine oregano with flowers that create a contrast of shape and color. For example, the purplish oregano flowers look striking alongside red roses, and they contrast beautifully with yellow and orange marigolds. For fresh arrangements, harvest just before the buds are in full flower. For drying, cut the stems while in full bloom and hang them in bundles away from direct sunlight. You may spray them with a preservative if you wish, but they will last for months or even years without it, as long as they're handled carefully.

Create a fragrant herbal potpourri by blending oregano leaves and flowers with rosemary, thyme, and bay leaves. Try adding other scents, such as floral or spice, to create your own unique blends. Since oregano blooms prolifically all summer, you should have an abundance of material for all your projects.

Most oregano plants are easy to grow, and they attract beneficial pollinators, like bees, to the garden. They're favored by butterflies as well. Other ornamental varieties to try are Marshall's Memory, Showy Pink, Kent Beauty, and Herrenhausen. Even some of the varieties that are known mainly as culinary herbs have lovely flowers you can use for decoration. Just remember to look at the scientific name of your plants when you purchase them so you know exactly which type you have! That's especially important when the plant has as many different varieties as oregano. Pretty and practical, oregano is essential for the crafty gardener.

Dyeing for Color

⤟ by Charlie Rainbow Wolf ⤞

Anyone who has ever tried to remove berry stains from their favorite garment knows that Mother Nature does indeed provide us with a wide variety of items from which we can create our own natural dyes. The process does not require a lot of equipment or technique in order for the colors to be successful. The main tools are a cooking pan, a wooden spoon, a plastic bucket, and water that is not treated water from a tap. Tap water often has additives that could affect the outcome of the dye project. Personally, I use distilled water.

The Equipment
The cooking pan needs to hold about five quarts of water, plus the material

that you are going to be dyeing. This pan is called a dye pan, and it is probably the most important piece of equipment you will use. This is where you boil your herbs and other ingredients to make your dyebath. Devote a pan specifically to this, because some of the inclusions are toxic if ingested. Ideally this pan should be stainless steel, as this will not react with any of your dye substances, but if cost prohibits this, aluminum is the next best thing. Remember that the material from which the pan is made could influence the outcome of the dye project. This is a greater concern once you're proficient in dyeing and need a particular outcome. I recommend starting with smaller projects and then working up to larger ones.

You'll want a long-handled wooden or plastic spoon, or lengths of dowel rod, for stirring the dyebath and lifting your item out of it. Wooden laundry tongs are awesome if you can find them. Remember that the dye will stain this item just as it will stain what you are dyeing. That's why I recommend dowel rods; they are inexpensive, and you can use a different one for different colors.

Rubber gloves are also essential. Not only will the dye stain your skin, but some of the substances can be irritants. Care and prevention are always better than cure. Remember, too, that the dyes and fixatives will fix the colors to things like your clothing, the kitchen counter, the floor, the dog, and anything else with which they come into contact. Using a plastic bucket when transferring items from the dyebath will help to keep things clean.

You will want to get marked cups and spoons for measuring your ingredients. Again, keep them solely for dyeing. I use a four-cup glass jug, as it is resistant to the heat. Scales to weigh dyestuffs, particularly those that can weigh tiny amounts, may be useful, but are not necessary. When weighing materials, place them on parchment paper and then on the scale, to avoid cross-contamination.

Other items don't need to be so specific, but they are necessary: a bucket for collecting dyestuffs from the wild, a knife to cut them into smaller pieces, and perhaps even a mortar and pestle (glass or marble, not wood) to crush ingredients. Muslin, which can be obtained at any craft store, is also recommended for straining substances from the dyebath.

Last but by no means least, you're going to need something to dye! Pure organic cotton or pure new wool is ideal for a first project. Synthetic fibers don't absorb the dye as well as natural ones, and should be avoided. Silk and linen can be expensive, but are also appropriate.

The Fixatives

In dyeing, the fixatives are called mordants, and they are the ingredient that binds the color to the material being dyed. This is the first step in the natural dyeing process, and takes as much time as the coloring. The right fixative for your dye is essential. Skipping this process could mean that your dye does not adhere to your material. Using the wrong mordant could change the color of the finished item. These chemical fixatives can be obtained from the pharmacy. Most are some kind of salt; in fact, salt is sometimes used as a mordant.

Choose a fixative that will work in harmony to create the color you desire. Alum is a common mordant, especially when working with yellow, because it tends to give a golden hue to the item being dyed. Tannic acid darkens colors and turns yellows into browns. Iron works as a fixative, but it dulls the colors and is not very commonly used. Table salt that has not been iodized can be used, but alum is a better choice and is nearly as common. I recommend 3 ounces alum in 5 quarts water is a good fixative recipe for beginners.

Make the mordant bath away from any food items. Ensure that your pan is large enough for the mordant and the material you are dyeing. It must be evenly submerged and well-soaked. Materials that are not properly mordanted could result in the dye not adhering evenly. Dissolve your mordant thoroughly, and wet the material to be dyed in rainwater or distilled water before immersing it in the dyebath. Stirring the fixative bath could cause your material to felt or chafe. Turn it over once, about halfway through the process. This will take about 45 minutes for a lightly woven fabric or spun yarn, and up to 90 minutes for something that is tightly woven. Cool the material in the mordant bath, then rinse it several times in tepid water without wringing or squeezing. It's possible to go right on to the dyeing process, for your fabric will need to be moist when you immerse it in the dyebath, but you can dry your fabric and dye it another day.

The Dyeing Process

Many things will give color, but not fastness. There are two elements to consider: will this fade when washed (think denim) and will this fade in light (think awnings). This is why we mordant first—it helps the color stick to the fabric. People who are really into their dyes make color swatches, placing them in the sunlight or washing them, to see how well the colors perform prior to doing a lot of dyeing.

It's also good to remember that the pretty colors found in nature's landscapes are not necessarily the colors that are going to be produced when dyeing. Yellows and golds are the most dependable colors. The hues will vary with the mordant used. Pinks and blues do not hold their colors as well as yellow tones.

The best time to forage for your dyestuffs is in the morning, after the dew is off the plant but before the sun has had a chance to warm it. Dried flowers don't yield as good a color as fresh ones, but dried leaves are preferred over fresh ones. Roots need to be harvested before the frosts in autumn or before the heat in summer.

Dyestuffs can also be purchased, which is useful when you need a large quantity of something very lightweight, or when you want to use something not native to your geographical area. Choose the supplier wisely; a good supplier will be able to provide quality ingredients, and you will be able to get repeat results by using them.

Different recipes will require different amounts of dyestuffs—we'll look at individual ingredients shortly. In general, to make the dyebath, put the quantity of dyestuffs in the required amount of pure water (not tap), boil for 15–45 minutes depending on the depth of color desired, then strain them from the dyebath through the muslin. Discard the muslin and its ingredients. The remaining liquid is your vegetable dye. I've found that it's best to soak roots and bark before boiling them, overnight for smaller, more tender items and up to a couple days for tougher ones. I also boil them a bit longer than I do the leaves and flowers.

The basic dyeing method is the same for all recipes. Prepare your dyebath as just described, and once it is strained, add your pre-moistened material. Remember not to crowd the dyebath; the dye needs to be able to get to all parts of the material to absorb the color. Simmer for half the required amount of time, turn, and finish simmering. Remove the item from the dyebath using the wooden spoon or dowel rod, and let it slop into the plastic bucket to be transported to the sink. Rinse the item in warm water, and wash gently in a natural soap rather than detergent. Rinse until the water is clear, and then dry away from a direct heat or light source.

Easy Recipes

These recipes are made from common ingredients easily found. Once you have determined that you enjoy dyeing, you can obtain more specialized ingredients from dye suppliers. For now, these are the materials that can be found in most kitchens, gardens, or grocery stores.

Coffee is a great introduction to natural dyeing. Store used coffee grounds in an old plastic container until you've saved about 1 pound of them (I err on the heavy side, as used grounds are wet and weigh more than dry ones). This yields a creamy brown dye when used with an alum fixative. To make the dyebath, soak the leftover grounds overnight in about 5 quarts of water. Boil for half an hour, then strain through the muslin. Add additional water to return the quantity to 5 quarts. Simmer your pre-moistened material in the bath for at least an hour, then rinse as previously discussed.

The flower heads of the dandelion make a bright yellow dye when used with alum. It takes a while to collect the 2 pounds of dandelion heads needed, but the color is worth it. Cover the flower heads in water, and boil them for 15–20 minutes. Strain through the muslin, add more water to return the quantity to 5 quarts, and add your damp material. Simmer in the dyebath for 45–60 minutes, turning once halfway through. Cool, and then remove your item, rinsing and washing as previously instructed.

Onion skin was one of my first great successes. I had all the local grocers saving their onion skins for me; not the red or the white onion skins, but just the rust-colored ones. The result, with an alum mordant, was a very pleasing autumn orange, but it took patience to collect 1 pound of onion skins! Fewer skins will produce a golden yellow. I boiled the skins for half an hour to make the dye, and dyed the material just short of an hour.

Rhubarb was my other great success. Be very careful handling the rhubarb leaves, as they are toxic if ingested. They make a lovely mustard yellow when using alum as a fixative. Rhubarb leaves are big and heavy, so it doesn't take any time to gather the 2 pounds needed. Cut them into smaller pieces before putting them into the dyebath. Boil for 45 minutes and don't be alarmed when they boil down to a sludge; this is normal—it just takes longer to strain. Dye the material for 45 minutes, and allow it to cool completely before rinsing and washing.

Tea can also be used. Save old tea leaves or tea bags until you have approximately 1 pound of them. Boil them for 30 minutes, strain, and simmer your material for about an hour. Again, cool your item completely before rinsing and washing.

Blackberries also make a good dye. Pick them when ripe and juicy. You'll want 1 pound of blackberries per gallon of dye, plus whatever you eat while you are picking them. Unlike some dyestuffs, blackberries can be used frozen without affecting the color. They produce a blue-gray color when used with alum as a fixative. Boil the fruit for 15 minutes, then strain through the muslin. Simmer your material for an hour, and allow it to cool completely before rinsing and washing.

Elderberries can be used the same way as blackberries. They yield a lovely pale-purple dye. Add a cup of vinegar to produce a more mauve shade of purple.

Blue dyes are the hardest to obtain, and I've purposely not discussed them here because they require a special process, one where the material is not exposed to oxygen until after it comes out of the dyebath. It's a fiddly process, and one in which I am not proficient. Likewise, to get a true green, yellow-dyed material has to be over-dyed with the blue indigo process.

These recipes will allow you to get started and make some wonderful experiments. I find that natural dyes do not have the harsh vibration that chemical dyes seem to have. I greatly appreciate the organic process of collecting the plants and turning them into a thing of joy into which I can wrap myself. There's an energy there, a connection, that is just not found in synthetic dyes and fabrics—one that I think you will find very rewarding when you enter the world of dyeing for yourself.

Herb History, Myth, and Lore

Does Your Green Grass Ever Feel Blue?

☙ by JD Hortwort ❧

At the head of a walking trail that encircles my home, I stop to admire one of the many beech trees on the property. Beech trees seem to me to have more character than any of the other, stately trees on the property. Their smooth gray bark is more inviting to the touch.

On this day, I'm temporarily distracted from my planned walk and head, instead, over to the edge of the yard. From this vantage point, I can see through the woods down to the lower loop of the trail. I reach out to brace myself against yet another beech as I gaze through the forest to the wetland beyond the trail.

The tree bark seems to tingle. For no reason, I lean closer and hug the trunk. The tree's outer skin feels cool and somehow reassuring against my cheek, the trunk, like one large muscle. Somehow happy, I push away and go back to the trailhead.

Just for the fun of it, I go to the first beech I see there and give it a hug. This one isn't as inviting, although I can't see any difference between the two mighty specimens. And, like a child in a kindergarten play yard, I wonder, why did the first beech like me and not the second?

Silly question, says the scientist. When people ask this sort of thing about any nonhuman thing, science tells us, they are anthropomorphizing the nonhuman thing—attributing human emotions and motives to something that clearly isn't human. We do it to everything from our cars to our stuffed animals.

People have emotions because people have brains. People can gather data, evaluate that data, and then react to it. No other nonhuman entity can do so, we are told.

That's what science says. The average person on the street is likely to be more generous with the gift of feeling. Most would say their pets can become depressed when left alone, that they grieve the passing of a loved one or become happy at the return of a human companion. But even these people might be reluctant to say their philodendron is moody because it was moved to a less desirable part of the living room or despondent because its favorite Tchaikovsky concerto was replaced by the latest Nicki Minaj track.

Do plants feel? Or perhaps we should ask, are they aware? Does the right music fill them with hope and aspiration? Do they tremble at the approach of the gardener with a hedge clipper?

We know our ancestors believed plants had living spirits. Sometimes those spirits were relatives; other times, the spirit was that of a once living person who had either been punished or honored by the gods. That belief fell from favor with the approach of the Age of Science. René Descartes said, "I think, therefore I am." Early scientists couldn't find a brain inside any plant they dissected and so felt safe in saying that plants have no brain, they cannot think, and therefore they cannot be aware of their existence.

That's not to say some nineteenth-century scientists didn't try to find a rationale for the thinking, self-aware plant.

Gustav Theodor Fechner, a German psychologist and father of experimental psychology, believed in panpsychism. He developed his theories between 1860 and the time of his death in 1887. Everything has some degree of mental awareness and spirit, he said, even rocks and plants.

Charles Darwin believed in at least a limited sort of plant awareness. After studying plants, he published a book in 1880 titled *The Power of Movement in Plants*. Plants were at least as aware as bacteria, he argued, saying: "It is hardly an exaggeration to say that the tip of the radical (root) thus endowed […] acts like the brain of one of the lower animals; the brain being situated within the anterior end of the body, receiving impressions from the sense-organs, and directing the several movements."

Indian scientist Sir Jagadish Chandra Bose did extensive experiments with plants. His work is often cited by modern-day believers when they postulate about the ability of plants to respond to music. Bose also believed plants could experience fear and joy.

Then there was Clive Backster, author of the 1960s classic *The Secret Life of Plants*. Backster, a layman, not a scientist, hooked lie-detector electrodes to plants to record their responses to perceived threats. He would have a person attack one plant with a lighter while another plant sat unharmed nearby. Then he would test for a reaction from the surviving plant later when the attacker reentered the room. Backster claimed to have recorded sharp spikes on the lie detector attached to the plant during the encounter, which he interpreted as the plant's fear of impending doom.

Unfortunately for supporters of the idea of plant sentience, Fechner's theory of panpsychism was seen as some of his less grounded work. Darwin's plant theory was dismissed. Bose's work was largely forgotten, and Backster was roundly criticized for not having proper scientific controls for his work.

The whole of idea of any flora registering the slightest quiver of emotion was relegated to the silly rants of New Agers and tree-hugging hippies.

Then the twenty-first century arrived. Suddenly, serious researchers were picking up on the idea that something beyond automated reactions was happening in the plant kingdom. What's more, they were and are performing the kind of "scientifically valid" research that, while many scientists still disagree with it, simply can't be dismissed with a huff and a wave of the hand.

Daniel Chamovitz, director of the Manna Center for Plant Biosciences at Tel Aviv University, has written a book titled *What a Plant Knows.* Plants experience life, he maintains. They learn, they remember (at least to a degree comparable to lower mammal life forms), and they smell—not just florally but each other.

Plants, Chamovitz says, aren't just inanimate objects. Their very evolutionary development—the fact that they are rooted to one place—has helped them develop what he described in one interview as "very sensual lives." About the only thing they can't do is hear, he says. What good would a sense of hearing do them? It's not like they can run away from the grazing cow or run after the gardener with the bag of plant food.

Scientists from the Department of Plant Physiology in Giessen and the Department of Structural Biology in Marburg, in Germany, have blurred the lines of distinction between humans and plants a bit further with a new understanding of how "phytochromes" work. A phytochrome molecule gets to the heart of what we think makes a plant, well, a plant. Reacting to light, it seems to trigger germination, growth, and flowering—making it a virtual light switch. The structure of this molecule is similar, researchers say, to that of structures in two enzymes in bacteria and humans that are responsible for signaling behavior.

Professor Stefano Mancuso goes to the next level with his studies of plant intelligence at the International Laboratory of Plant Neurobiology (LINV) near Florence, Italy. Not a few of his colleagues wince at the term "plant neurobiology." Mancuso and his associates believe plants "talk" to one another about food sources and predators, among other important topics for survival. He is even revisiting the impact of music on plants—not that he thinks plants can hear. But he does believe they can sense and react to vibrations in an intelligent manner.

Anthony Trewavas, a British biologist, defines intelligence as "an aspect of adaptive behavior that provides a capacity for problem solving." And, he says, plants have it. Plants actively search out food and water sources in an intelligent manner, he says. Plus, using what he calls "phenotypic plasticity," plants adapt to and anticipate upcoming conditions in their surroundings, not in a haphazard manner, but in a calculated way to ensure they live to grow another day.

To be clear, none of these researchers argue for evidence of feelings in plants. Chamovitz specifically argues that feelings, in a human sense, aren't necessary for plants to qualify as intelligent, aware, sentient entities.

And still.

I walk around my landscape, making plans for the next Saturday workday. I stop to consider a large skip laurel and instinctively reach out to stroke the leaves.

"I need to cut you back, baby," I explain. "You're getting a little too far out into the walkway."

When it comes time to cut out the mulberry tree that has volunteered in a nearby flower bed, I will apologize and probably feel a little guilty. I can't help myself. I've always talked to plants. I don't think I've ever expected that they can "hear" me in a traditional sense. But I like to think they understand the sentiment and appreciate the fair warning.

I don't think plants feel. I hope they don't. What a terrible world that would be! Imagine the horror of being tied to one spot and experiencing the menacing blade of a lawn mower week after week as it cruelly slices away one-third of your existence with every whirl of the blade. Imagine the sorrow of knowing that thousands and thousands of your offspring will fall to your roots, never reaching their full potential. Or the ravages of bugs and squirrels and fungi that relentlessly gnaw at your body.

Someone asked once if I thought plants had an opinion about the human beings who swarm around them, plucking leaves and flowers. Do you think they resent it? he asked. No, I replied, I think this is their existence and they just accept it.

Plants simply are. In their own unique way, they exist. Their existence is not a human existence. We should respect them for that.

Avocado Appreciation 101

☙ by Susan Pesznecker ❧

The avocado *(Persea americana)* is a member of the laurel (Lauraceae) family, the same plant family that gives us bay leaves and cinnamon. Also known as the avocado pear or the alligator pear, avocados grow on a large evergreen tree that may reach seventy feet in height. Considered a tropical plant, the trees thrive in tropical or subtropical climates.

The plant has been around for a long time—the oldest known avocado evidence was found in Mexico and dates back some ten thousand years. Paul C. Barry records the finding of an avocado-shaped ceramic jar, dated to 900 C.E., in the remote pre-Incan city of Chan Chan. In a more modern expression, the avocado first appeared in the English language in 1696, listed in an indexing of Jamaican plants.

The avocado is a plain-appearing ovoid or pear-shaped fruit weighing several ounces and covered by a pebbly black or dark green skin. Its name comes from a Spanish word (from Nahuatl, an Aztec dialect) meaning "testicle," no doubt reflecting the heavy, ovoid shape of the fruit. This name origin may also account for traditional associations of the avocado with love, lust, and sensuality.

The avocado's flesh is pale green under the skin, lightening to a yellowish or greenish-yellow interior that surrounds a large central pit—the avocado's seed. The soft, ripe flesh is eaten; the peel and seed are not. All parts of the avocado can be used medicinally.

Avocado's Chemical Constituents

Avocado's leaves and bark contain flavonoids; rich in antioxidant chemicals, these help repair cell damage and slow the effects of aging. They also contain tannins, harsh astringents that tend to tighten and contract tissues, stop bleeding, and dry up excessive watery secretions. The leaves and bark also contain volatile oils; also called essential oils, these have a deep scent and diffuse and evaporate quickly.

The flesh (fruit pulp) of avocado contains protein, which is essential for building healthy bones and tissues, as well as sesquiterpenes, which are important biological building blocks. The flesh also contains vitamins and minerals, which are important for tissue growth and repair and cellular actions, and unsaturated fatty acids, mostly monounsaturated—the so-called good fats that promote health and may help prevent cardiovascular disease.

Avocados are rich in riboflavin (vitamin B2), which is important for cell growth, cellular metabolism and energy function, and healthy skin and mucous membranes. Avocados also contain thiamine (vitamin B1) and niacin (aka nicotinic acid or vitamin B3), which are well-known for their effects on neurotransmitter synthesis and energy maintenance, respectively. The avocado also contains vitamin K, which is important for blood clotting.

Avocado is probably best known as a source of natural, healthful fats and oils—primarily plant-based oils, which are a key energy source and aid in the absorption of fat-soluble vitamins. These oils also help maintain the softness and vitality of our skin, hair, and nails. The avocado contains more available plant protein (up to 25 percent of the flesh is protein) than any other fruit. Avocado oil—which is pressed from the pulp rather than the seed—is high in vitamin E (tocopherol), an important antioxidant.

The avocado is a good source of a number of trace minerals, including magnesium (a critical element in protein metabolism), phosphorus (essential in brain, nerve, and muscle function), and sulfur (supports bone growth, blood clotting, and muscle strength). Further, the flesh is rich in fiber, which is known for its health benefits.

Avocado as a Healer

Although avocado leaves are not used as a food source, a leaf infusion (dried leaves) or decoction (fresh leaves) may be useful for diuresis (i.e., stimulating the release of retained fluid through the urine), liver cleansing, and moderation of high blood pressure. A decoction of bark and leaves has been used to treat stomach problems, dysmenorrhea, and cough. Avocado remains, today, a traditional folk remedy in Guatemala, where all parts of the avocado are widely used in various types of health and healing practices. For example, Guatemalans use the flesh to stimulate hair growth and the skin as a vermifuge (for expulsion of worms and other parasites). A decoction made from the seed is widely used throughout Central and South America for treating bowel problems, diarrhea, and dysentery. The seed has also been ground and used as a female contraceptive by some Amazonian tribes.

The avocado's flesh provides a moisturizing effect when applied to the skin, and may be used as a poultice to "draw" a wound. The fruit may have general health benefits as well; at least one study showed a reduction in serum cholesterol levels in association with an avocado-rich diet (Lopez, et al.), and avocados are routinely prescribed as part of a healthful diet because of their plant proteins and monounsaturated fats.

Avocado as a Beauty Boost

The avocado's rich, creamy texture has long linked it to cosmetic use, with avocado pulp and oil frequently used in commercial skin creams, lotions, and conditioners. You can add avocado to your personal beauty regimen with spectacular results.

- Mash fresh avocado with coarse sea salt for a moisturizing scrub. Massage it into your skin, remove the excess with a paper towel (don't let it go down the bathroom drain!), then rinse with cool water.

- Combine mashed avocado and warm olive oil for a cleansing and moisturizing face mask; apply liberally and allow to sit for 30 minutes before removing. It will moisten and nourish your skin and provide a topical dose of vitamin A as well.

- Add a few drops of avocado oil to your post-shampoo conditioner.

Avocado in Your Kitchen

Avocados are harvested and transported while still unripe and continue to ripen after they're picked. This is fortunate, as ripe avocados are very fragile and would be hard to transport without being crushed. Allow unripe fruit to sit on the kitchen counter until it ripens and softens. For faster results, place the avocados in a small, closed paper bag with a ripe apple; the apple emits ethylene gas, which encourages the avocados to ripen more quickly. Once ripe, store them in the refrigerator for up to a week or two. Handle the ripe fruit gently, as it bruises if bumped.

Ripe avocados may be sliced or chunked, mashed, puréed, or even spread like butter. In fact, in India, the avocado is often called "butter fruit." Up to 75 percent of avocado's calories come from monounsaturated fats; although calorie-dense (the typical avocado has around 225–250 calories), monounsaturated fats have a number of health benefits and are well worth adding to one's diet.

Avocados may be added to salads or eaten as a side dish. A well-known and much-loved preparation is guacamole, a dish combining mashed avocado, chopped tomatoes, onions, hot peppers, and cilantro. Avocados are also often added to sandwiches, where their richness and moisture replace mayonnaise, butter, and other spreads. The pulp may even be mashed and used as a simple baby food.

A favorite recipe in some Asian countries is the avocado smoothie—a mixture of ripe avocado, sweetened condensed milk, and spices, whirled into a velvety smoothie that is creamy, lightly sweet, and gorgeously pale green.

When an avocado is cut in half and the seed removed, each half becomes a "boat" to be filled with all sorts of goodies and eaten either raw or baked. An egg baked in an avocado boat is a tasty breakfast treat, especially if sautéed chopped mushroom and a little cheese are sprinkled atop just before the egg finishes cooking. Use the Haas cultivar for cooking—some of the others may be bitter when heated.

Avocado oil can be used for cooking, as its smoking point is very high. It's also lovely as an ingredient in salad dressing or mayonnaise.

Grow an Avocado Tree

Each avocado tree grows from one of the large seeds inside a fruit, and it's easy to grow an avocado tree at home.

Begin by saving the intact pit from a ripe avocado. Rinse clean under cool running water and blot dry with a paper towel.

Carefully push three toothpicks about ½ inch into the thickest width of the pit (imagine this as the pit's "equator"). Angle the toothpicks up slightly; they will suspend the pit across the mouth of a drinking glass or small jar, with the slender top part of the pit in fresh air and the fat base of the pit in the water.

Adjust the water level in the glass to ensure water covers the base of the pit.

Place the glass in a bright windowsill. In 3–6 weeks, the top of the avocado pit will begin to split, a sprout will emerge from the top, and roots will begin to grow at the base. (If nothing has happened in 6–7 weeks, throw it out and try again.)

When the stem grows to about 5–6 inches, pinch out the top set of leaves. In another 2–3 weeks, new leaves will sprout.

When the new leaves show, it's time to pot the young avocado tree. Fill a large flowerpot with enriched potting soil to about an inch from the top. Make a hole in the center of the soil and place the pit, root-side down, into the depression so that the upper half of the pit is above the soil line. Use care so as not to injure the roots. Add some more soil around the pit to fill in any air holes by the roots and then firm it into the soil by gently pushing the soil around the base of the pit.

Water generously to moisten the soil. Keep your young tree in a warm, sunny room and keep the soil surface slightly moist. If you live in a temperate location, you may move the plant outdoors. Otherwise, you're now the proud owner of a lovely avocado tree houseplant.

Sources Consulted

Barry, Paul C. "Avocado: The Early Roots of Avocado History." *Canku Ota*. April 7, 2001: Issue 33. http://www .turtletrack.org/Issues01/Co04072001/CO_04072001 _Recipes.htm.

Bremness, Lesley. *Herbs: The Visual Guide to More Than 700 Herb Species from Around the World.* London: Dorling Kindersley, 1994.

Chevallier, Andrew. *Encyclopedia of Herbal Medicine: The Definitive Home Reference Guide to 550 Key Herbs with all Their Uses as Remedies for Common Ailments.* London: Dorling Kindersley, 2000.

Lopez Ledesma, R., A. C. Frati Munari, B. C. Hernandez Dominguez, S. Cervantes Montalvo, M. H. Hernandez Luna, C. Juarez, and S. Moran Lira. "Monounsaturated Fatty Acid (Avocado) Rich Diet for Mild Hypercholesterolemia." *Arch-Med-Res.* 996 Winter; 27 (4): 519–23. http://www.ncbi.nlm.nih.gov/pubmed/8987188.

Lust, Dr. John. *The Herb Book: The Complete and Authoritative Guide to More Than 500 Herbs.* New York: Beneficial Books, 2005.

Oxford English Dictionary. London: Oxford University Press, 2009.

All About Mullein

⤳ by Calantirniel ⤲

Great mullein *(Verbascum thap-sus)* and other species like black mullein *(V. negra)* are extremely plentiful, yellow-flowered "weeds" that taste very mild and have a long history of safe medicinal use. All are biennial and in the Scrophulariaceae (figwort) family. Common names include beard plant, mullein rod, and Indian tobacco.

If you type *Verbascum* in Google's image-search function, you will find hundreds of photo examples, making it much easier to identify the species in your area. Please make sure you use plants that are far enough from the roads and free of herbicides, pesticides, and other toxins.

Native to Europe, mullein is easily identified by its foot-long, broad

yet lanceolate leaves that are very thick, hairy, and velvety, creating in its first year a rosette. By the second year, a rather stout, sturdy, and fuzzy stalk rich with resin shoots easily to six to eight feet tall. The top of this stalk features clusters of small five-petaled yellow flowers very close to its stalk that bloom by mid- to late summer. Sometimes this strong stalk will splinter, having more than one offshoot for these clusters. Other species may have variations. For instance, moth mullein *(Verbascum blattaria)* has pointed and jagged-edged leaves without fuzz, and larger flowers, sometimes white with purple centers.

Mullein is very accessible and can be found all over Europe, Asia, North Africa, and nearly all of North America, as well as Australia and New Zealand, it does best in temperate climates. Whether found in the wild or along roadsides and other disturbed areas, it is a known soil regenerator. In some areas, it is regarded as a noxious weed—making it quite sustainable for medicinal use.

History and Lore

The name mullein is derived from a Latin word *mollis*, meaning "soft." It is also said to have come from a Celtic-originated French word, *moleine*, that means "yellow." The resinous staffs when dead lit a sustaining fire easily, so were dipped in tallow and used as torches, particularly for funerals or other ceremonial use. They were also once used as candlewicks. Once brought to the New World, the Native Americans heartily embraced this amazing plant, easily integrating it into their herbal medicinal knowledge, and administering it often for its amazingly wide range of healing qualities.

Herbal Qualities and Medicinal Use

Mullein is described as a tonic nervine that is analgesic, antispasmodic, demulcent, emollient, expectorant, vulnerary, pectoral, cough-suppressant, diuretic, and somewhat diaphoretic. As an anodyne, it is also slightly sedative and narcotic.

Mullein is one of the most versatile medicinal herbs you can implement in your herbal arsenal. The best-known use is to infuse the flowers in oil to remedy ear infections.

For the respiratory system, mullein helps clear mucous, soothes sore throats, and reaches deep where many herbs cannot. It softens areas that have hardened due to dryness, and tends to have an upward motion (resonant of the plant shooting up a tall stalk in its second year). At times, cough can worsen, but in these instances the cough becomes more productive to rid toxins that were not releasing before, and then subsides when toxins are released. Mullein is one of the best herbal treatments for asthma and bronchitis and in the past was even implemented for relieving tuberculosis. For those who make smoking mixtures (or even loose incense), mullein is an excellent base herb.

For the kidney and urinary tract, mullein helps generally balance, soothe, and heal these areas. For the nervous system, it has excellent pain-relieving and antispasmodic properties. The resin in the stem has the best healing properties for this use. If the pain relates to back or neck alignment or injury, mullein is an excellent herb not just for pain but also for helping the body to regain proper structure, and is a great herb for muscular-skeletal uses, including a softening of creaky joints. Internal and external applications are both used; consider implementing the root or the first-year basal leaves.

The best use of mullein is for anything (and I mean anything!) glandular or lymphatic. If lymph nodes feel like hard knots or are not working properly, creating systemic sluggishness, mullein is great at softening these up to move energy, healing these conditions. It works very well for sore or lumpy breasts, swollen thyroid, stunted pituitary, and painful/cysted ovaries/testicles; any gland that is overactive or underactive for any reason, acute or chronic, is helped greatly with mullein. Because of mullein's herbal actions, many systemic skin conditions are greatly improved by applying a poultice or fomentation, particularly if the skin condition is linked to the lymphatic system (i.e., scrofula, an external form of tuberculosis that was more common in the past, is rooted in the neck's lymph nodes). Herbalist Michael Moore has successfully used mullein with herpes simplex.

Contra-indications: According to the *Physician's Desk Reference (PDR) for Herbal Medicines*, while mullein is quite mild and generally safe, it could cause issues if absolutely copious and rather improbable amounts are administered. Two particular chemical constituents, coumarin and rotenone, would be reasons to ensure that only moderate amounts are consumed. *Do not consume the seeds for medicine*, since they are very high in rotenone—in fact, the seeds were historically used by a few Native American tribes to paralyze fish for easier fishing!

Harvesting to Create Herbal Medicine

Though you can harvest mullein before it blooms, it is most common to harvest when the blooming season occurs, which is usually later in the summer. The parts used for creating medicine are the leaves, flowers, root, and even the resin in the stalks. The root is only good medicine when the first-year plant is harvested in the autumn; after dieback or basal leaf harvest is fine.

If there is an immediate need and the plant is available and in season, use the fresh uppers, any part, to make tea. A good rule is to use lower plant parts for lower body issues, and higher plant parts for higher body issues. Just fill the teacup with plant material and pour boiling water over, then cover and steep for 15 minutes. Make sure to strain out fibers by pouring through a good filter, because the hairs from the plant that fall loose can really irritate the throat. The taste is rather bland and, if some of the plant resin is present, can be a bit salty or vanilla-ish. If needed, sweeten with raw honey, agave juice, or stevia, or flavor with tamari sauce or liquid amino acids if you prefer a salty taste.

For making tea or infusions later on, you can dry flowers by gently removing from the stalks for drying in a paper-lined wicker basket, or by gathering the stalks and placing them upside-down loosely inside a paper bag in a dry place away from the sun. You can also harvest and dry the leaves from the plant (first or second year) and lay flat and non-overlapped in the paper-lined wicker basket. The tiny insects will leave the dried herbs, falling to the bottom. Drying can take a week or so in dry areas to about two weeks in more humid areas. I recommend keeping a heater nearby (not too close) to dry the air and avoid mold and mildew issues. Keep in an airtight container (I like glass jars) away from light, and it should have a shelf life of 2–4 years.

To create a vinegar tincture, place as much of the fresh plant material (leaves or flowers are probably best here) as possible in a glass jar, fill to the top with Bragg or Spectrum raw apple cider vinegar, seal, and allow to sit (even in the fridge) for 6–8 weeks, shaking the jar periodically. Filter (I use an unbleached coffee filter or untreated fabric with a screen colander) into a glass bottle, label (along with date made), and keep the vinegar in the fridge for medicinal use. This method is good for those who wish to avoid alcohol, and it should last a few years.

If I must tincture, I prefer an alcohol-based tincture, as it will pull more resin, is stronger medicinally, and doesn't need refrigeration. It will also last nearly indefinitely. Again, place as much of the harvested plant material (root and stalk along with leaves and flowers) as possible into a glass jar, and fill to the top with vodka or brandy (50 percent alcohol or higher, if possible), seal, and let sit on the kitchen counter for 6–8 weeks, shaking occasionally. Filter as for vinegar tincture, label (along with date made), and keep in an herbal tincture-type dark bottle with a glass dropper. Any extra can be placed in a small jar in a dark place.

Either tincturing method can be enhanced by adding more fresh plant material after the filtering process, which creates the same healing power in smaller doses.

You can cover fresh plant material with local raw honey, if available (perhaps with a splash or more of vodka, brandy, or vinegar as well to help liquefy and later facilitate filtering). This can be an easy way to store medicinal herbs as well as a great way to administer herbs (especially to kids!). For dosing, use proportions similar to herbal vinegar.

For those interested in making mullein flower oil for ear infections (or for making salve for external use), you can place fresh flowers into some olive oil by gently separating them from their stalk. Apply gentle heat to allow the flowers to permeate the oil, and filter. The oil will keep for about a year.

Many herbalists prefer to tincture the flowers in alcohol (which stores for many years), and to use 2–3 drops each of the tincture mixed with olive oil at the time of use (treating both ears is ideal—drain onto cotton ball or washcloth). This method is also easier, and there is less chance of spoilage.

Medicinal Dosages

Fresh plant directions were just described. To use dried plant matter to make an infusion (tea), use 1 heaping teaspoon of herbs per 8 ounces of near-boiling water, pour over and steep for 15 minutes (if root or stalk, make a decoction—keep on low heat for 30–60 minutes), strain, and drink. The tea is rather bland, even flavorless; nonetheless, this ought to help make it easy to consume. This is also likely the best way if administering to an infant or child. If the mother is nursing, she can drink the tea and pass the medicinal properties to the child through her milk.

To use the vinegar tincture, use 1–2 tablespoons and ingest straight, or in water. To use the vodka tincture, use 10–30 drops in some hot water to boil off some of the alcohol, and add some cooler water to help you swallow.

For acute conditions that are likely painful, 1–2 doses may be enough; make sure to wait an hour or two between doses. For more chronic issues, use 2–4 times per day, 6 days per week, as long as needed for improvement or elimination of conditions.

For external applications, use a strong infusion or hot water with tincture, and when cool enough, moisten a cloth with the mixture (called a fomentation) and apply to areas where glandular or lymphatic tissue is blocked, especially if these areas feel hard when touched. If you have access to fresh mullein leaves, you can create a poultice by scalding the leaves in water and applying when slightly cooled to these areas.

If you are more advanced, you can also create a salve by skillfully mixing mullein-infused olive oil with melted beeswax in proportion with the weather (more beeswax if weather is warmer), and when cool, apply salve. Ear infection use was noted earlier.

I hope you find mullein to be a cornerstone of your herbal medicine cabinet, particularly if you are a beginner. This is a wonderful, versatile herb to first study and use!

Resources

Harvey, Clare G. *The Encyclopedia of Flower Remedies*. London: Watkins Publishing, 2007.

McIntyre, Anne. *Flower Power*. New York: Henry Holt and Co., 1996.

Physicians Desk Reference for Herbal Medicines. 3d ed. Montvale, NJ: Thompson PDR, 2004.

Wood, Matthew. *The Earthwise Herbal: A Complete Guide to Old World Medicinal Plants*. Berkeley, CA: North Atlantic Books, 2008.

Internet Resources

DeVries, Lynn. *Medicinal Herb Info*. http://medicinalherb info.org/herbs/Mullein.html.

Rose, Kiva. "A Golden Torch: Mullein's Healing Light." *Bear Medicine Herbals*. http://bearmedicineherbals .com/a-golden-torch-mullein's-healing-light.html.

History and Folklore of the Rose

≈ by Ellen Dugan ≈

All the lovely and beautiful times we had,
All the garlands of violets and roses...
—Sappho

Roses have an extensive and enchanting history. The origin of the rose is
ancient beyond recorded history, as
the first known roses to science are,
in fact, fossils. According to fossil
evidence, the species of the rose is 35
million years old. The first known
rose fossil was found in Austria in
1848. Other rose fossils came from
China, Japan, France, Germany, and
the Czech Republic. There were
also rose fossils found in the western
United Sates, specifically in Alaska,
California, Colorado, and Oregon.

All of the roses from all over the
world in their many fabulous varieties

descend from wild roses. The genus *Rosa* has over 150 species throughout the Northern Hemisphere, from Alaska to Mexico, and in northern Africa. In truth, garden cultivation of roses probably began in China some five thousand years ago.

Roses in Mythology and Legend

Roses have been immortalized in literature and folklore for centuries. They are emblems of love, beauty, war, and politics. This flower has played an important role in art, religion, and commerce for thousands of years.

The ancient Greeks and Romans linked the rose to love, beauty, and passion. There were large public rose gardens in ancient Rome. The rose was used medicinally and for perfumes, of course, and the rose petals were used as confetti for celebrations.

According to Greek mythology, all roses were white in the beginning. The flower was born when the goddess Aphrodite rose from the ocean and the sea foam that dropped from her body fell upon the earth and became the first white rose. Interestingly, it was later when Aphrodite tried to help her wounded lover, Adonis, that she scratched herself on the thorns of a rose. As her blood splattered on the flower petals, the rose was so ashamed at having wounding the goddess that it turned its petals to red as an apology. So touched was Aphrodite by this gesture that she adopted the rose as her own flower, and it became known henceforth as the flower of love.

To the Romans, the rose was the emblem of the goddess of flowers, Flora. In Flora's tale, the rose was created when one of Flora's favorite friends died. Her friend was a nymph, and Flora asked the other gods to change her fallen friend into a beautiful flower. The story goes that Apollo, the god of light, gave the flower the breath of life. The god of the vine, Bacchus, gifted it with nectar. The god of gardens and gardening, Vertumnus, gifted the flower with a beautiful perfume. The apple goddess Pomona granted the new plant fruit (the rose hips), and finally Flora gave the flower a crown of petals.

As to the thorns on the rose plant, they have a legend as well. The thorns are rumored to have come from the son of Aphrodite when he was a child. The young god Eros, or Cupid, as he was known to the Romans, apparently was shooting arrows at the bees, hovering around the rose, that had stung him. The thorns grew from the rose stems where his arrows missed the bees and instead hit the flowers.

In another, darker tale, Apollo, the god of the sun, turned an upstart wanna-be deity named Rhodanthe into a rose—and her attendants into thorns, for daring to try to usurp his sister Diana as the goddess of the hunt and a protector of women.

To the Egyptians, the rose was sacred to the goddess Isis, the supreme goddess of magick and marriage. According to legend, Cleopatra, who was a priestess of Isis, was said to have had a field day with roses when she set out to seduce Marc Antony. When she set out to meet him, she wreathed herself in roses, had barges decorated with them, and had fragrant roses strewn about the palace, floating on lakes and fountains. It's a pretty safe bet that roses were in her boudoir as well.

As history marched on, sadly, there were many rose varieties that were lost in the period of time between the fall of the Roman Empire and the Muslim invasion of Europe. For a while, the cultivation of roses waned as civilization changed.

After the conquest of Persia in the seventh century, a fondness for the rose was reborn. The Muslim empire ranged from India to Spain then, and many varieties of roses were reintroduced to Europe at that time. The ancestor of most European roses—and one that would have been familiar to gardeners in the ancient world—is *R. Gallica.*

The cultivation and use of roses was closely associated with old Pagan Rome and thus was frowned upon by the Church during the Dark Ages, as they considered the rose to be a symbol of secrecy, magic, and trickery. Eventually the Church adopted the rose as a symbol for Mary, and she became called the "Mystical Rose." During the Dark Ages, roses found refuge in monasteries. It was a rule that at least one monk per monastery should be well-versed in botany and familiar with the medicinal and healing virtues of plants.

During the Dark Ages, the tales of the rose and its power became darker. The rose was classically used to ward off the evil eye. Worn as a chaplet (wreath of flowers around the head) or pinned onto clothing, it was a protective charm against evil. The rose and its thorns became wrapped up in the legend of Arthur and Merlin as well.

Viviane, the Lady of the Lake, who some say was a faery and others say was a priestess of the Old Ways, trapped Merlin in a tower of white roses. The story goes that as Merlin grew old, he let slip some of his magic secrets to Viviane. While he was enamored of her, she, on the other hand, wanted to keep Merlin's magic safe from the church and the wizard all to herself. So she cast a spell and created a tower of white roses, thorns, and other flowers to keep Merlin safe and all to herself. There Merlin remains under Viviane's spell.

The Rose: Symbol of Passion and Politics

The rose eventually became an important heraldic symbol. During the fifteenth century, the rose was used as a symbol for the feuding houses of Plantagenet for the control of England. This was known as the "War of the Roses." The House of York was symbolized by a white rose, and the House of Lancaster by a red rose. The final victory went to Henry Tudor, who defeated the last Yorkist king and then married Elizabeth of York to unite the two houses. He also united their symbols with a new rose motif: the "Tudor Rose," a large five-petaled red rose with a smaller white five-petaled rose in the center. The House of Tudor then went on to rule England for over a hundred years.

According to history, the rose was in such demand that during the seventeenth century royalty considered roses and in some cases rose water as legal tender. The Empress Josephine of France, the first wife of Napoleon, started her rose collection at Chateau de Malmaison in Paris in the 1800s. Within a decade, by 1814, her garden contained every species of rose known at the time. By 1829 her rose garden contained 2,562 different roses. This garden became the setting for Pierre-Joseph Redouté, a botanical illustrator. In 1824 he finished his watercolor collection entitled *Les Roses*. This is still considered one of the finest records of botanical illustration.

It is believed that modern hybridization of roses also began with Josephine's horticulturalist André Dupont. This would have been accomplished through both artificial and controlled pollination. Before this, most new rose cultivars were "spontaneous mutations," or accidental bee-induced hybrids, so they occurred rarely.

In the late eighteenth century, cultivated repeat-bloomer roses were introduced into Europe from China. They were different from the once-a-season blooming roses, and hybridizers were fascinated and set out to breed these new roses with the native varieties. They worked to make the plants winter-hardy, with a long bloom season. These hybridized roses became the parents of the roses we enjoy today.

Roses for Everyone

A rose for every home, a bush in every garden.
—Motto of the American Rose Society

Today there is a variety of rose for just about everyone. Try a polyantha rose named "The Fairy" and treat yourself to miniature clusters of blossoms, in a low-maintenance rose bush that sprawls six feet wide and three feet tall.

Roses can be used for hedging or as a specimen plant. Climbers and ramblers scramble over fences, trellises, and arbors, and ground-cover roses creep along the ground. Old-fashioned roses are grown for their fruits and heady perfume. Stately hybrid teas produce their beauties on single long stems, and floribundas, with their clusters of roses, grow side by side in gardens ranging from the cultured botanical garden to the carefree cottage-style gardens at home. Patio and miniature roses are perfect for pots and containers, and there are multitudes of colors, scents, and blossom shapes for everyone to enjoy.

Enjoy them all, their history, tales, and legends, for roses do bring their own magic into the garden in many fragrant and colorful ways.

The Hollyhock: Startling the Gods

❧ by Linda Raedisch ❧

When it comes to getting noticed, the hollyhock is right up there with the giant sunflower and the dinner plate dahlia. At thirteen feet, some of the oldest varieties might even stop traffic. Our forebears made cough syrup from the milky stems, and in Japan the mucilage is used in the traditional papermaking process. Early American settlers made a blue dye from the petals—another excuse, if you needed one, for keeping these extravagantly pretty flowers in an otherwise serious kitchen or medicinal garden.

At their most practical, hollyhocks serve as the garden's wallpaper. Traditionally, they were the boldly patterned drapes that screened the

smokehouse, outhouse, or broken stone wall. To my knowledge, no one has ever tried to breed a more mucilaginous hollyhock, but seed sellers have played with the height, the number of petals, and the colors, engineering a wide range of varieties, from white to yellow to the midnight burgundy that is the black hollyhock.

Older books give the hollyhock's Latin name as *Althaea rosea*, while more recent publications call it *Alcea rosea*. (I will refer to it simply as *A. rosea*, leaving it to the reader to lisp or not to lisp.) Those older books will also tell you that the *halig hoc*, or "holy mallow," was brought to England by returning Crusaders. Later writers like to stress that hollyhocks originated in China and did not appear in England until 1548. When it did arrive, it joined its less showy cousin, the native mallow *(A. officinalis)*, which had long grown in the northern salt marshes and whose even milkier roots were the source of the first "marsh mallows." By 1543, England was already lapsing into Modern English and had left the mallow's ancient name of *hoc* far behind. Had *A. rosea* still been a novelty at that time, surely they would have dubbed it "Chinese mallow" instead of reverting back to the Old English *hoc*. So, while *A. rosea* undoubtedly had its ultimate origins in China, I'm going to agree with those older writers that the hollyhock entered northern Europe via the Middle East, and that it was already well ensconced in English gardens by the thirteenth century or so.

A less common name for the hollyhock is "Spanish Rose," lending support to the argument that it worked its way to England along a westward route, across North Africa and up through Moorish Spain. There, in the fountain-fed courtyards of sprawling palaces like the Alhambra, the educated classes had both the sunshine and the leisure to grow a great variety of plants for both beauty's and curiosity's sake.

In a more fanciful scenario, the first hollyhock seeds reached English shores in the baggage of a returning Crusader who, whilst fleeing from the Saracens, had found the time to grab a stalk of ripe seed heads for his lady wife. One wonders what the lady's first impression might have been when, come Midsummer, the first blushing pink blossoms opened in her kitchen garden. Did she clap her hands in delight, or did she consider these holy hocs too exotic, too wanton as they spread their petals wide for the bumblebees?

A handful of legends once current in England tell of a Crusader who returns home with a Saracen wife in his baggage, even though he already has an English one waiting for him at home. In one variant, the Middle Eastern princess, left behind by her lover, makes her own way to London, where she strolls up and down the crowded streets, dark eyes flashing above her jeweled veil. She does not have to stroll for long before someone notices her poised on the corner, like a nodding *A. rosea nigra*, and reunites her with her Christian beau. In another take, the foreign princess is locked away in her own wing of the knight's castle, where she goes slowly mad before expiring. Her spirit having taken root, she stays on to haunt the place like the ghostly white *A. rosea alba*.

Many of the treasures that made their way from the Holy Land into the British Isles were later attributed to the fairies, like the silken Fairy Flag of Dunvegan Castle and the Luck of Edenhall, a Syrian-made enameled glass beaker that was supposedly snatched from the fairies as they danced in a ring near St. Cuthbert's Well. The hollyhock, too, became a fairy creation: according to one legend, the first hollyhock was a little girl whom the fairies had transformed in retribution for picking flowers from their garden on Midsummer Eve. And the "budds of hollyhocke" were one of the principal ingredients in the complicated charm "To Enable One to See Fairies," now in the Ashmolean Museum at Oxford.

From its original home in China, the hollyhock also migrated eastward to the isles of Japan, where it eventually won a starring role in the sixth-century *Aoi Matsuri*, or Hollyhock Festival. Had the medieval English cottager had the occasion to witness the pageantry of the Aoi Matsuri, he would certainly have mistaken it for a fairy procession. The Hollyhock Festival still takes place each year on May 15, the streets of Kyoto filling with a slow, eerily beautiful parade of women and girls dressed in the many-layered silk robes and trailing trousers of the ancient Heian court. With black wigs and powdered faces, they make their solemn way to the Kamigamo Shrine to ask the gods, or *kami*, for protection against famine, earthquakes, and other natural disasters. In order to hedge humanity's bet, each of the more than five hundred supplicants is adorned with dark green hollyhock leaves, which are believed to act as talismans against such calamities.

The word *matsuri* is almost always translated as "festival," but, whereas our "festival" stems from the Latin *festum*, "a feast," matsuri comes from the verb *matsuru*, meaning "to worship, serve, offer, sacrifice." This includes serving up an eyeful, for the purpose of a matsuri is to capture the gods' attention, even to startle them. This can be done with drumming and dancing, or with a dignified procession of antique court ladies whose pastel layers of silk kimono peek out at the sleeves like the folded petals of the *A. rosea* variety "April Peach Parfait."

My own first impression of the hollyhock was not made in a garden but in the pages of a book: the Platt & Munk Company's 1953 edition of *Mother Goose Nursery Rhymes*, "illustrated by Eulalie." There was plenty going on in that book, including four and twenty very lively blackbirds being forced into a pie dish. There were silver bells and cockleshells, but what I remembered most fondly were the hollyhocks peeping in through the window in the illustration for "Hush-a-Bye, Baby." While writing this article, I looked back at that illustration for the first time in years and was surprised to find that the flowers that had loomed so large and long in my imagination were mere blots of the watercolor brush, tiny dabs of pale burgundy-pink in the background. Somehow, they had captured my attention and held it across all those decades, the sable tip of Eulalie's brush speaking to me in the shape of the hollyhock.

So if you want to turn a few heads, divine or otherwise, install some hollyhocks against your garden fence. Even if you're in the habit of growing only what you can eat, distill, or use to scent your laundry, surely you can make room for a towering "Black Watchman" or a few of Eulalie's heirloom "Indian Spring"—probably not yet "heirloom" when she painted them. If, on the other hand, you want your garden to go unnoticed, plant hostas.

Bibliography

Cooke, Steve. "Aoi Matsuri." *Green Tour Kyoto*. http://www .greentour-kyoto.net/events/aoi-matsuri.

Gardner, Jo Ann. *The Heirloom Garden*. Pownal, VT: Storey Communications, 1992.

Gonick, Gloria Granz. *Matsuri!: Japanese Festival Arts*. Los Angeles, CA: UCLA Fowler Museum of Cultural History, 2002.

Jacob, Dorothy. *A Witch's Guide to Gardening*. New York: Taplinger Publishing Company, 1965.

Taylor, Raymond L. *Plants of Colonial Days*. Mineola, NY: Dover Publications, 1996.

Ward, Bobby J. *A Contemplation upon Flowers: Garden Plants in Myth and Literature*. Portland, OR: Timber Press, 2005.

Moon Signs, Phases, and Tables

The Quarters and Signs
of the Moon

Everyone has seen the moon wax and wane through a period of approximately 29½ days. This circuit from new moon to full moon and back again is called the lunation cycle. The cycle is divided into parts called quarters or phases. There are several methods by which this can be done, and the system used in the *Herbal Almanac* may not correspond to those used in other almanacs.

The Quarters

First Quarter

The first quarter begins at the new moon, when the sun and moon are in the same place, or conjunct. (This means the sun and moon are in the same degree of the same sign.) The moon is not visible at first, since it rises at the same time as the sun. The new moon is the time of new beginnings of projects that favor growth, externalization of activities, and the growth of ideas. The first quarter is the time of germination, emergence, beginnings, and outwardly directed activity.

Second Quarter

The second quarter begins halfway between the new moon and the full moon, when the sun and moon are at a right angle, or a 90° square, to each other. This half moon rises around noon and sets around midnight, so it can be seen in the western sky during the first half of the night. The second quarter is the time of growth and articulation of things that already exist.

Third Quarter

The third quarter begins at the full moon, when the sun and moon are opposite one another and the full light of the sun can shine on the full sphere of the moon. The round moon can be seen rising in the east at sunset, then rising a little later each evening. The full moon stands for illumination, fulfillment, culmination, completion, drawing inward, unrest, emotional expressions, and hasty actions leading to failure. The third quarter is a time of maturity, fruition, and the assumption of the full form of expression.

Fourth Quarter

The fourth quarter begins about halfway between the full moon and the new moon, when the sun and moon are again at a right angle, or a 90° square, to each other. This decreasing moon rises at midnight and can be seen in the east during the last half of the night, reaching the overhead position just about as the sun rises. The fourth quarter is a time of disintegration and drawing back for reorganization and reflection.

The Signs

Moon in Aries

Moon in Aries is good for starting things and initiating change, but actions may lack staying power. Activities requiring assertiveness and courage are favored. Things occur rapidly but also quickly pass.

Moon in Taurus

Things begun when the moon is in Taurus last the longest and tend to increase in value. This is a good time for any activity that requires patience, practicality, and perseverance. Things begun now also tend to become habitual and hard to alter.

Moon in Gemini
Moon in Gemini is a good time to exchange ideas, meet with people, or be in situations that require versatility and quick thinking. Things begun now are easily changed by outside influences.

Moon in Cancer
Moon in Cancer is a good time to grow things. It stimulates emotional rapport between people and is a good time to build personal friendships, though people may be more emotional and moody than usual.

Moon in Leo
Moon in Leo is a good time for public appearances, showmanship, being seen, entertaining, drama, recreation, and happy pursuits. People may be overly concerned with praise and subject to flattery.

Moon in Virgo
Moon in Virgo is good for any task that requires close attention to detail and careful analysis of information. There is a focus on health, hygiene, and daily schedules. Watch for a tendency to overdo and overwork.

Moon in Libra
Moon in Libra is a good time to form partnerships of any kind and to negotiate. It discourages spontaneous initiative, so working with a partner is essential. Artistic work and teamwork are highlighted.

Moon in Scorpio

Moon in Scorpio increases awareness of psychic power and favors any activity that requires intensity and focus. This is a good time to conduct research and to end connections thoroughly. There is a tendency to manipulate.

Moon in Sagittarius

Moon in Sagittarius is good for any activity that requires honesty, candor, imagination, and confidence in the flow of life. This is a good time to tackle things that need improvement, but watch out for a tendency to proselytize.

Moon in Capricorn

Moon in Capricorn increases awareness of the need for structure, discipline, and patience. This is a good time to set goals and plan for the future. Those in authority may be insensitive at this time.

Moon in Aquarius

Moon in Aquarius favors activities that are unique and individualistic and that concern society as a whole. This is a good time to pursue humanitarian efforts and to identify improvements that can be made. People may be more intellectual than emotional under this influence.

Moon in Pisces

Moon in Pisces is a good time for any kind of introspective, philanthropic, meditative, psychic, or artistic work. At this time personal boundaries may be blurred, and people may be prone to seeing what they want to see rather than what is really there.

January Moon Table

Date	Sign	Element	Nature	Phase
1 Wed	Capricorn	Earth	Semi-fruitful	New 6:14 am
2 Thu 12:03 pm	Aquarius	Air	Barren	1st
3 Fri	Aquarius	Air	Barren	1st
4 Sat 11:58 am	Pisces	Water	Fruitful	1st
5 Sun	Pisces	Water	Fruitful	1st
6 Mon 2:45 pm	Aries	Fire	Barren	1st
7 Tue	Aries	Fire	Barren	2nd 10:39 pm
8 Wed 9:24 pm	Taurus	Earth	Semi-fruitful	2nd
9 Thu	Taurus	Earth	Semi-fruitful	2nd
10 Fri	Taurus	Earth	Semi-fruitful	2nd
11 Sat 7:26 am	Gemini	Air	Barren	2nd
12 Sun	Gemini	Air	Barren	2nd
13 Mon 7:25 pm	Cancer	Water	Fruitful	2nd
14 Tue	Cancer	Water	Fruitful	2nd
15 Wed	Cancer	Water	Fruitful	Full 11:52 pm
16 Thu 8:00 am	Leo	Fire	Barren	3rd
17 Fri	Leo	Fire	Barren	3rd
18 Sat 8:23 pm	Virgo	Earth	Barren	3rd
19 Sun	Virgo	Earth	Barren	3rd
20 Mon	Virgo	Earth	Barren	3rd
21 Tue 7:43 am	Libra	Air	Semi-fruitful	3rd
22 Wed	Libra	Air	Semi-fruitful	3rd
23 Thu 4:43 pm	Scorpio	Water	Fruitful	3rd
24 Fri	Scorpio	Water	Fruitful	4th 12:19 am
25 Sat 10:13 pm	Sagittarius	Fire	Barren	4th
26 Sun	Sagittarius	Fire	Barren	4th
27 Mon	Sagittarius	Fire	Barren	4th
28 Tue 12:04 am	Capricorn	Earth	Semi-fruitful	4th
29 Wed 11:33 pm	Aquarius	Air	Barren	4th
30 Thu	Aquarius	Air	Barren	New 4:39 pm
31 Fri 10:45 pm	Pisces	Water	Fruitful	1st

February Moon Table

Date	Sign	Element	Nature	Phase
1 Sat	Pisces	Water	Fruitful	1st
2 Sun 11:55 pm	Aries	Fire	Barren	1st
3 Mon	Aries	Fire	Barren	1st
4 Tue	Aries	Fire	Barren	1st
5 Wed 4:47 am	Taurus	Earth	Semi-fruitful	1st
6 Thu	Taurus	Earth	Semi-fruitful	2nd 2:22 pm
7 Fri 1:44 pm	Gemini	Air	Barren	2nd
8 Sat	Gemini	Air	Barren	2nd
9 Sun	Gemini	Air	Barren	2nd
10 Mon 1:33 am	Cancer	Water	Fruitful	2nd
11 Tue	Cancer	Water	Fruitful	2nd
12 Wed 2:15 pm	Leo	Fire	Barren	2nd
13 Thu	Leo	Fire	Barren	2nd
14 Fri	Leo	Fire	Barren	Full 6:53 pm
15 Sat 2:26 am	Virgo	Earth	Barren	3rd
16 Sun	Virgo	Earth	Barren	3rd
17 Mon 1:23 pm	Libra	Air	Semi-fruitful	3rd
18 Tue	Libra	Air	Semi-fruitful	3rd
19 Wed 10:33 pm	Scorpio	Water	Fruitful	3rd
20 Thu	Scorpio	Water	Fruitful	3rd
21 Fri	Scorpio	Water	Fruitful	3rd
22 Sat 5:12 am	Sagittarius	Fire	Barren	4th 12:15 pm
23 Sun	Sagittarius	Fire	Barren	4th
24 Mon 8:50 am	Capricorn	Earth	Semi-fruitful	4th
25 Tue	Capricorn	Earth	Semi-fruitful	4th
26 Wed 9:55 am	Aquarius	Air	Barren	4th
27 Thu	Aquarius	Air	Barren	4th
28 Fri 9:53 am	Pisces	Water	Fruitful	4th

Times are in Eastern Time.

March Moon Table

Date	Sign	Element	Nature	Phase
1 Sat	Pisces	Water	Fruitful	New 3:00 am
2 Sun 10:40 am	Aries	Fire	Barren	1st
3 Mon	Aries	Fire	Barren	1st
4 Tue 2:12 pm	Taurus	Earth	Semi-fruitful	1st
5 Wed	Taurus	Earth	Semi-fruitful	1st
6 Thu 9:37 pm	Gemini	Air	Barren	1st
7 Fri	Gemini	Air	Barren	1st
8 Sat	Gemini	Air	Barren	2nd 8:27 am
9 Sun 9:33 am	Cancer	Water	Fruitful	2nd
10 Mon	Cancer	Water	Fruitful	2nd
11 Tue 10:09 pm	Leo	Fire	Barren	2nd
12 Wed	Leo	Fire	Barren	2nd
13 Thu	Leo	Fire	Barren	2nd
14 Fri 10:17 am	Virgo	Earth	Barren	2nd
15 Sat	Virgo	Earth	Barren	2nd
16 Sun 8:46 pm	Libra	Air	Semi-fruitful	Full 1:08 pm
17 Mon	Libra	Air	Semi-fruitful	3rd
18 Tue	Libra	Air	Semi-fruitful	3rd
19 Wed 5:13 am	Scorpio	Water	Fruitful	3rd
20 Thu	Scorpio	Water	Fruitful	3rd
21 Fri 11:39 am	Sagittarius	Fire	Barren	3rd
22 Sat	Sagittarius	Fire	Barren	3rd
23 Sun 4:03 pm	Capricorn	Earth	Semi-fruitful	4th 9:46 pm
24 Mon	Capricorn	Earth	Semi-fruitful	4th
25 Tue 6:39 pm	Aquarius	Air	Barren	4th
26 Wed	Aquarius	Air	Barren	4th
27 Thu 8:10 pm	Pisces	Water	Fruitful	4th
28 Fri	Pisces	Water	Fruitful	4th
29 Sat 9:54 pm	Aries	Fire	Barren	4th
30 Sun	Aries	Fire	Barren	New 2:45 pm
31 Mon	Aries	Fire	Barren	1st

April Moon Table

Date	Sign	Element	Nature	Phase
1 Tue 1:20 am	Taurus	Earth	Semi-fruitful	1st
2 Wed	Taurus	Earth	Semi-fruitful	1st
3 Thu 7:48 am	Gemini	Air	Barren	1st
4 Fri	Gemini	Air	Barren	1st
5 Sat 5:40 pm	Cancer	Water	Fruitful	1st
6 Sun	Cancer	Water	Fruitful	1st
7 Mon	Cancer	Water	Fruitful	2nd 4:31 am
8 Tue 5:50 am	Leo	Fire	Barren	2nd
9 Wed	Leo	Fire	Barren	2nd
10 Thu 6:08 pm	Virgo	Earth	Barren	2nd
11 Fri	Virgo	Earth	Barren	2nd
12 Sat	Virgo	Earth	Barren	2nd
13 Sun 4:33 am	Libra	Air	Semi-fruitful	2nd
14 Mon	Libra	Air	Semi-fruitful	2nd
15 Tue 12:20 pm	Scorpio	Water	Fruitful	Full 3:42 am
16 Wed	Scorpio	Water	Fruitful	3rd
17 Thu 5:44 pm	Sagittarius	Fire	Barren	3rd
18 Fri	Sagittarius	Fire	Barren	3rd
19 Sat 9:28 pm	Capricorn	Earth	Semi-fruitful	3rd
20 Sun	Capricorn	Earth	Semi-fruitful	3rd
21 Mon	Capricorn	Earth	Semi-fruitful	3rd
22 Tue 12:18 am	Aquarius	Air	Barren	4th 3:52 am
23 Wed	Aquarius	Air	Barren	4th
24 Thu 2:55 am	Pisces	Water	Fruitful	4th
25 Fri	Pisces	Water	Fruitful	4th
26 Sat 6:01 am	Aries	Fire	Barren	4th
27 Sun	Aries	Fire	Barren	4th
28 Mon 10:23 am	Taurus	Earth	Semi-fruitful	4th
29 Tue	Taurus	Earth	Semi-fruitful	New 2:14 am
30 Wed 4:56 pm	Gemini	Air	Barren	1st

Times are in Eastern Time.

May Moon Table

Date	Sign	Element	Nature	Phase
1 Thu	Gemini	Air	Barren	1st
2 Fri	Gemini	Air	Barren	1st
3 Sat 2:13 am	Cancer	Water	Fruitful	1st
4 Sun	Cancer	Water	Fruitful	1st
5 Mon 1:55 pm	Leo	Fire	Barren	1st
6 Tue	Leo	Fire	Barren	2nd 11:15 pm
7 Wed	Leo	Fire	Barren	2nd
8 Thu 2:24 am	Virgo	Earth	Barren	2nd
9 Fri	Virgo	Earth	Barren	2nd
10 Sat 1:19 pm	Libra	Air	Semi-fruitful	2nd
11 Sun	Libra	Air	Semi-fruitful	2nd
12 Mon 9:07 pm	Scorpio	Water	Fruitful	2nd
13 Tue	Scorpio	Water	Fruitful	2nd
14 Wed	Scorpio	Water	Fruitful	Full 3:16 pm
15 Thu 1:44 am	Sagittarius	Fire	Barren	3rd
16 Fri	Sagittarius	Fire	Barren	3rd
17 Sat 4:12 am	Capricorn	Earth	Semi-fruitful	3rd
18 Sun	Capricorn	Earth	Semi-fruitful	3rd
19 Mon 5:58 am	Aquarius	Air	Barren	3rd
20 Tue	Aquarius	Air	Barren	3rd
21 Wed 8:18 am	Pisces	Water	Fruitful	4th 8:59 am
22 Thu	Pisces	Water	Fruitful	4th
23 Fri 12:01 pm	Aries	Fire	Barren	4th
24 Sat	Aries	Fire	Barren	4th
25 Sun 5:28 pm	Taurus	Earth	Semi-fruitful	4th
26 Mon	Taurus	Earth	Semi-fruitful	4th
27 Tue	Taurus	Earth	Semi-fruitful	4th
28 Wed 12:47 am	Gemini	Air	Barren	New 2:40 pm
29 Thu	Gemini	Air	Barren	1st
30 Fri 10:13 am	Cancer	Water	Fruitful	1st
31 Sat	Cancer	Water	Fruitful	1st

June Moon Table

Date	Sign	Element	Nature	Phase
1 Sun 9:43 pm	Leo	Fire	Barren	1st
2 Mon	Leo	Fire	Barren	1st
3 Tue	Leo	Fire	Barren	1st
4 Wed 10:20 am	Virgo	Earth	Barren	1st
5 Thu	Virgo	Earth	Barren	2nd 4:39 pm
6 Fri 10:01 pm	Libra	Air	Semi-fruitful	2nd
7 Sat	Libra	Air	Semi-fruitful	2nd
8 Sun	Libra	Air	Semi-fruitful	2nd
9 Mon 6:38 am	Scorpio	Water	Fruitful	2nd
10 Tue	Scorpio	Water	Fruitful	2nd
11 Wed 11:23 am	Sagittarius	Fire	Barren	2nd
12 Thu	Sagittarius	Fire	Barren	2nd
13 Fri 1:04 pm	Capricorn	Earth	Semi-fruitful	Full 12:11 am
14 Sat	Capricorn	Earth	Semi-fruitful	3rd
15 Sun 1:27 pm	Aquarius	Air	Barren	3rd
16 Mon	Aquarius	Air	Barren	3rd
17 Tue 2:26 pm	Pisces	Water	Fruitful	3rd
18 Wed	Pisces	Water	Fruitful	3rd
19 Thu 5:26 pm	Aries	Fire	Barren	4th 2:39 pm
20 Fri	Aries	Fire	Barren	4th
21 Sat 11:03 pm	Taurus	Earth	Semi-fruitful	4th
22 Sun	Taurus	Earth	Semi-fruitful	4th
23 Mon	Taurus	Earth	Semi-fruitful	4th
24 Tue 7:05 am	Gemini	Air	Barren	4th
25 Wed	Gemini	Air	Barren	4th
26 Thu 5:05 pm	Cancer	Water	Fruitful	4th
27 Fri	Cancer	Water	Fruitful	New 4:08 am
28 Sat	Cancer	Water	Fruitful	1st
29 Sun 4:43 am	Leo	Fire	Barren	1st
30 Mon	Leo	Fire	Barren	1st

Times are in Eastern Time.

July Moon Table

Date	Sign	Element	Nature	Phase
1 Tue 5:24 pm	Virgo	Earth	Barren	1st
2 Wed	Virgo	Earth	Barren	1st
3 Thu	Virgo	Earth	Barren	1st
4 Fri 5:43 am	Libra	Air	Semi-fruitful	1st
5 Sat	Libra	Air	Semi-fruitful	2nd 7:59 am
6 Sun 3:33 pm	Scorpio	Water	Fruitful	2nd
7 Mon	Scorpio	Water	Fruitful	2nd
8 Tue 9:24 pm	Sagittarius	Fire	Barren	2nd
9 Wed	Sagittarius	Fire	Barren	2nd
10 Thu 11:24 pm	Capricorn	Earth	Semi-fruitful	2nd
11 Fri	Capricorn	Earth	Semi-fruitful	2nd
12 Sat 11:07 pm	Aquarius	Air	Barren	Full 7:25 am
13 Sun	Aquarius	Air	Barren	3rd
14 Mon 10:40 pm	Pisces	Water	Fruitful	3rd
15 Tue	Pisces	Water	Fruitful	3rd
16 Wed	Pisces	Water	Fruitful	3rd
17 Thu 12:07 am	Aries	Fire	Barren	3rd
18 Fri	Aries	Fire	Barren	4th 10:08 pm
19 Sat 4:43 am	Taurus	Earth	Semi-fruitful	4th
20 Sun	Taurus	Earth	Semi-fruitful	4th
21 Mon 12:36 pm	Gemini	Air	Barren	4th
22 Tue	Gemini	Air	Barren	4th
23 Wed 10:59 pm	Cancer	Water	Fruitful	4th
24 Thu	Cancer	Water	Fruitful	4th
25 Fri	Cancer	Water	Fruitful	4th
26 Sat 10:55 am	Leo	Fire	Barren	New 6:42 pm
27 Sun	Leo	Fire	Barren	1st
28 Mon 11:37 pm	Virgo	Earth	Barren	1st
29 Tue	Virgo	Earth	Barren	1st
30 Wed	Virgo	Earth	Barren	1st
31 Thu 12:09 pm	Libra	Air	Semi-fruitful	1st

August Moon Table

Date	Sign	Element	Nature	Phase
1 Fri	Libra	Air	Semi-fruitful	1st
2 Sat 10:57 pm	Scorpio	Water	Fruitful	1st
3 Sun	Scorpio	Water	Fruitful	2nd 8:50 pm
4 Mon	Scorpio	Water	Fruitful	2nd
5 Tue 6:19 am	Sagittarius	Fire	Barren	2nd
6 Wed	Sagittarius	Fire	Barren	2nd
7 Thu 9:38 am	Capricorn	Earth	Semi-fruitful	2nd
8 Fri	Capricorn	Earth	Semi-fruitful	2nd
9 Sat 9:52 am	Aquarius	Air	Barren	2nd
10 Sun	Aquarius	Air	Barren	Full 2:09 pm
11 Mon 8:55 am	Pisces	Water	Fruitful	3rd
12 Tue	Pisces	Water	Fruitful	3rd
13 Wed 9:00 am	Aries	Fire	Barren	3rd
14 Thu	Aries	Fire	Barren	3rd
15 Fri 11:58 am	Taurus	Earth	Semi-fruitful	3rd
16 Sat	Taurus	Earth	Semi-fruitful	3rd
17 Sun 6:41 pm	Gemini	Air	Barren	4th 8:26 am
18 Mon	Gemini	Air	Barren	4th
19 Tue	Gemini	Air	Barren	4th
20 Wed 4:45 am	Cancer	Water	Fruitful	4th
21 Thu	Cancer	Water	Fruitful	4th
22 Fri 4:49 pm	Leo	Fire	Barren	4th
23 Sat	Leo	Fire	Barren	4th
24 Sun	Leo	Fire	Barren	4th
25 Mon 5:33 am	Virgo	Earth	Barren	New 10:13 am
26 Tue	Virgo	Earth	Barren	1st
27 Wed 5:54 pm	Libra	Air	Semi-fruitful	1st
28 Thu	Libra	Air	Semi-fruitful	1st
29 Fri	Libra	Air	Semi-fruitful	1st
30 Sat 4:53 am	Scorpio	Water	Fruitful	1st
31 Sun	Scorpio	Water	Fruitful	1st

Times are in Eastern Time.

September Moon Table

Date	Sign	Element	Nature	Phase
1 Mon 1:17 pm	Sagittarius	Fire	Barren	1st
2 Tue	Sagittarius	Fire	Barren	2nd 7:11 am
3 Wed 6:15 pm	Capricorn	Earth	Semi-fruitful	2nd
4 Thu	Capricorn	Earth	Semi-fruitful	2nd
5 Fri 7:59 pm	Aquarius	Air	Barren	2nd
6 Sat	Aquarius	Air	Barren	2nd
7 Sun 7:47 pm	Pisces	Water	Fruitful	2nd
8 Mon	Pisces	Water	Fruitful	Full 9:38 pm
9 Tue 7:33 pm	Aries	Fire	Barren	3rd
10 Wed	Aries	Fire	Barren	3rd
11 Thu 9:17 pm	Taurus	Earth	Semi-fruitful	3rd
12 Fri	Taurus	Earth	Semi-fruitful	3rd
13 Sat	Taurus	Earth	Semi-fruitful	3rd
14 Sun 2:26 am	Gemini	Air	Barren	3rd
15 Mon	Gemini	Air	Barren	4th 10:05 pm
16 Tue 11:24 am	Cancer	Water	Fruitful	4th
17 Wed	Cancer	Water	Fruitful	4th
18 Thu 11:10 pm	Leo	Fire	Barren	4th
19 Fri	Leo	Fire	Barren	4th
20 Sat	Leo	Fire	Barren	4th
21 Sun 11:54 am	Virgo	Earth	Barren	4th
22 Mon	Virgo	Earth	Barren	4th
23 Tue 11:59 pm	Libra	Air	Semi-fruitful	4th
24 Wed	Libra	Air	Semi-fruitful	New 2:14 am
25 Thu	Libra	Air	Semi-fruitful	1st
26 Fri 10:29 am	Scorpio	Water	Fruitful	1st
27 Sat	Scorpio	Water	Fruitful	1st
28 Sun 6:50 pm	Sagittarius	Fire	Barren	1st
29 Mon	Sagittarius	Fire	Barren	1st
30 Tue	Sagittarius	Fire	Barren	1st

October Moon Table

Date	Sign	Element	Nature	Phase
1 Wed 12:41 am	Capricorn	Earth	Semi-fruitful	2nd 3:33 pm
2 Thu	Capricorn	Earth	Semi-fruitful	2nd
3 Fri 4:00 am	Aquarius	Air	Barren	2nd
4 Sat	Aquarius	Air	Barren	2nd
5 Sun 5:24 am	Pisces	Water	Fruitful	2nd
6 Mon	Pisces	Water	Fruitful	2nd
7 Tue 6:07 am	Aries	Fire	Barren	2nd
8 Wed	Aries	Fire	Barren	Full 6:51 am
9 Thu 7:44 am	Taurus	Earth	Semi-fruitful	3rd
10 Fri	Taurus	Earth	Semi-fruitful	3rd
11 Sat 11:51 am	Gemini	Air	Barren	3rd
12 Sun	Gemini	Air	Barren	3rd
13 Mon 7:30 pm	Cancer	Water	Fruitful	3rd
14 Tue	Cancer	Water	Fruitful	3rd
15 Wed	Cancer	Water	Fruitful	4th 3:12 pm
16 Thu 6:29 am	Leo	Fire	Barren	4th
17 Fri	Leo	Fire	Barren	4th
18 Sat 7:08 pm	Virgo	Earth	Barren	4th
19 Sun	Virgo	Earth	Barren	4th
20 Mon	Virgo	Earth	Barren	4th
21 Tue 7:12 am	Libra	Air	Semi-fruitful	4th
22 Wed	Libra	Air	Semi-fruitful	4th
23 Thu 5:10 pm	Scorpio	Water	Fruitful	New 5:57 pm
24 Fri	Scorpio	Water	Fruitful	1st
25 Sat	Scorpio	Water	Fruitful	1st
26 Sun 12:40 am	Sagittarius	Fire	Barren	1st
27 Mon	Sagittarius	Fire	Barren	1st
28 Tue 6:03 am	Capricorn	Earth	Semi-fruitful	1st
29 Wed	Capricorn	Earth	Semi-fruitful	1st
30 Thu 9:52 am	Aquarius	Air	Barren	2nd 10:48 pm
31 Fri	Aquarius	Air	Barren	2nd

Times are in Eastern Time.

November Moon Table

Date	Sign	Element	Nature	Phase
1 Sat 12:37 pm	Pisces	Water	Fruitful	2nd
2 Sun	Pisces	Water	Fruitful	2nd
3 Mon 1:53 pm	Aries	Fire	Barren	2nd
4 Tue	Aries	Fire	Barren	2nd
5 Wed 4:33 pm	Taurus	Earth	Semi-fruitful	2nd
6 Thu	Taurus	Earth	Semi-fruitful	Full 5:23 pm
7 Fri 8:45 pm	Gemini	Air	Barren	3rd
8 Sat	Gemini	Air	Barren	3rd
9 Sun	Gemini	Air	Barren	3rd
10 Mon 3:38 am	Cancer	Water	Fruitful	3rd
11 Tue	Cancer	Water	Fruitful	3rd
12 Wed 1:44 pm	Leo	Fire	Barren	3rd
13 Thu	Leo	Fire	Barren	3rd
14 Fri	Leo	Fire	Barren	4th 10:16 am
15 Sat 2:08 am	Virgo	Earth	Barren	4th
16 Sun	Virgo	Earth	Barren	4th
17 Mon 2:30 pm	Libra	Air	Semi-fruitful	4th
18 Tue	Libra	Air	Semi-fruitful	4th
19 Wed	Libra	Air	Semi-fruitful	4th
20 Thu 12:31 am	Scorpio	Water	Fruitful	4th
21 Fri	Scorpio	Water	Fruitful	4th
22 Sat 7:19 am	Sagittarius	Fire	Barren	New 7:32 am
23 Sun	Sagittarius	Fire	Barren	1st
24 Mon 11:31 am	Capricorn	Earth	Semi-fruitful	1st
25 Tue	Capricorn	Earth	Semi-fruitful	1st
26 Wed 2:23 pm	Aquarius	Air	Barren	1st
27 Thu	Aquarius	Air	Barren	1st
28 Fri 5:03 pm	Pisces	Water	Fruitful	1st
29 Sat	Pisces	Water	Fruitful	2nd 5:06 am
30 Sun 8:14 pm	Aries	Fire	Barren	2nd

December Moon Table

Date	Sign	Element	Nature	Phase
1 Mon	Aries	Fire	Barren	2nd
2 Tue	Aries	Fire	Barren	2nd
3 Wed 12:15 am	Taurus	Earth	Semi-fruitful	2nd
4 Thu	Taurus	Earth	Semi-fruitful	2nd
5 Fri 5:28 am	Gemini	Air	Barren	2nd
6 Sat	Gemini	Air	Barren	Full 7:27 am
7 Sun 12:34 pm	Cancer	Water	Fruitful	3rd
8 Mon	Cancer	Water	Fruitful	3rd
9 Tue 10:14 pm	Leo	Fire	Barren	3rd
10 Wed	Leo	Fire	Barren	3rd
11 Thu	Leo	Fire	Barren	3rd
12 Fri 10:19 am	Virgo	Earth	Barren	3rd
13 Sat	Virgo	Earth	Barren	3rd
14 Sun 11:05 pm	Libra	Air	Semi-fruitful	4th 7:51 am
15 Mon	Libra	Air	Semi-fruitful	4th
16 Tue	Libra	Air	Semi-fruitful	4th
17 Wed 9:52 am	Scorpio	Water	Fruitful	4th
18 Thu	Scorpio	Water	Fruitful	4th
19 Fri 4:55 pm	Sagittarius	Fire	Barren	4th
20 Sat	Sagittarius	Fire	Barren	4th
21 Sun 8:25 pm	Capricorn	Earth	Semi-fruitful	New 8:36 pm
22 Mon	Capricorn	Earth	Semi-fruitful	1st
23 Tue 9:52 pm	Aquarius	Air	Barren	1st
24 Wed	Aquarius	Air	Barren	1st
25 Thu 11:07 pm	Pisces	Water	Fruitful	1st
26 Fri	Pisces	Water	Fruitful	1st
27 Sat	Pisces	Water	Fruitful	1st
28 Sun 1:35 am	Aries	Fire	Barren	2nd 1:31 pm
29 Mon	Aries	Fire	Barren	2nd
30 Tue 5:56 am	Taurus	Earth	Semi-fruitful	2nd
31 Wed	Taurus	Earth	Semi-fruitful	2nd

Times are in Eastern Time.

Dates to Destroy Weeds and Pests

Dates	Sign	Quarter
Jan 16, 8:00 am–Jan 18, 8:23 pm	Leo	3rd
Jan 18, 8:23 pm–Jan 21, 7:43 am	Virgo	3rd
Jan 25, 10:13 pm–Jan 28, 12:04 am	Sagittarius	4th
Jan 29, 11:33 pm–Jan 30, 4:39 pm	Aquarius	4th
Feb 14, 6:53 pm–Feb 15, 2:26 am	Leo	3rd
Feb 15, 2:26 am–Feb 17, 1:23 pm	Virgo	3rd
Feb 22, 5:12 am–Feb 22, 12:15 pm	Sagittarius	3rd
Feb 22, 12:15 pm–Feb 24, 8:50 am	Sagittarius	4th
Feb 26, 9:55 am–Feb 28, 9:53 am	Aquarius	4th
Mar 16, 1:08 pm–Mar 16, 8:46 pm	Virgo	3rd
Mar 21, 11:39 am–Mar 23, 4:03 pm	Sagittarius	3rd
Mar 25, 6:39 pm–Mar 27, 8:10 pm	Aquarius	4th
Mar 29, 9:54 pm–Mar 30, 2:45 pm	Aries	4th
Apr 17, 5:44 pm–Apr 19, 9:28 pm	Sagittarius	3rd
Apr 22, 12:18 am–Apr 22, 3:52 am	Aquarius	3rd
Apr 22, 3:52 am–Apr 24, 2:55 am	Aquarius	4th
Apr 26, 6:01 am–Apr 28, 10:23 am	Aries	4th
May 15, 1:44 am–May 17, 4:12 am	Sagittarius	3rd
May 19, 5:58 am–May 21, 8:18 am	Aquarius	3rd
May 23, 12:01 pm–May 25, 5:28 pm	Aries	4th
May 28, 12:47 am–May 28, 2:40 pm	Gemini	4th
Jun 13, 12:11 am–Jun 13, 1:04 pm	Sagittarius	3rd
Jun 15, 1:27 pm–Jun 17, 2:26 pm	Aquarius	3rd
Jun 19, 5:26 pm–Jun 21, 11:03 pm	Aries	4th
Jun 24, 7:05 am–Jun 26, 5:05 pm	Gemini	4th
Jul 12, 11:07 pm–Jul 14, 10:40 pm	Aquarius	3rd
Jul 17, 12:07 am–Jul 18, 10:08 pm	Aries	3rd

Dates to Destroy Weeds and Pests

Dates	Sign	Quarter
Jul 18, 10:08 pm–Jul 19, 4:43 am	Aries	4th
Jul 21, 12:36 pm–Jul 23, 10:59 pm	Gemini	4th
Jul 26, 10:55 am–Jul 26, 6:42 pm	Leo	4th
Aug 10, 2:09 pm–Aug 11, 8:55 am	Aquarius	3rd
Aug 13, 9:00 am–Aug 15, 11:58 am	Aries	3rd
Aug 17, 6:41 pm–Aug 20, 4:45 am	Gemini	4th
Aug 22, 4:49 pm–Aug 25, 5:33 am	Leo	4th
Aug 25, 5:33 am–Aug 25, 10:13 am	Virgo	4th
Sep 9, 7:33 pm–Sep 11, 9:17 pm	Aries	3rd
Sep 14, 2:26 am–Sep 15, 10:05 pm	Gemini	3rd
Sep 15, 10:05 pm–Sep 16, 11:24 am	Gemini	4th
Sep 18, 11:10 pm–Sep 21, 11:54 am	Leo	4th
Sep 21, 11:54 am–Sep 23, 11:59 pm	Virgo	4th
Oct 8, 6:51 am–Oct 9, 7:44 am	Aries	3rd
Oct 11, 11:51 am–Oct 13, 7:30 pm	Gemini	3rd
Oct 16, 6:29 am–Oct 18, 7:08 pm	Leo	4th
Oct 18, 7:08 pm–Oct 21, 7:12 am	Virgo	4th
Nov 7, 8:45 pm–Nov 10, 3:38 am	Gemini	3rd
Nov 12, 1:44 pm–Nov 14, 10:16 am	Leo	3rd
Nov 14, 10:16 am–Nov 15, 2:08 am	Leo	4th
Nov 15, 2:08 am–Nov 17, 2:30 pm	Virgo	4th
Nov 22, 7:19 am–Nov 22, 7:32 am	Sagittarius	4th
Dec 6, 7:27 am–Dec 7, 12:34 pm	Gemini	3rd
Dec 9, 10:14 pm Dec 12, 10:19 am	Leo	3rd
Dec 12, 10:19 am–Dec 14, 7:51 am	Virgo	3rd
Dec 14, 7:51 am–Dec 14, 11:05 pm	Virgo	4th
Dec 19, 4:55 pm–Dec 21, 8:25 pm	Sagittarius	4th

Times are in Eastern Time.

About the Authors

Elizabeth Barrette has been involved with the Pagan community for more than twenty-three years. She served as Managing Editor of *PanGaia* for eight years and Dean of Studies at the Grey School of Wizardry for four years. Her book *Composing Magic: How to Create Magical Spells, Rituals, Blessings, Chants, and Prayers* explains how to combine writing and spirituality. She enjoys magical crafts, historic religions, and gardening for wildlife. Visit her blog, *The Wordsmith's Forge* (http://ysabetwordsmith .livejournal.com), or her website, *PenUltimate Productions* (http:// penultimateproductions.weebly.com).

Calantirniel has practiced many forms of natural spirituality since the early 1990s. She is a professional astrologer, tarot card reader, dowser, flower essence creator and practitioner, and Usui Reiki Master and became a ULC Reverend and a Master Herbalist in 2007. She has an organic garden, crochets professionally, and is co-creating the spiritual path Tië eldaliéva, meaning "the Elven Path." Please visit http://astroherbalist.com for more information.

Dallas Jennifer Cobb lives a magical life, manifesting meaningful and flexible work, satisfying relationships, and abundant gardens. She enjoys a balance of time and money, which support her deepest desires: a loving family, time in nature, self-expression, and a healthy home. She lives in paradise, in a waterfront village in rural Ontario. Contact her at jennifer.cobb @live.com.

Sally Cragin is the author of *Born on the Cusp: Birthdays Between the Signs* and *The Astrological Elements*, both published by Llewellyn. She writes the "Moon Signs" forecasts for the *Boston Phoenix* and also sees clients in her astrology and tarot work. She teaches history and writing at Fitchburg (MA) State University, and is the only professional astrologer elected to public office in Massachusetts, as she serves on the Fitchburg School Committee.

Alice DeVille is an internationally known astrologer, writer, and metaphysical consultant specializing in relationships, health, real estate, government affairs, career and change management, and spiritual development. An accomplished cook, Alice enjoys preparing American, Italian, French, Tex-Mex, and Southern cuisine and enjoys creating new recipes. Contact Alice at alice@astrologyondemand.com and visit her website, AstrologyonDemand.com.

Ellen Dugan, the "Garden Witch," is an award-winning author and psychic-clairvoyant. She is the author of many Llewellyn books, including *Garden Witchery* and *Herb Magic for Beginners.* Ellen wholeheartedly encourages folks to go outside and get their hands dirty, so they can discover the wonder and magick of the natural world. Ellen and her family live in Missouri. Visit her popular syndicated blog at ellendugan.blogspot.com and her website at ellendugan.com.

Emyme resides in a multigenerational, multi-cat household in southern New Jersey. Past and present writing projects include a human interest column for the local paper, a self-published book on blended families, and poetry about strong women of mythology and fairy tales. Currently, Emyme is writing a series of articles on bed & breakfasts from the point of view of the over-fifty-five, single female traveler. Questions or comments: catsmeow24@verizon.net.

Darcey Blue French—Devotee of Wildness, Wildcrafter of Botanical Wonders, Herbal Matchmaker, and Shamana Flora—is a shamanic and clinical herbalist in southern Arizona. Darcey has been using and learning from plants, both wild and cultivated, since childhood. She works privately with clients and students who are eager to learn from the plants a healing way as old as time itself. Visit her at shamanaflora.com.

Ember Grant has been contributing to the Llewellyn annuals since 2003. She is also a poet and photographer, and her work explores the topics of nature, spirituality, folklore, and mythology. She lives in Missouri with her husband and their extremely spoiled feline companion.

Jill Henderson is an artist, author, and world traveler with a penchant for wild edible and medicinal plants, herbs, and nature ecology. A lifelong organic gardener and seed saver, Jill gives workshops on the global challenges presented by bioengineered food crops and how participants can grow and save their own open-pollinated seeds. Jill also writes and edits the blog *Show Me Oz* (showmeoz.wordpress.com) and is the author of three books: *The Healing Power of Kitchen Herbs*, *A Journey of Seasons*, and *The Garden Seed Saving Guide*. She and her husband, Dean, live in the heart of the Ozark Mountains.

JD Hortwort resides in North Carolina. She is an avid student of herbology and gardening, a professional writer, and an award-winning magazine editor and journalist.

James Kambos has had an interest in plants and herbs since childhood. He raises an extensive collection of herbs, vegetables, and wildflowers in his Ohio garden. When not writing for Llewellyn's annuals, he is also a folk artist who paints in the American primitive style.

Esthamarelda McNevin (Missoula, MT) is the founding Priestess and Oracle of the "Eastern Hellenistic" magickal order Opus Aima Obscuræ (OAO). She is a professional spiritual tutor, healer, tarot reader, and intuitive, as well as a campus lecturer, baker, writer, organic gardener, and psychic intermediary. She hosts esoteric and culinary classes, seasonal events, fundraisers, and temple rituals. Contact her at facebook.com /opusaimaobscurae or Esthamarelda@gmail.com.

Susan Pesznecker, M.S., is a child of the natural world and a student of astronomy, herbology, healing, stonework, green magicks, and folklore. A degreed writer, Sue teaches writing and literature at two universities and teaches herbalism in the online Grey School (greyschool.com). She is the author of *Crafting Magick with Pen and Ink* and *The Magickal Retreat* (both from Llewellyn). Contact Sue at susanpesznecker.com or facebook .com/SusanMoonwriterPesznecker.

Linda Raedisch is the author of *Night of the Witches: Folklore, Traditions and Recipes for Celebrating Walpurgis Night* (2011) as well as an upcoming Christmas book for Llewellyn. She lives, works, and writes in northern New Jersey, where she grows a variety of impractical ornamentals.

Charlie Rainbow Wolf—also known as "the stonetalker"—is of English and Cherokee heritage, and has studied the mysteries of both cultures. She is a member of the American Tarot Association and is a certified professional reader. Charlie is also the Dean of Faculty, Psychic Arts, and Assistant Dean of Divination at the Grey School (greyschool.com). A published author and recorded singer/songwriter/storyteller, she feeds her creative muse with writing, pottery, knitting, soapmaking, and organic gardening. Please visit charlierainbow.com.

Diana Rajchel took an interest in herbs since planting a cucumber patch the summer before kindergarten. You can find out more about her by visiting http://blog.dianarajchel.com. Remember that *j*.

Suzanne Ress has been writing fiction and nonfiction for over twenty-five years. She is an accomplished self-taught herb gardener, beekeeper, silversmith, and mosaicist. She lives at the foot of the Alps in northern Italy with her husband, daughter, three dogs, three horses, and many wild animals.

Laurel Reufner's mother can verify that she grew up a "wild child" in farming country. Laurel has been earth-centered for over twenty years now and really enjoys writing about topics that grab her attention. Laurel has always lived in Southeastern Ohio and currently calls Athens County home, where she lives with her wonderful husband and two wild children of her own. Visit her website at http://laurelreufner.blogspot.com.

Anne Sala is a freelance journalist based in Minnesota. This summer, she had a thriving pot of cilantro growing on her balcony until her one-year-old daughter decided it was her favorite plant to yank out by the roots.

Tess Whitehurst (Venice, CA) is an intuitive counselor, energy worker, feng shui consultant, and speaker, and the author of five Llewellyn titles, including *The Magic of Flowers: A Guide to Their Metaphysical Uses & Properties*. She has appeared on the Bravo TV show *Flipping Out*, and her writing has been featured in such places as the AOL welcome page, *Writer's Digest*, and the *Whole Life Times* blog. To learn about her workshops, writings, and appearances, and to sign up for her free monthly newsletter, visit her at tesswhitehurst.com.